ZONED IN THE USA

ZONED IN THE USA

The Origins and Implications of American Land-Use Regulation

Sonia A. Hirt

CORNELL UNIVERSITY PRESS   ITHACA AND LONDON

First published 2014 by Cornell University Press
First printing, Cornell Paperbacks, 2014
Printed in the United States of America

Library of Congress Cataloging-in-Publication Data

Hirt, Sonia, author.
  Zoned in the USA : the origins and implications of American land-use
regulation / Sonia A. Hirt.
     pages cm
  Includes bibliographical references and index.
  ISBN 978-0-8014-5305-2 (cloth : alk. paper)
  ISBN 978-0-8014-7987-8 (pbk.)
  1. Land use—United States—Planning—History. 2. City planning—United
States—History. I. Title.
  HD191.H57   2014
  333.77′170973—dc23   2014022378

Cornell University Press strives to use environmentally responsible suppliers and
materials to the fullest extent possible in the publishing of its books. Such materials
include vegetable-based, low-VOC inks and acid-free papers that are recycled,
totally chlorine-free, or partly composed of nonwood fibers. For further
information, visit our website at www.cornellpress.cornell.edu.

Cloth printing   10 9 8 7 6 5 4 3 2 1
Paperback printing   10 9 8 7 6 5 4 3 2 1

To Oliver

Contents

Acknowledgments

I will never forget my first encounter with an American zoning code. This may not sound like an exciting thing to remember for most people, but for me it was eye-opening. I was trained as an architect in a faraway country and was generally oblivious to American city planning (and culture in general) until I stepped on American soil in 1993. Working as intern in a nonprofit organization focused on redesigning old neighborhoods, I had to quickly familiarize myself with local planning law. A zoning ordinance was the first American legal document I ever read (followed closely by the Constitution). For this reason, it became one of the windows through which I could look into American culture. What a document this ordinance was! So full of surprises! Such a stunning level of regulatory detail: your houses must be a certain size—and in each zone they must be different; no, this lot is too small here, it must be at least one acre (this regulation caused further confusion, since I didn't know what an acre was!); no, you cannot sell cookies here, this area is for *living* only; no, here you cannot rent your third floor to your sister-in-law or build an apartment block, this is for *single-family* homes only; here is a long list of permitted uses in this district—note that these include tattoo shops but not shops for hypnotists. And if something is not on the list of permitted uses, if it did not happen to have entered the mind of the wise regulator, then you are out of luck—it is prohibited. How could Americans, whose reputation for being independent and freedom-loving and respecting private property was worldwide put up with such tedious laws governing the building of their everyday environments and way of life? I thought I must be misunderstanding what America is all about. Twenty years later, I finally wrote this book to try to understand.

I am indebted to a very large number of people who helped me make sense of U.S. planning law. It begins with my professors at the University of Michigan: Jonathan Levine, who inspired my interest in land-use regimes; and Robert Fishman, who inspired my interest in planning history. I am extremely grateful to all my colleagues at Virginia Tech, who have tolerated me for nine years, especially Theodore Koebel, who was stuck with reading many of my papers before I send them for journal review. Many ideas came from delightful conversations and other correspondence with some of the greatest experts in the fields of U.S. land-use planning and planning history, who shared their thoughts with me out of pure generosity. These include Jerold Kayden at Harvard University, William Fischel at Dartmouth, Raphael Fischler at McGill University, Robert Bruegmann at the University of Illinois, and Christopher Silver at the University of Florida. The book was supported by the inaugural Senior Fellowship from Virginia Tech's Institute for Society, Culture and the Environment, which is led by Karen Roberto. Much of the archival research was conducted at the Frances Loeb Library at Harvard's Graduate School of Design. Special thanks to Dean Mohsen Mostavafi and Professors Rahul Mehrotra, Alex Krieger, Peter Rowe, and Susan Fainstein, who in 2011 kindly invited me to serve as visiting associate professor at Harvard.

Julie Steiff, Kate Babbitt, and Karen Laun read and commented on the entire manuscript, for which I will be forever grateful. I thank the journals that published shorter versions of some of the book chapters: the *Journal of Planning Education and Research*, the *Journal of Planning Literature*, and *Planning Practice & Research*. Their editors and reviewers provided me with superb input. I received extremely thoughtful comments from Michael McGandy, Cornell's acquisitions editor. His help through the writing and publication process was invaluable. I am also heavily indebted to my research assistants, Cynthia Lintz, Shraddha Nadkarni, and Kate Oldrey. Above all, I am thankful to my family on both sides of the North Atlantic for their unconditional love and support.

AN AMERICAN MODEL
OF LAND-USE CONTROL

Nobody loves zoning but the people.

—Richard Babcock[1]

Ernst Freund was only technically a New Yorker. Born in the great city while his German parents were on a brief American tour, he spent his childhood in Dresden and Frankfurt and, in 1884, immigrated to the country of his birth as a young man. Freund eventually became a distinguished professor and one of the founders of the University of Chicago Law School. He also became one of the first and most prominent scholars of U.S. and European administrative law. Among many other subjects, his scholarship covered a novel legal practice of his time— municipal zoning. The practice was ostensibly invented by the Germans in the 1870s and had been spreading with great vigor throughout the United States in the early 1900s, when Freund did much of his writing. Like Alexis de Tocqueville nearly a century earlier, Freund was able to offer unique insights on U.S. society because he retained the capacity to scrutinize it with a fresh, outsider's eye. In 1926, Freund made the following observation on the contrasts between American and European cities and their land-use laws:

> The whole zoning problem in this country is affected by two factors which I should like myself to learn more about than I know. They are in a sense peculiarly American. [There is an] ... extraordinary sensitiveness of property to its surroundings. I know something about foreign cities. As a boy, I lived in two German cities, and I have travelled somewhat in Europe. Conditions there are very different. People do not mind a little store around the corner a bit. When you go to Vienna, you find that the

palace of one of the great aristocratic families has a big glass works display room on the lower floor. The family has a glass business in its Bohemian estates, and thinks nothing of advertising the fact in its residence. We wouldn't have that in this country because it is not comfortable to our ideas. One of the millionaires in Frankfurt built his house right across the way from an amusement establishment where there were concerts given twice a day. We [Americans] wouldn't do that. (Freund 1926, 78–79)

For all his accomplishments, Freund was no Tocqueville. He proposed no broad theory on why the differences exist. But he alluded, if vaguely, to some deeply rooted features of the American "national temperament" and its impact on America's laws and America's cities.

In this book I explore some ways in which America's cities[2] and landscapes are, as Freund suspected, shaped by land-use laws and policies grounded in America's "national temperament," whatever this elusive term may mean. Are these laws and policies indeed peculiarly American? Are American cities and city environs exceptional, partially because of these laws and policies? Is there a "distinctive geographical character" to American urbanism (Conzen 1996)? If so, does the peculiarity, the "American-ness" of U.S. built forms and the laws that guide them persist nearly a century after Freund wrote? There can hardly be clear answers to these complex questions. Still, travelers and scholars seem to agree that compared to cities in most other parts of the industrialized world, such as those in Europe, U.S. urban and suburban landscapes tend to have some specific geographic features (see Coppa 1976). These features include lower densities and greater distances; neat, geometric layouts; an abundance of green space, especially green space organized in private yards; a clearer separation between living and working spaces; a greater overall uniformity and orderliness; a greater level of social segregation reflected in space; a greater share of individual, single-family detached housing, and so forth (Conzen 1996). In contrast, cities and regions in other parts of today's industrialized world are messier, denser, and more mixed in terms of people meeting each other and activities occurring simultaneously in smaller spaces (Beatley 2000; Musterd 2005; Pichler-Milanovic 2007). Assuming there is empirical evidence to prove that these differences exist, what explains them? What laws and policies affect them? Like Freund, with whom I share the immigrant, European-turned-American life story, "I should like myself to learn more about [this] than I know" (1926: 79).

One important mechanism through which human environments are shaped is the public control of private activities, including building and land use. In the United States, the most common means and the best-known form of land-use control is municipal zoning—the subject of Freund's interest—although a number of other tools (e.g., design review, development agreements, subdivision controls, parking requirements) are also in play (Levy 2011; Cullingworth 1993; Kayden 2004; Lewyn 2005). Here is a typical definition: "Zoning entails separating the land in a particular [municipal] area into sections, or zones, with different rules governing activities on that land" (Pendall, Puentes, and Martin 2006, 2–3). Some 95 percent of American locales, including almost all cities,[3] use zoning, ostensibly to serve the public interest.

Land-use control and zoning in particular are crucially important to our every-day lives (Platt 2004). Zoning defines the rules governing what and where people and institutions can and cannot build and operate in our cities, suburbs, and towns. By regulating what gets built and where, it sets the basic spatial parameters of where and thus *how* we live, work, play, socialize, and exercise our rights to citizenship. By imposing spatial constraints on social behavior, zoning "affects the basic organiza-tion of our human environment" (Haar and Kayden 1989, xi). Furthermore, like other sometimes invisible but influential human institutions, zoning serves as "a shorthand of the unstated rules governing what are widely regarded as correct social categories and relationships" (Perrin 1977, 3). In fact, zoning not only expresses our societal consensus on the "correct" relationships and categories, it also shapes it. Not only does it tell us what we can and cannot do in certain places, it also cements, both metaphorically and literally, our ideas of the *proper* categories and relationships that occur in space. It conveys to us messages of the places in the city where we can and should meet each other, the streets we can and should travel on, how many cars we can and should have, and the kinds of homes we can and should live in. It tells us about the activities we can and should perform at home and the kinds of people we can and should live near. Even where the Occupy Wall Street protesters could and could not go had a lot to do with zoning (Kayden 2011). In governing our building practices, zoning solidifies in our minds what is normal and expected, decent, and desirable. It thus imposes a moral geography on our cities. The ubiquity of zoning makes it so commonplace as to be invisible, but in this invisibility lies power—the power to shape daily practices and the power to shape ideas and ideals.

It is no wonder that public meetings about zoning changes often spark fiery emo-tions, controversy, and outright anger and that in many U.S. locales such changes can be enacted only after referenda. Clashes over building rules, especially around the American home, touch upon issues that are at the heart of Americans' percep-tions of democracy: citizens' freedom, choice, and control over their own lives. The blog exchange from the Wellington neighborhood of Woodinville, Washington, is one among thousands of examples of the high-pitched passions that rezoning pro-posals arouse across the country in public meetings and in the blogosphere (espe-cially when they pertain to a neighborhood's status quo, its residential character, and the perceived threat of intrusion from other, unwelcome uses; see the textbox). Note how the debate goes straight to the core of what people think American democracy is all about and includes references to the Constitution and several presidents.

TEXTBOX 0.1   Excerpts and Blog Exchanges from the Website of Concerned Neighbors of Wellington (CNW), Dedicated to Preserving the Rural Character of the Wellington Neighborhood

The exchange followed a proposal to permit uses such as daycare centers, home occupations, higher-density housing, schools, and emergency shelters in the Wellington neighborhood of Woodinville, Washington, which is occupied primarily by single-family homes.

Excerpts from the Website's Front Page

One morning you awaken to the sound of bulldozers as a neighbor's lot is subdivided and your view changes from woods to the back of four to eight houses!

CNW wants to insure the City of Woodinville's promise of "preserving our Northwest woodland character, our open space, and our clean environment." We believe high-density housing, and the resulting increased traffic through our neighborhoods, are in direct conflict with the City's vision. The R-1 [single-family residential] district lies inside a Washington State Urban Growth Area which mandates a minimum of R-4, or four homes per acre, in total density. Numerous projects have been proposed which have an irreversible impact on our quiet rural neighborhood and our property values.

Blog Exchanges

If I wanted to live in a crowded neighborhood in Lynnwood I would have moved there!

I was informed today that the roaming homeless encampment of Tent City has applied for a permit at North Shore United Church adjacent to Leota Junior High and Wellington Elementary Schools. I'm unsure whether this should be posted here or in the Crime Reports section! The City has a moratorium preventing the creation of high impact, non-R1 [single-family residential] uses in the Wellington . . . [but] watch our council roll-over with this travesty of zoning.

Citizens lining up to address their elected officials—what the First Amendment calls "to petition the government for redress of grievances"—is as American as apple pie. Democracy in action and at its best! But it seems that some on the Woodinville City Council don't share this sentiment. . . . Just so you'll know, democracy isn't served when you snap back at or chide a

citizen for exercising the absolute Constitutional right to hold you accountable for the performance of your public duties or criticize you in a public
setting.... President Harry Truman ... had a few choice words to say about
holding office that you should consider. He said, "If you can't stand the heat,
get out of the kitchen." No one held a gun to your head and forced you to
run for the Council.... He also said, "The buck stops here!" ... Politics isn't
a municipal group hug even in a city of 10,000 and especially when you're
faced with tough issues like Brightwater and Tent City 4.... The next elec-
tion may be a long way away, but it will come eventually. As Lincoln said,
"You can't fool all of the people all of the time."

Source: Concerned Neighbors of Wellington n.d.

For most American citizens and city-building professionals, the American
land-use planning and regulation system, especially zoning, has long held an
aura of normalcy, inevitability, and even universality (Light 1999; Wickersham
2001). Most Americans have at some point of their lives dealt (often passionately,
as in the Wellington example) with their local building or zoning authorities. I
would be surprised if any American is unfamiliar with the basic zoning categories: residential, commercial, industrial, and so forth. As Levine (2006) points
out, the model seems virtually self-evident to the point that justification is rarely
demanded. But common perceptions that the U.S. land-use control system is
normal and inevitable are wrong, as I argue throughout the book.

So here is my first main point: the zoning system that we have in the United
States, as "normal" as it may seem to those who grew up with it, may be *particularly* American.[4] The ways that Americans or, more accurately, U.S. municipal
governments plan and regulate the form of cities, towns, and suburbs is fairly
unique in the world.[5] It is different from the models used by other countries that
are commonly compared to the United States—the countries of the so-called
industrialized or western world. These countries regulate the structure of their
settlements with strictness and sophistication that is by no means less than what
we find in the United States. But they do it differently.[6] In fact the contrasts are so
fundamental that "comparisons between the planning model in the US and other
countries often provoke bewilderment because the planning system in the US
seems unique, if not incomprehensible to planners from other countries. Likewise, US planners often react with incredulity to the planning system of other
countries, citing the vast structural and cultural differences that exist" (Schmidt
and Buehler 2007, 55).

To begin with, the differences are *procedural*. The U.S. model relies to a degree larger than elsewhere on the public regulation of the activities of the private sector through zoning and other rules. This tends to shock Europeans. In one of my favorite books, *The Political Culture of Planning: American Land Use Planning in Comparative Perspective*, the esteemed English scholar Barry Cullingworth described the American model as "resistant to description, let alone explanation" (1993, 1). One can perhaps infer from the fact that the first part of Cullingworth's tome is titled "Zoning" that he not only fully grasped the importance of zoning as an American institution but also saw it as a key to understanding the planning contrasts between the United States and his native England. In *Town and Regional Planning*, Peter Hall, another Englishman, similarly commented on both the strangeness (as he saw it) of U.S. planning and the key role of U.S. zoning: "To many Europeans, even well-informed ones, planning in the United States is a contradiction in terms" (2002, 189). He also noted that "the real core of the American system of land-use control is not planning, but zoning" (205). The reason both Cullingworth and Hall were surprised is that while public regulation of private building activities is the core of the U.S. system, in West European countries, England included, governments often regulate less rigidly but their level of public intervention in urban development is higher because they plan and construct more (e.g., they own higher shares of city land and thus can mold it as they wish,[7] they build and distribute housing directly,[8] and they are less constrained by national laws in telling the private sector what and what not to do[9]). There are other, equally fundamental procedural contrasts. Most land-use planning and regulation in the United States occurs at the level of the municipality, whereas elsewhere in the western world we find stronger interventions coming from higher-tier governments (regional and national). The U.S. model relies on explicit, relatively strict and uniform rules to issue or deny planning permissions. This does not mean that U.S. governments are deprived of discretion; on the contrary, their discretionary powers have only grown over time (Kayden 2004). But they do have less discretion as compared to the governments of European countries. In England, especially, zoning—a tool that virtually guarantees the rights of private actors to build on their land as long as they follow the rules—does not even exist and the entire planning system is often referred to as "discretionary" (Booth 2003).

In addition to the procedural differences, the U.S. model is distinct *substantively* in the sense that it aims to produce a distinct type of built forms. Partially as a result of the peculiarity of the U.S. land-use planning and regulation model, U.S. built environments are unusual in the western world. The U.S. model works to create urbanized environments that are strikingly low in population density, from an international point of view. Further, it focuses on strictly separating the basic land-use classes (residential, commercial, industrial, etc.) in ways we don't commonly find in other countries. It also gives a highly preferential treatment to a particular spatial form—the single-family home with the private yard—in ways we don't easily find elsewhere. The last point deserves further reflection. In U.S. zoning, the single-family residential district is omnipresent. I have yet to find a single U.S. zoning ordinance that does *not* include a single-family category. But here is the peculiar thing. The idea of legally designating areas exclusively for residential structures, areas where home is separated from all that is not home, appears to be an aberration in the history of the world's building regulations, even though the regulations date back thousands of years. The single-family category is not too common in the countries I surveyed even today, except in Canada. Of course, this is not to say that there are no single-family homes in other countries—there are plenty of them and in many locations, urban and suburban. But I could find no evidence in other countries that this particular form—the detached single-family home—is *routinely*, as in the United States, considered to be so incompatible with all other types of urbanization as to warrant a legally defined district all its own, a district where all other major land uses and building types are outlawed.

Thus, what is ubiquitous (and therefore assumed normal) in the United States—an omnipresent district dedicated exclusively to single-family housing—is an international rarity, historically and today. Why? Scholars have for a long time argued—sometimes with appreciation and sometimes as a critique—that isolating the single-family home from all else was the primary reason for the popularity of zoning in early twentieth-century America (Pollard 1931; Babcock 1966; Logan 1976) in ways we do not seem to find in other nations (including where zoning was first used, in Germany and England). This appears to be the case to this day, as I try to show in this book.

Perhaps the strangest thing about the U.S. land-use regulation model is that it exists. At first glance, the model contradicts what may be the most fundamental feature of the American "national temperament," to use Freund's words one more time. We are talking about the United States here, the country where freedom from government action has always been a virtue. This is the country whose cultural and political trajectory has been shaped by the intellectual insights of the likes of Ralph Waldo Emerson in *Self-Reliance* ([1841] 2010) and Herbert Hoover in *American Individualism* (1922). This is the country where "that government is best which governs least," as Henry Thoreau put it ([1849] 2000), and where "the chief business" of the people is business, as Calvin Coolidge put it (1925). This is the country where political individualism—the idea that success comes from the actions of autonomous individuals free from government intrusion— has perpetually been a mainstream conviction (Zelinsky 1973; Elazar 1988), an integral part of what we often call the American Dream (Truslow [1931] 1941; Cullen 2003; Jillson 2004).[10] One needs only to listen to contemporary political debates on the role of the public versus the private sector in such activities as generating wealth and providing education, health care, and services for seniors to get this impression.[11] International surveys further prove that when it comes to attitudes toward public and private, individual and community, people and government, Americans espouse views that differ from those of the citizens of most other western countries. Americans are generally more appreciative of individual autonomy, initiative, and competition and less supportive of collectivist, government-led solutions.[12]

Here is a paradox. In seeming contradiction to these core values, American zoning not only exists but thrives. Yet it is a case of restrictive government intrusion into the activities of individuals, of the private sector. For anyone who doubts this, please read any zoning code. How could such heavy government regulations be acceptable in the land of political individualism? One way of thinking about this is as follows. There are many sides to American individualism. In addition to political individualism (the autonomy of individuals from political authority), there is also economic individualism. I refer here to the idea that each individual should be free to pursue advancement through the accumulation of private property and material wealth.[13] This has been another cornerstone of American culture and politics, of the American idea of democracy, of the American Dream, if you will (see Cullen 2003; Jillson 2004). As Tocqueville put it, "I know of no other country where the love of money has such a grip on men's hearts" ([1838] 1966, 47).[14] And then there is spatial individualism. By this I mean Americans' fascination with generous spaces to be conquered and subjugated to human will (Zelinsky 1973; Conzen 1996), whether on the homestead of the yeoman farmer or in the suburban family compound. This fascination with space can be traced to the writings of many of America's founding fathers (e.g., Benjamin Franklin and Thomas Jefferson) and many of America's most iconic intellectuals (e.g., Henry Thoreau and Frank Lloyd Wright). The twentieth-century version of this ideal—the middle-class suburban home with the lush green yard—may well be the most commonly held image, the perceived lynchpin and crown jewel of the American Dream (Dolce 1976; Shlay 1986; Kostof 1987; Kelly 1993; Archer 2005; Beauregard 2006; Samuelson 2010; Forman 2011; Lowenthal and Curzan 2011).[15]

The different sides of individualism are related. In all cases, we are talking about carving out and preserving autonomous, individual spaces, whether political, economic, or material. But they sometimes conflict. During the late nineteenth and early twentieth centuries—times of phenomenal urban growth and limited government regulation in the United States—this conflict was, in some sense, exactly what was going on. The tradition of political individualism was undermining the traditions of economic and spatial individualism. The value of many people's major assets—their land and buildings—was being severely depreciated as the surroundings of properties were perpetually "invaded" by uses and structures perceived as less desirable. (Of course, there was a strong class- and race-based element in this story: some people held far more assets than others and the "undesirables" who were threatening them were, generally, the poor and minorities.) Comfortable living in cities was becoming increasingly harder for the well-to-do, whose mansions were under constant siege by the booming industries and the "undesirables" these industries brought in (the class- and race-based element in this story is again obvious). Without limits on political individualism (e.g., without increased government regulation), economic and spatial individualisms were in danger. But how did increased government regulation of private land and property ever become acceptable to a nation that ostensibly cherished the opposite?

One answer is suggested by economists.[16] The argument goes as follows: real-estate markets in late nineteenth- and early twentieth-century America were experiencing a range of failures due to negative externalities (see Wheaton 1989). Public regulations such as zoning emerged to control these externalities and improve the operation of the markets. Since individuals could not effectively ensure the stability of their property values, they turned to a certain legal instrument—municipal zoning—that performs a function similar to that of personal property rights but at the collective level (Nelson 1977).[17] A noteworthy contemporary addition to this line of thinking is provided by William Fischel (2001b). Like Freund, who wished to make sense of the "extraordinary sensitiveness of [U.S.] property to its surroundings," Fischel seeks to explain the proclivity of U.S. zoning to mandate strictly controlled residential-only environments. His well-known and superbly articulated "homevoter hypothesis" points to home-ownership as a key variable that accounts for the popularity of U.S. zoning.[18] The argument is that since homes are the greatest financial asset of the American middle class, their owners—the largest voting bloc in the United States—exercise rational choice by supporting local policies such as zoning that protect their homes' financial values. These financial values are threatened by decline following changes in the homes' environs.[19] (Such changes may include the entry of denser housing, retail establishments, offices, and industries, which may lead to noise, traffic, pollution, and other negative consequences.) In the absence of homeowners' insurance against neighborhood change, homeowners embrace the next best thing: zoning, which freezes the environs of the homes, excluding everything except other homes of a similar type. Fischel's conclusion is that: "Local politics [including mass political support for zoning] is thus driven by real-estate economics" (2001b, 19).

To give the homevoter hypothesis its due, we should clarify that in addition to homeownership, it takes into account the importance of local government structure. It is well known that U.S. metropolises are highly fragmented: most are comprised by hundreds of independent suburban locales surrounding a central city.[20] Metropolitan Pittsburgh, for example, consists of some 400 locales. U.S. local governments rely heavily on local property taxes. It could be inferred that American homeowners wield significant political power in their small communities because hundreds of locales are competing to attract the "good" tax-paying homeowners.[21] If local governments do not serve their residents well by providing the desired policies, the residents "shop" among competing locales.[22] Protecting property values through restrictive zoning may be regarded as one of these desirable policies. If we are to ground our explanation of the differences between American and European urban land-use laws in government structure alone, we would need to prove that U.S. governments are more politically and fiscally decentralized than their European counterparts.[23] The latter statement appears to be a point of consensus among scholars if we compare the United States to countries such as England and Germany (Cullingworth 1993; Newman and Thornley 1996). But by some measures today's French government system, for example, is also quite fragmented,[24] as are the systems of East European countries such as the Czech Republic (United Cities and Local Governments 2008). Yet despite evidence of some urban sprawl and exclusionary practices in these countries (see Le Goix and Callen 2010; Stanilov and Sykora 2012), we do not find in their metropolises densities as low as those in the United States, a comparable dominance of detached homes, or zoning laws that so decisively favor monofunctional patterns and single-family housing. If government structure is not the answer, could the U.S.-European contrast be attributable only to real-estate economics and property values?

Certainly there is plenty of historic and contemporary evidence that protecting private property values was an important factor in making zoning acceptable to the American public. In fact, I will provide much historic evidence of the key role of property in early zoning debates in chapter 6. (My argument in this chapter is that constraining political individualism through zoning became acceptable in the early 1900s partially because the new legal tool was justified as a means of achieving greater economic individualism: i.e., as means of increasing private property values.) But the economic explanation is not enough. If real-estate economics was and continues to be the key factor, if residential property values inevitably decline in surroundings where multiple land uses and housing types are allowed,[25] shouldn't people in the other capitalist democracies be equally fearful about their home's environs and their home's values? In principle, it should not make much difference whether a privately owned dwelling is located in a single-family structure (as is more common in the United States) or in a multifamily structure (as is more common in Europe). As long as the dwelling constitutes a person's major financial asset, it could be assumed that he or she would strive to protect it. Thus, the question remains: Shouldn't other countries with high homeownership rates (and there are many, as chapter 2 shows) embrace similarly restrictive laws guarding the environs of their residential properties—properties that also must comprise major financial assets of their respective national middle classes? Yet they don't—and apparently they didn't in the past, either. Freund's Frankfort millionaire must have felt confident that his mansion's worth would not decrease if it were next to an amusement park. His Viennese aristocratic family must not have feared imminent financial ruin from the combination of its place of dwelling with its place of business. Why? Freund's answer was simple: the Europeans had different spatial preferences; they were more accustomed to urban density and mixture. Yet density and mixture were "not comfortable with our [American] ideas" at the time when zoning was spreading across in the United States.

> If you live in a big apartment [as in European cities] . . . you don't care who your neighbors are. The sensitiveness is only restricted to the private house [assuming] your neighbors are close by. If you go into bigger buildings, just as in Europe, that disappears. . . .
>
> In Frankfurt, property was very much mixed, but it didn't interfere with the building of very handsome houses next to apartment houses. People simply didn't think about it; it didn't make much difference. People were not sensitive. (Freund 1926, 79–80)

My simple proposal is that, much as Freund suspected, certain ideals (or "sensitivities" in his terms) that were widely shared among the founders of U.S. zoning—ideals as to what constitutes proper, desirable living space[26]—bolstered and, as a matter of fact, continue to bolster the popularity of the traditional U.S. zoning system, which so strictly guards the privacy of single-family homes from all else. These were (and are) essentially pastoral ideals that value generous private family domains immune from the chaos and intensity of dense collective living (Lees 1994). Of course, not everyone in the United States wishes (or can afford) to live in a low-density environment of spacious detached homes. Yet many do, as surveys of housing preferences continue to show. And this is, I think, partially why U.S. real-estate markets operate the way they do. Yes, the values of residential properties may often decline when their environs are less controlled, but they decline to a large extent because people do not like living in mixed, uncontrolled environs. The property markets do not work under some universal real-estate laws (an implicit assumption of many economists); they are deeply embedded in culture (see also Light 1999).[27]

My second main point, then, is that U.S. zoning is at its base a cultural institution: it was built to reflect the values of its founders, values that have been and,
arguably, continue to be in alliance with popular American ideals of good government and good urbanism. This cultural claim may seem self-evident. Of course
zoning is a cultural institution; aren't they all? The idea that institutions have cultural underpinnings goes back at least to Plato, who noted in *The Republic* (360
BCE) that "governments vary as the dispositions of men vary," and it has been
brilliantly defended by a long line of scholars from Max Weber (1930) to Robert
Putnam (1993). But there is also a long line of scholars throughout modern history,
both Marxist and not, who have sought to minimize cultural values as an explanatory variable; in our case, by singling out the role of either real-estate economics or
government structure. Surely both economics and institutions play a major part,
but both are framed by the set of historically conditioned decisions on how to
make zoning—initially, a European tool—fit American social and cultural realities
of the 1900s. The question is whether these early decisions are nearly as socially or
culturally appropriate today as they were decades ago. Or is an early-twentieth-
century invention trapping us, by the force of habit, into practices whose questionable impacts we understand today much better than we did in the past?

A similar culture-based argument can also be advanced about the underpinnings of many—possibly all—U.S. policies that have a spatial effect. And many of
them (not just zoning) work toward creating low-density built forms dominated
by private spaces. These include policies in the realms of transportation, housing,
and taxation, which are carried out at state and federal levels. As I discuss in chapter 1, such policies favor certain housing types and tenure (e.g., the ownership
of single-family homes rather than the renting of apartments), certain transport
modes (cars rather than mass transit), certain consumer behaviors (e.g., the purchase of bulky and energy-consuming items such as large houses and large cars
over smaller, more ecologically friendly ones), and so forth (Nivola 1999). These
policies can all be interpreted through economic or institutional lenses. But if we
miss the cultural part of the story, we would be missing a lot.

Throughout this book, my main method is the comparison. I highlight the contrasts that exist between the U.S. land-use control model and those of select other
countries. I also show that certain elements of U.S. land-use control may well be
unprecedented; they constitute a break with land-use practices globally and in
history. My goal is not to prove that "others do it better" (certain policies may
work better in other nations only because they are a better cultural or institutional fit) or to "learn" from other nations directly. As Charles Haar (1984: 204)
put it, the main value of foreign explorations lies not so much in the discovery of
directly transferable tools (that rarely happens) but in "the stimulus of insightful
reflection of culture and experiences."

A few words on what the book is not. This is not a comprehensive textbook on U.S. land-use planning of the type provided by Godschalk et al. (2006). I focus only on a few key points that distinguish the U.S. land-use regulation model from others and try to show how and why the contrasts emerged. I use historical evidence, but this is not a classic history book. If I were to write a comprehensive history of zoning that explains how it became culturally acceptable in the early twentieth century, I would have to pay much closer attention to various legitimate motivations behind it: for example, concerns about public health and safety. (For an excellent and much more comprehensive account of the emergence of zoning, the reader should review Toll's [1969] classic, *Zoned American*.) Further, I would also have to pay greater attention to the most sinister intent behind zoning: sheer racism (Silver 1997 and Fischler 1998a, b have done brilliant work in this area). While I integrate these factors into the narrative (it would be impossible to do otherwise), I focus on how and why American land-use control is exceptional in guarding residential exclusivity, and I do not think that any single factor—health, safety, racism, or economics—can explain it all. If this were a history book, it would be strangely lopsided and organized. I search for the origins of urban land-use control far back in world history and discuss the emergence of zoning in the United States, but I do not review post–World War II U.S. zoning history in detail (Richard Babcock [1966] and John Delafons [1969] are the classic sources on the time period). My focus is on what I call the formative years of zoning: between about 1905, when the first comprehensive zoning proposals emerged, and about 1935, when most American cities and suburbs were fully zoned. It is during these years that zoning's key constructs, including the basic land-use categories, were formed. I do away with chronology: I first explain how the system works today and then return to history. My logic is this: let us first pose an empirical puzzle—that the U.S. model of land-use control is distinct from the models used in other nations—and then let us reflect on how this potentially unique system emerged. And since my goal is to show how the basic U.S. distinctions developed as they did during the first half of the twentieth century, it is this historic period that I analyze in depth.

The book updates and extends existing knowledge on land-use regulation from an international, comparative perspective. I am building on the solid foundation provided by Delafons (1969), Haar (1984) and Cullingworth (1993). I hope that the book will enrich the reflective insights of Babcock (1966), Nelson (1977), Haar and Kayden (1989), and, more recently, Platt (2004), Levine (2006), Wolf (2008), and Talen (2012a) on American land-use regulation. Still, I believe that there are several points that distinguish this book from others and that may make it a valuable read not only for urban planning scholars but also for scholars in urban history, geography, sociology, anthropology, and comparative law. These points include an expanded comparative scope (thus far, England and

Germany have been the "usual suspects" for comparison with the United States); an extended historical timeline (land-use control is a very old idea, although its histories are often written starting with the industrial age); a stronger empirical basis for the claim that the U.S. urban land-use regulation model (and, more broadly, the U.S. model of urbanism) is distinct, especially in terms of the residential settings it creates; and a focus on explaining some of the peculiar aspects of the U.S. model through historical investigation.

Chapters 1, 2 and 3, which discuss contemporary land-use controls, are based primarily on a review of U.S. and foreign laws (including select municipal ordinances), most of which are available online, as well as a review of the literature and available secondary data. Sources for the historical chapters (4, 5 and 6) include literature and available documents pertaining to the history of urban land-use regulation worldwide, plus primary U.S. (and, to a lesser extent, foreign) sources from the early 1900s, such as key early planning reports and zoning ordinances; planning tractates and textbooks widely used at the time (especially those written by such prominent land-use lawyers as Edward Bassett, Ernst Freund, and Frank Backus Williams); court cases, media reports, and scholarly articles; and the full set of transcripts from the National Conferences on City Planning over a 25-year period from 1909 (when the first conference took place) to 1934 (when zoning was an established institution nationally).

I have structured my argument as follows. In chapter 1, I build a case for the distinct nature of American urbanism, specifically for its exceptionally low density and the predominance of the detached single-family home with the large private yard. In chapter 2, I outline how the U.S. land-use regulation system works. In chapter 3, I compare the U.S. system of land-use control to the systems of other industrialized nations, particularly with regard to treating residential areas. My argument is that far from being exceptional as a "nation of homeowners," the United States is exceptional in being a "nation of homezoners." By this I mean that Americans have an unusual proclivity to impose strict legal barriers around the single-family home and protect it from interaction with all other forms of urbanization, including all other housing types as well as other nonhousing built forms. In so doing, Americans tend to severely limit the variety of behaviors and activities that can occur in the vicinity of single-family housing and the types of people who can be in that vicinity. Partially as a result of policy, the detached single-family home is more dominant in the United States than in almost all other nations, it is larger than what we find elsewhere, it is enveloped by unusually bountiful chunks of privately owned open space (by most of the world's standards), and it is legally shielded from all else to a degree hard to find anywhere else that a study of municipal land-use laws can take us. In sum, American single-family housing areas are characterized not only by their striking spatial generosity but also by their exceptional social and functional purity, which is legally protected by mechanisms such as zoning laws. This purity has been critiqued on social, economic, environmental, and aesthetic grounds by a long line of writers of the magnitude of Jane Jacobs (1961) and Richard Sennett (1970) for more than five decades. In response, the legal system has changed to some extent. I discuss some of its most popular recent alternatives. But, as chapter 2 shows, the empirical evidence suggests that these changes have touched the margins rather than the substance, the core of the legal system. The marginality of the reforms is best illustrated by a comparison between the prevailing U.S. model of zoning and what we see in other countries. Yes, the current U.S. zoning model seems different if we compare it to itself, say, during the 1930s, 40s or 50s, but it seems remarkably stable if we compare it to the models of other industrialized nations (e.g., in Europe).

The peculiarities of the current U.S. zoning system, with its focus on strict order, land-use segregation, and exclusive private spaces limited to particular family types and particular physical configurations, can be gauged in another way: by placing it in a historic context. Chapters 4, 5, and 6 review the historical evidence. Here is the story in short. Today, as I noted earlier, most of us in the United States consider it normal, routine, and virtually inevitable to split urban space into various functional categories, of which single-family residential is especially prominent. However, the notion was actually invented at a particular historic moment. Although some seeds of the idea can be found in Greek and Roman times, in the history of the Western world, at least, this moment does not arrive until the full effects of the industrial revolution hit cities during the late nineteenth century and the Enlightenment-born spirit of high modernity brought about a previously unknown impulse to control space by intricate division and classification. But the negative effects of the industrial revolution and the rising modern Zeitgeist did not lead to identical land-use-separation systems in all industrializing societies: the U.S. system became the strictest. In chapter 4, I look for the roots of land-use separation through regulation in the very long history of urban building laws around the world. In chapter 5, I study the emergence of a potentially distinct land-use regulation model in the United States against the background of the models developing in Western Europe (mostly Germany and England) during the nineteenth century. In chapter 6, I analyze historical materials from the formative years of zoning in the United States (1905–1935). I address the question of how zoning—a government instrument with such restrictive powers—could ever become culturally acceptable in a country where political individualism was a mainstream philosophy. My answer has three parts. I highlight the extent to which the new regulation system was presented as a tool that constrains government bureaucrats just as it restricts private parties (this helped make the system acceptable in a nation dominated by political individualism). I underscore how the system was justified as a means of defending private property values (i.e., as a means of advancing economic individualism). Finally, I emphasize the invention of the legal tool that implements Americans' spatial individualism in built form: the exclusive single-family zoning district.

In the concluding chapter, I summarize the promises and paradoxes of the American model of land-use control. And I argue that Ernst Freund may have been right: there is something peculiarly American about our land-use practices, something perhaps as quintessentially American as baseball and apple pie.

AMERICA'S HOUSING TRADEMARK

America has long prided itself on being a "nation of home owners," as FDR once put it (quoted in Kelly 1993, 171). This statement is true in the sense that most American families—two-thirds of them—own their homes. But the phrase also implies something else: that in its success in securing mass homeownership, America is exceptional among other nations. This notion, however, is inaccurate. True, homeownership rates were dramatically higher in the United States than in other parts of the western world some 100 years ago. In the late 1800s, 48 percent of families owned their homes, a figure reflecting the unusual affluence of American middle-class society at the time. After a dip during the Great Depression, the rates grew steadily to reach the current figure of about 65 percent by 1970 (e.g., Gale, Gruber, and Stephens-Davidowitz 2007). By contrast, in the early 1900s, the homeownership rate in England was only 10 percent (Hicks and Allen 1999; Home 2009). The situation was similar in most other West European countries, where homeownership rates did not increase significantly until after World War II. However, the historic contrast no longer stands. In homeownership, today's America is but a middle-range country (Munjee n.d.), ranked seventeenth out of twenty-six "economically advanced countries" covered in a recent report (Pollock 2010). The report shows, in fact, twelve "economically advanced" countries whose homeownership rates are at or exceed 70 percent, with Singapore (89 percent) leading the pack, as figure 1.1 illustrates. The average homeownership rate among the European Union's (EU) twenty-eight members is over 70 percent as

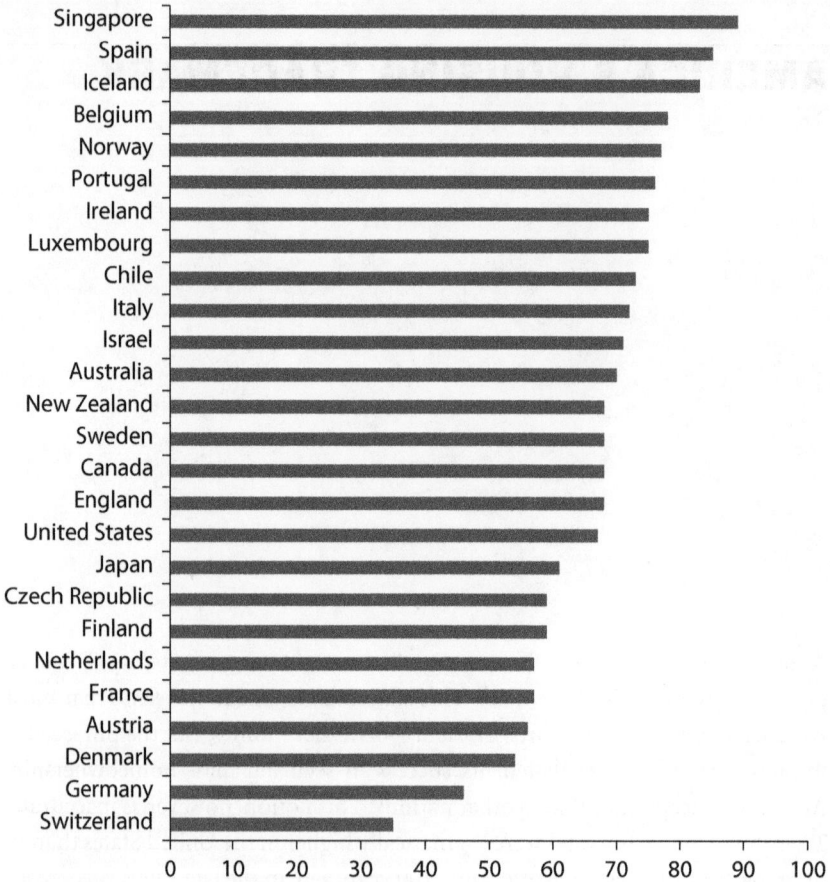

FIGURE 1.1 International comparison of homeownership rates.

Source: Pollock (2010). Prepared by Cynthia Lintz.

table 1.1 shows. The United States, at 65 percent, would come nearly at the tail end of the chart, following most European nations, as well as Canada and Australia.[1] But if not in ownership per se,[2] are U.S. housing patterns distinct at all, and if so, in what way?

Home, Sweet (Single-Family) Home

What makes Americans special is not their homeownership rates but the fact that they reside, in unusually high numbers, in *detached single-family homes*. As Table 1.2 shows, over two-thirds of American housing comprises single-family homes. True, some of the European numbers are higher, on both sides of the former Iron Curtain (e.g., in Ireland, the UK, Norway, Belgium, the Netherlands, Hungary, Croatia and

TABLE 1.1 Percentage of households in owner-occupied and rental housing in the United States and select western nations

	OWNER-OCCUPIED HOUSING			RENTAL HOUSING	OTHER	TOTAL HOUSING
	WITH MORTGAGE	WITHOUT MORTGAGE	TOTAL PERCENT OF OWNER-OCCUPIED HOUSING			
United States	45.4	19.7	65.1	34.9	0	100
Europe						
EU-28	27.4	43.4	70.8	29.2	0	100
Austria	25.7	31.8	57.5	42.5	0	100
Belgium	41.9	29.9	71.8	28.2	0	100
Bulgaria	1.5	85.7	87.2	12.8	0	100
Croatia	2.6	89.5	92.1	8.0	0	100
Cyprus	15.3	58.5	73.8	26.1	0	100
Czech Republic	18.1	61.9	80.0	19.9	0	100
Denmark	52.7	14.4	67.1	32.9	0	100
Estonia	16.7	66.9	83.6	16.5	0	100
Finland	41.9	32.2	74.1	25.9	0	100
France	29.4	33.7	63.1	36.9	0	100
Germany	28.1	25.3	53.4	46.6	0	100
Greece	15.7	60.1	75.8	24.1	0	100
Hungary	23.1	66.7	89.8	10.2	0	100
Iceland	62.7	15.1	77.8	22.1	0	100
Ireland	34.6	35.7	70.3	29.8	n/a	100
Italy	15.6	57.3	72.9	27.1	0	100
Latvia	8.3	74.2	82.5	17.5	0	100
Lithuania	6.7	85.6	92.3	7.8	0	100
Luxembourg	40.0	28.2	68.2	31.8	0	100
Malta	17.7	63.1	80.8	19.2	0	100
Netherlands	59.6	7.6	67.2	32.9	0	100
Norway	63.0	21.0	84.0	16.0	0	100
Poland	8.4	73.7	82.1	18.0	0	100
Portugal	34.0	41.0	75.0	25.0	0	100
Romania	0.6	96.0	96.6	3.4	0	100
Slovakia	8.2	82.0	88.2	9.8	0	100
Slovenia	7.7	69.8	77.5	22.5	0	100
Spain	32.8	49.8	82.7	17.3	0	100
Sweden	65.9	3.7	69.6	30.3	0	100
Switzerland	39.5	4.4	43.9	56.1	0	100
United Kingdom	41.9	26.0	67.9	32.1	0	100
Other countries						
Australia	34.9	32.1	67.0	29.6	3.4	100
Canada	n/a	n/a	68.7	31.3	0	100
Japan	n/a	n/a	61.9	38.1	n/a	100

Sources: Australia Bureau of Statistics (2013); Eurostat (2014b); Canada Mortgage and Housing Corporation (2013); Statistics Japan (2010); U.S. Census Bureau (2010c). EU-28 stands for the 28 members of the European Union. Iceland, Norway, and Switzerland are not EU members, but included in the EU datasets. Numbers in last column are rounded to nearest whole number.

TABLE 1.2 Percentage of housing by dwelling type in the US and select western nations

	SINGLE-FAMILY HOMES			MULTIFAMILY BUILDINGS	OTHER	TOTAL
	DETACHED SINGLE-FAMILY HOMES	ATTACHED SINGLE-FAMILY HOMES	TOTAL SINGLE-FAMILY HOMES			
United States	63.3	5.4	68.7	24.5	6.7	100
Europe						
EU-28	34.7	23.6	58.3	40.9	0.8	100
Austria	43.2	13.7	56.9	42.2	0.9	100
Belgium	36.9	41.9	78.8	20.6	0.6	100
Bulgaria	47.6	9.4	57.0	42.4	0.6	100
Croatia	71.7	6.3	78.0	21.8	0.2	100
Cyprus	47.0	29.2	76.2	22.8	1.0	100
Czech Republic	37.3	10.1	47.4	52.4	0.2	100
Denmark	59.2	0.0	59.2	27.6	13.2	100
Estonia	30.0	4.9	34.9	64.5	0.6	100
Finland	47.1	19.0	66.1	33.2	0.7	100
France	44.6	22.3	66.9	33.0	0.1	100
Germany	28.8	16.1	44.9	53.6	1.5	100
Greece	31.8	8.5	40.3	59.6	0.1	100
Hungary	64.7	5.4	70.1	29.2	0.7	100
Iceland	35.0	19.1	54.1	45.4	0.5	100
Ireland	35.7	59.9	95.6	4.4	0.0	100
Italy	24.4	26.7	51.1	48.4	0.5	100
Latvia	30.9	3.5	34.4	65.3	0.3	100
Lithuania	35.3	6.8	42.1	57.4	0.5	100
Luxembourg	41.5	25.1	66.6	33.0	0.4	100
Malta	5.6	46.5	52.1	47.2	0.7	100
Netherlands	16.0	61.2	77.2	18.4	4.4	100
Norway	62.3	19.2	81.5	7.5	11.0	100
Poland	48.8	4.4	53.2	46.7	0.1	100
Portugal	40.7	19.2	59.9	39.7	0.4	100
Romania	60.8	1.5	62.3	37.7	0.0	100
Slovakia	49.5	2.0	51.5	48.4	0.1	100
Slovenia	66.8	4.0	70.8	28.9	0.3	100
Spain	14.1	21.0	35.1	64.9	0.0	100
Sweden	50.9	8.6	59.5	40.1	0.4	100
Switzerland	24.5	12.2	36.7	60.3	3.0	100
United Kingdom	26.5	58.9	85.4	14.4	0.2	100
Other countries						
Australia	75.6	9.9	85.5	13.6	0.9	100
Canada	55.2	10.4	65.6	34.4	0.0	100

Sources: Australia Bureau of Statistics (2013); Eurostat (2014a); Canada Mortgage and Housing Corporation (2013); U.S. Census Bureau (2011a). EU-28 stands for the 28 members of the European Union. Iceland, Norway, and Switzerland are not EU members, but included in the EU datasets. In the U.S. data, mobile home units are shown in the "other" column of this table; however; mobile homes are typically detached single-family homes, which means the percentage of single-family homes in the U.S. is likely closer to 70. Numbers in last column are rounded to nearest whole number.

Slovenia), but note that these numbers generally drop sharply when we separate the detached from the attached family homes. In detached single-family homes—homes with private yards—the United States shoots nearly to the top, reaching nearly twice the EU average (63 as compared to 34 percent).[3] And perhaps surprisingly, although the United States rate of single-family housing is similar to, say, that of Norway or post-communist nations such as Hungary or Romania, it dwarfs that of the United Kingdom, which stands at only 26 percent. Moreover, one can dig into the high European numbers a bit deeper and detect a different story. For various historic, geographic, and economic reasons, Eastern Europe and Scandinavia, the two primary regions with high detached single-family housing rates, have been less urbanized than the rest of the continent and the United States (e.g., Bairoch and Goertz 1986; Szelenyi 1996). Notwithstanding some recent trends toward urban decentralization, in Eastern Europe and Scandinavia detached single-family housing is often associated with small towns and villages, with the rural way of life. In contrast, large metropolitan areas are dominated by multifamily buildings. In the large cities of nations that were once under the Soviet thumb, multifamily buildings constructed of prefabricated panels after World War II house the majority of the population: in the Romanian capital of Bucharest, for instance, 82 percent of people live in such buildings (Hirt and Stanilov 2009). In the large cities of central and western Europe, Spartan mass housing is typically less dominant, but the large majority of the population dwells in multifamily structures: 81 percent in Berlin, 97 in Rome and in Madrid, and 99 in Paris[4] (Urban Audit n.d.). Compare this to cities in the United States. Only New York comes close, with 80 percent of its population residing in multifamily housing (the number drops, though, to 62 if we consider New York's metropolis as a whole). In Chicago, the respective numbers are 65 percent (city) and 37 (metropolis), in Seattle 46 (city) and 29 (metropolis), in New Orleans 31 (parish) and 21 (metropolis), and in Philadelphia only 25 (city) and 20 (metropolis) (U.S. Census Bureau 2011b).[5] (Figures 1.2 and 1.3 illustrate the

FIGURE 1.2 Urban sprawl in northern Virginia. Except for in the central urban cores, housing in the region consists primarily of single-family units (attatched and detached). According to the U.S. Census Bureau (2011a), 69 percent of households in the area reside in such units. Photo by Cynthia Lintz.

FIGURE 1.3   A view of Marseille, France, where individual homes (attached and detached) comprise only 31 percent of housing in the agglomeration and 17 percent in the city itself (INSEE 2012). Photo by Cynthia Lintz.

contrast between European and American housing patterns.) The differences between Europe and the United States grow sharper if we take into account that even in U.S. cities where a significant percentage of the population lives in multifamily housing, this type of housing occupies only a minor portion of the total urban land area (the rate is typically in the single digits), whereas a very large part of the area designated for residential uses is taken by land zoned specifically for detached single-family homes— often about half the city, and the number is much higher in the suburbs.[6] (More on this in the next chapter.)

Americans are also champions when it comes to the *size* of the homes they live in: from the viewpoint of almost the entire rest of the world, American homes are unusually spacious. The average size of a new dwelling has more than doubled since the 1950s, from about 1,000 to 2,300 square feet (even though the average household size has shrunk; Wilson and Boehland 2005). The latest reported median is about 1,700 square feet (U.S. Census Bureau 2011a).[7] This well exceeds most of the available numbers for European countries and those for other nations for which I could find data (only the New Zealand statistic comes close to that of the United States; see figure 1.4).[8] American dwellings are also surrounded by ever-expanding private yards featuring what is practically a mythical entity around the world: the perfectly manicured green American lawn.[9] The average size of American residential lots has increased from about 6,000 square feet in the 1930s (Adams 1934, 65) to about 14,000 square feet in 1982 to about 18,000 square feet in 2008—a generous figure.[10]

To the unusually spacious individual houses positioned on unusually large private lots, add America's millions of other large buildings built at large distances from each other and the extraordinary amount of space created to support another aspect

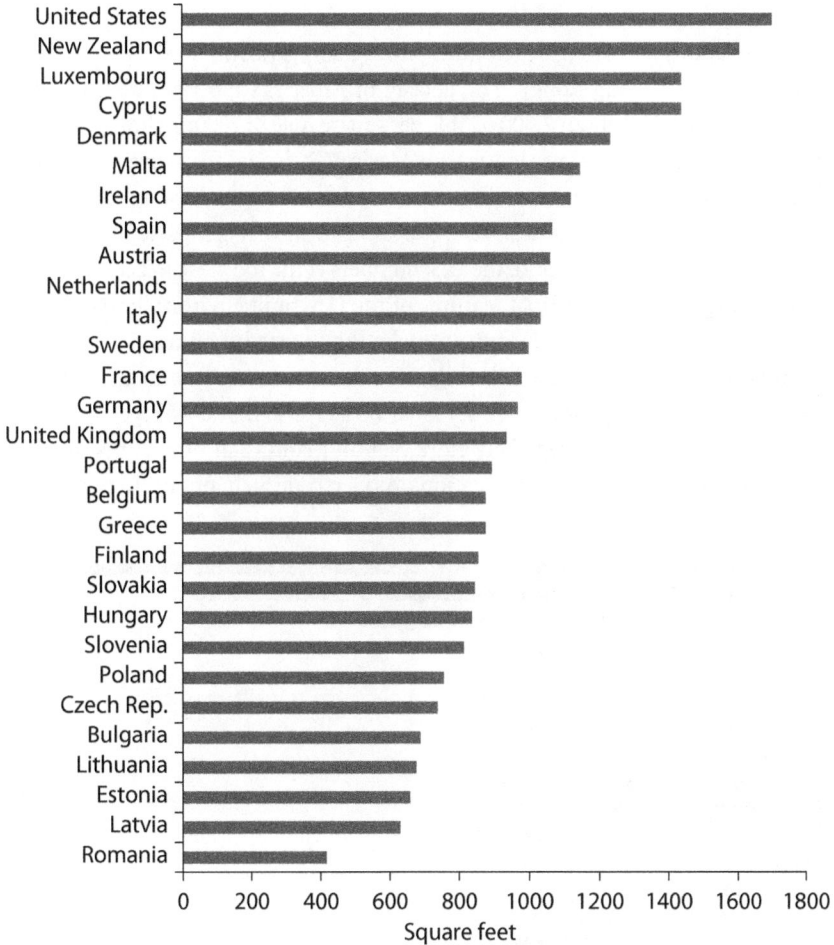

FIGURE 1.4 Dwelling size in the United States (median) and select other nations (averages).

Sources: Dol and Haffner (2010); Core Logic New Zealand (2011); U.S. Census Bureau (2011a). Prepared by Cynthia Lintz.

of Americans' private lifestyles—the ability to travel vast distances alone (i.e., in an automobile).[11] In some estimates, "car-architecture" (spaces taken by highways, roads, parking, driveways, gas stations, etc.) in U.S. cities and suburbs occupies well over a quarter of the total built landscape (Ellin 2006, 47). The result is a potentially distinct U.S. model of urbanism (or suburbanism, to be more precise): an urbanism of such low density that it could well be seen as nonurban by outsiders. Forget America's image as a land of downtowns with skyscrapers (these occupy a miniscule portion of the total built landscape, as they do, of course, in many other countries) and look at overall densities. Metropolitan Atlanta's density is about 700 people per square mile; this is more than ten times lower than Moscow's and Paris's and 100 times lower than Hong Kong's. The density of America's most populated Metro, New York, which had about 2,000 people per square mile in 2000, is about five times lower than Prague's, ten times lower than Mexico City's, and forty-five times lower than Dhaka's. In fact, as figure 1.5 illustrates, it is difficult to graphically represent the population densities of American metro areas in a way that compares them to that of other cities around the world: the U.S. numbers come too close to zero.

What explains these distinct features of the U.S. built environment? Why the unusually low population density? And why the unusual domination of a particular housing form, the detached single-family home, placed at an arm's-length distance from its neighbors? Ask a casual observer and you will get the same answer:[12] America has always had more plentiful land than others; this is what distinguishes America from other nations. As Gertrude Stein put it, "In the United

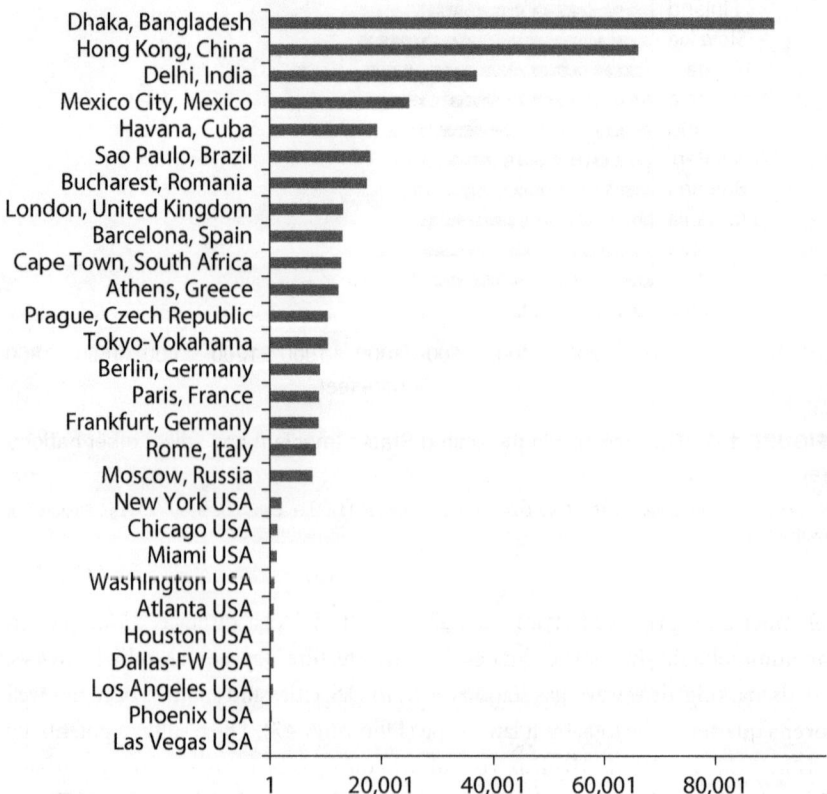

FIGURE 1.5   Population densities in select metropolises in the United States and the world (people per square mile).

Sources: U.S. Census Bureau (n.d., a); Demographia (2013). Prepared by Cynthia Lintz.

States there is more land where nobody is than where anybody is. This is what makes America what it is" (quoted in Platt 2004, 6). There is certainly a long history of such perceptions. American land developers of all eras learned to capture and play with such perceptions again and again, to their benefit (Figure 1.6 offers a contemporary illustration of how developers use these perceptions).

FIGURE 1.6   A real-estate company advertising its products by referring to Americans' fascination with open space and its conquest. Courtesy of Ruger Ranch and Arizona Land & Ranches, Inc.

At the dawn of the twentieth century, when the English and the Germans were beginning to seriously worry about sprawling cities and preserving the countryside, American urban policy makers could still proudly proclaim that there is "no danger [in America, unlike in Europe] that this great urban population will cause a national land shortage" (Ihlder 1927, 73). I will discuss the relationship between the perception of limitless land and the development of America's early land-use laws in greater depth in chapter 5, but here I should just note that more than one excursion into U.S. urban forms, laws and institutions has started with land:

> The existence of free land, its continuous recession, and the advance of American settlement westward, explain American development. . . . The peculiarity of American institutions is, the fact that they have been compelled to adapt themselves to the changes of an expanding people. (Turner [1893] 2008)

> Land has never been a scarce resource in America. Its great abundance has been a powerful influence on American attitudes toward the land, its development, and attempts by government to control its use. . . . The general unconcern for the rate at which land is consumed by new development, born out of the confidence that the supply is virtually unlimited, has been called "the prairie psychology." And it is not altogether fanciful to see a persistence of the [prairie farmer's] log-cabin tradition in the overwhelming American preference for the detached house on a large plot. The customs and attitudes of the frontier still flourish. (Delafons 1969, 1, 4)

> Of all the modern industrialized nations, the United States is the only one that began with what originally seemed to be an endless supply of land. . . . One of the important foundations of this country was that everyone was free to do what he wanted, partly because of the abundance of land. And that freedom certainly included control of the use of one's own land. (Abeles 1989, 122)

Land by itself cannot make people do one thing or another, build one type of landscape or another.[13] The issue at hand is what American cultural historian Leo Marx (1991) has called an American "ideology of space" and Dutch comparative geographer Gerrit Wissink (1962) has called the unusual space-relatedness of American culture: the high value that Americans tend to assign to vast spaces and their subjugation to human will (see also Beauregard 2006, 15). The seed of this explanation dates back at least to Frederick Jackson Turner's ([1893] 2008) famous, if highly controversial, essay in which he sought to link America's

geography with the American "character." Turner's argument was that continuous exposure to the raw edge of civilization made Americans uniquely reliant on
self and family. It also made them hostile to government control.[14] Gerrit Wissink
continued this interpretation. He identified a set of distinctly American spatial
credos that overlap substantially with what I referred to in the introduction as
America's tradition of spatial individualism. These credos include a sentiment
favoring a rustic way of life "on one's own," a taste for large spaces and faraway
distances, and a belief that there will always be plenty of everything (including
land) for everybody. To those ideals, Wilbur Zelinsky (1973) and Michael Conzen
(1996) add Americans' love of spatial orderliness and perfectionism and the cult
of domesticity—the tendency to divide life into a work sphere and a domestic
sphere, assuming that their mixture could endanger serene family lifestyles and is
thus profane (also Perrin 1977; Hayden 1981; Frug 1996). Examples of how these
ideals came together in the urban visions and landscape laws proposed by early
Americans abound (I will discuss some of them in chapter 5). Here is just one,
from William Penn, the founder of Philadelphia. In 1681, Penn, the leading real-
estate magnate of his time, a man who owned more land in seventeenth-century
America than any other nonroyal, saw the future of America's towns as nothing
similar to what existed in Europe: "Let every house be placed . . . in the middle
of its plat, as to the breadthway of it, so that there may be ground on each side
for gardens or orchards, or fields, that it may be a greene country towne." Penn's
town for "country gentlemen" was to be made of neat geometric boxes filled with
a few public squares and many more orderly private residential lots filled with
freestanding individual homes, each separated from its neighbors by generous
chunks of lush greenery (quoted in Skaler and Keels 2008, 44).[15] Ignoring for a
moment the complexity of American urbanism that followed in the 300 years
thereafter, we could say that the principal elements of Penn's vision still stand.
From the viewpoint of foreigners, most contemporary American towns and cities (not just suburbs and exurbs) are country-like in their population density,
in the generosity of their open spaces (even if some of these spaces are taken by
un-country-like wide roads and parking lots), and in the extent to which they are
dominated by individual homes.

It is true, of course, that a certain generosity of urban space follows from
economic growth, from improving living standards (e.g., Mieszkowski and Mills
1993). Poverty and crowding are positively related. Any review of housing statistics from around the world will show that richer countries tend to have larger
average dwelling-sizes and that wealthier cities tend to have larger suburban
belts dominated by individual homes. As urban historian Robert Bruegmann
has argued, today the trend toward greater spatial consumption is "visible in
affluent cities worldwide" (2007, 10).[16] Yet the brief evidence presented above

suggests that we observe a notable difference in *extent*: settlement densities in the United States are significantly lower than those of almost all countries in the same economic bracket. America has exceeded historic and international precedent to build what may well be the lowest-density settlements *in the history of the world*. This American model of urbanism, of "greene" country towns (and town surroundings) made of single-family homes with neatly cut front lawns and barbeque patios in the backyard has become, especially since the prosperous post–World War II years, a powerful national identity builder, a potent symbol of U.S. exceptionalism, an integral part of the very idea of what America is (Beauregard 2006).

Federal Aid

No matter how uniquely powerful America's historic fascination with "greene" country towns may have been, it is unlikely that it could have been realized as it exists today, on a mass scale, solely as a result of market forces and cultural preferences. The massive industrialization of the nineteenth century and the shock urbanization that followed certainly did away with the pastoral visions of the likes of William Penn. Quaint towns were overrun by growth, green public spaces vanished, and the majority of the people that set foot in the swelling cities, whether they came from the American countryside or from other countries, landed in overcrowded tenements. Initially, the country-gentleman lifestyle could be restored to only a few members of the industrial class, who began to exit the city for greener suburban pastures in the mid-1800s (Warner 1962; Fishman 1987).

Making the "greene-towne" vision accessible to the American masses required government help. Some of this help came in the form of municipal regulations such as zoning laws that protected the "nice" residential areas from the intrusion of undesirable uses and people. More help came from the federal government beginning in the 1930s. At that time consensus emerged in federal circles that a particular housing tenure (homeownership) and a particular housing form (the detached single-family home) should be targets of concerted government effort (Archer 2005). As earlier noted, at the time, the United States was already a world leader in homeownership (the rate then was about 50 percent). But the goal of New Deal policy makers and their post–World War II successors was much more ambitious: to enable the large majority of the U.S. population to build equity and wealth through the ownership of single-family homes. The widely held belief was—and arguably continues to be—that homeownership, viewed as synonymous with *single-family* homeownership, is an inherent civic virtue; the ultimate realization of Americans' aspirations for privacy, property, and independence; and an integral component of the American model of democracy (Kelly 1993; McGinn 2008; Lucy 2010). America's leaders at the time virtually competed with each other to endorse the idea in the most powerful terms. For example, Herbert Hoover declared that "to own one's home is a physical expression of [American] individualism, enterprise, of independence, and of the freedom of spirit" (quoted in Archer 2005, 295); Franklin Delano Roosevelt proclaimed that "a nation of home owners, of people who own a real share in their own land, is unconquerable" (quoted in Kelly 1993, 171).[17] Recent presidents have continued this tradition. President George W. Bush, for example, spoke of his vision of an "ownership society." "We want everybody in America to own their own home," Bush said in 2002 (quoted in Lucy 2010, 24).[18]

Since the 1930s, the federal government has set in motion myriad policies promoting the single-family home (some scholars list them under the umbrella term "residential protectionism"; see Stern 2009). These policies have continued to exist in one form or another, and many newer ones have been adopted over time. In the paragraphs below, I will briefly summarize some of the key historic and contemporary federal policies that favor the building of low-density urban and suburban landscapes in general and of single-family homes in particular. Each of these policies certainly each deserves its own book (for an overview, see Knaap et al. 2001).

To begin with, the 1930s gave Americans the Federal Housing Administration (FHA) and the Home Owners' Loan Corporation, with the idea to provide federal mortgage insurance to prevent homeowners from defaulting and foreclosures. This was followed by the Federal National Mortgage Association (FNMA, or Fannie Mae), which established a secondary market for mortgages. These policies did not nominally favor certain settlement patterns or housing types. But since most land available for new housing construction was along the edges of cities, the de facto effect of these policies was to propel the growth of suburbs dominated by single-family dwellings. Post–World War II policies were even more aggressive. The Veterans Administration encouraged the buying of homes (primarily single-family ones) by insuring mortgages for veterans that had minimal down payments. Equally important was the Federal Highway Act of 1962, which resulted in the construction of the largest infrastructure project in world's history—the U.S. highway system. Like the housing policies, the act was not thought of as a policy that would favor suburban over urban areas, but it did just that by enabling the movement of large middle-class populations toward low-density suburban areas where single-family dwellings could be built with much greater ease. The residential movement was promptly followed by industries and services. Along with other federal transport policies (e.g., a low gas tax),[19] the act ensured the supremacy of the car over mass transit, thus encouraging low-density settlements via other means. Another key policy has been the homeowner mortgage deduction program (Green 1999), which allows the deduction of interest on homeowners' mortgages on federal tax returns. No equivalent tax break exists for renters.[20] American tax policy is important in another way: as everyone knows, the United States has no federal consumption tax, and the bulk of individual taxation falls on income. It can be argued that a consumption tax, like the VAT (the value-added tax that exists in the European countries) would penalize the purchase of large durables such as single-family homes on large lots filled with large consumer goods. But the U.S. tax system tends to have the opposite effect by encouraging large-scale consumption. And, unlike most European governments today, the U.S. federal government does not penalize "anti-environmental" consumer choices (e.g., buying gas-guzzlers) with high taxes; this amounts to another federal incentive to produce low-density environments. Jointly, these policies have not led toward higher homeownership rates than those in Europe. But they may well have contributed to creating the sprawling pattern that generally distinguishes U.S. settlements from their European counterparts (e.g., see Nivola 1999).[21]

Doubtless, the Great Recession challenged the U.S. model of perpetual urban expansion. There was evidence that whether for economic or for cultural reasons, Americans were becoming more interested in living in denser, more mixed urban settings even before the onset of the recession, in the 1990s and early 2000s (e.g., Levine 2006). Since the recession, however, preferences have continued to evolve further in favor of denser living (Nelson 2012). Patterns of development have also notably changed: many existing low-density suburbs are in trouble and the growth of exurbs has significantly slowed down (Yen 2012).[22] Recent studies suggest that although most Americans (80 percent, according to a 2010 survey by the National Association of Realtors) prefer to live in detached single-family homes, nearly half would like these homes to be located closer to transit, jobs, and services. Still, according to the same survey, the privacy afforded by the single-family home remains the quality most sought after by prospective homebuyers (Reed 2011).[23] Americans continue to be suspicious of European-like urban densities (Talen 2009a), and according to a recent *New York Times* poll, 90 percent still view private homeownership as an integral part of the American Dream (Streitfeld and Thee-Brenna 2011).

   In the next chapter, I focus on how municipal land-use policies in the form of zoning work in the United States and how they relate to some of the ideas of space discussed above, especially the idea of low-density housing forms separated from other types of urbanization.

HOW THE SYSTEM WORKS

Most stories are told chronologically. As I said in the Introduction, this one I will be telling backward. First, in this and the next chapter, I will define the basic terminology related to land use and advance my primary empirical claim: that contrary to implicit conventional assumptions of the normalcy of the U.S. zoning model, it is quite distinct from the models used in the rest of the West. This U.S. distinction is the empirical puzzle that later chapters try to explain by examining the adaptation of the original zoning idea, which was first applied in Europe and inspired U.S. reformers of the early 1990s, to fit American conditions. This structure of the argument—first empirical claim, then historical or theoretical explanation—justifies the otherwise counterintuitive chronological arrangement of the book.

To begin though, let us first establish a baseline by identifying the principal tenets of the traditional land-use control system in the United States. The following questions will also be addressed: Why is the traditional system attracting so much criticism lately? And if this criticism is justified, what contemporary alternatives have emerged? Finally, what is the current state of affairs of the American system: Has the traditional land-use-based zoning approach been substantially modified or do its basic principles persist?

What Zoning Is and How It Works

In the United States, zoning is the "the mother lode of city rules" (Talen 2012a, 3). It is used almost universally across American cities, towns, suburbs, and villages.

As mentioned earlier, zoning is a law adopted by a local government that separates the land in a particular locale into sections, or zones, with different rules governing the activities on that land (Pendall, Puentes, and Martin 2006, 2–3; Levy 2006, 121).[1] In each zoning district, the rules address three main aspects of land and buildings (Kayden 2004, 2):[2] their use (function) or the activities that occur within them (typically categorized as residential, commercial, industrial, etc.), their shape (their two- or three-dimensional configuration on land or in the air; for example, building height), and their bulk (the amount of building that can be placed on a unit of land). Common techniques include defining a ratio of built to open space, or floor-to-area ratio (FAR[3]), defining the maximum number of buildings that could be built on a land unit, and defining the minimum size of the land unit on which a building could be placed.[4] Although all these techniques exert powerful influence on the built environment, it is the first aspect of traditional U.S. zoning regulation—land use or function—that forms its "structural core" (Kwartler 1989, 195). The surest thing that would doom a development application in front of a planning commission would be failure to comply with the list of permitted uses in the pertinent land-use district. It is debatable whether human activities on the land should inevitably be classified into the popular land-use categories of residential, commercial, industrial, and so forth (as we will see later, they are a product of the nineteenth-century imagination). But the fact remains that these categories are the standard fare of zoning, and they are often presented as part of its definition. For example, according to Kelly and Becker (2000, 203–204), zoning is a system of local regulations that defines "districts by uses and intensities," where the "basic use categories" are "agricultural, residential, commercial (or business), industrial (or manufacturing)." Such contemporary definitions are almost identical to definitions written seventy years ago:

> Zoning is the division of a city or town by authority of law into districts, in each of which there is prohibited the use of the land for any purpose, which though harmless in itself, impairs the public welfare by interfering with the devotion of the district to the use for which it is best adapted. Zoning usually also includes restrictions upon the size of lots, the height and bulk of buildings, and density with which land may be occupied, which differ in the different districts, so as to be appropriate to the uses permitted in each district. . . . The use of districts almost invariably established by zoning are: respectively, residential, business or commercial, industrial or manufacturing. (Nichols 1943, 143)

Today, municipal zoning of the type described above may seem routine and commonsensical, but at the beginning of the twentieth century, many American lawyers, politicians, and citizens questioned both its wisdom and its legality. The controversy, which I discuss in greater depth in the historical chapters, was grounded in the fact that zoning is an exercise of *public* control over the *private* sector. Under zoning doctrine, if private-sector losses result from the regulatory restrictions, as they inevitably do on many occasions, the government enforcing the zoning law is not necessarily obliged to provide compensation to the private party. Yet as most U.S. citizens surely know, the U.S. Constitution constrains the government's ability to take over private property without due process and compensation. (And the decrease of private property value from regulation *could* fit under the umbrella of a government takeover.) The Fourth Amendment states in part that "the right of the people to be secure in their persons, houses, papers, and effects, against unreasonable searches and seizures, shall not be violated"; the Fifth Amendment states in part that "nor [shall any person] be deprived of life, liberty, or property, without due process of law; nor shall private property be taken for public use, without just compensation"; the Fourteenth Amendment states in part that "nor shall any state deprive any person of life, liberty, or property, without due process of law." Applying zoning (or other) regulations that tie the hands of private property owners could be construed as a "regulatory taking,"[5] and the story of land-use debates in the United States has been very much the story of what the courts have said about these takings—more so than in any other nation.

This is exactly where the case for U.S. exceptionalism in land-use control begins. Most other western countries lack strong "taking" clauses in their constitutions. Private property is protected in all democratic nations, and the core legal documents in those nations do contain language restricting government takeovers (for an excellent in-depth comparative analysis, see Alterman 2010). International conventions also protect private property: for example, the 1948 UN Universal Declaration of Human Rights states, among other things, that "no one shall be arbitrarily deprived of his property." Some scholars claim that many western countries have recently moved to strengthen the protection of private property rights by changing or reinterpreting their core legal texts (Jacobs 2006, 2009). Still, some obvious differences with the U.S. case remain. Take, for example, the German Constitution. Article 14 (1) states that "property and the right of inheritance shall be guaranteed. Their content and limits shall be defined by the laws." This is immediately followed in Article 14 (2) by the statement "Property entails obligations. Its use shall also serve the public good," suggestive language that is absent from the U.S. Constitution.[6] The difference likely underpins in part, the greater role the German government at all levels plays in shaping urban environments and constraining urban sprawl (see Schmidt and Buehler 2007). The Dutch constitution guards against expropriation without full compensation but lacks explicit language that protects private property from being taken by regulation. The Dutch government, again at all levels, has tools for guiding urban development that far exceed what would be politically or legally acceptable in the United States (e.g., preemptive buyouts of farmland on the outskirts of urban areas at relatively low values in anticipation of future growth, thus limiting the ability of private parties to make a profit by converting rural land to urban uses; see Lefcoe 1979;

Thornley and Newman 1996; Alterman 1997; van der Krabben and Jacobs 2013). England, of course, has no written single constitutional document. English planning doctrine stipulates no direct legal right to compensation for financial loss caused by the particular designation of land in a development plan (Purdue 2006)—the type of financial loss that could lead to a charge of regulatory taking in the United States. In fact, English doctrine prevents local authorities from considering loss of private property value when making decisions. Planning Policy Guidance 1 states this:

> The planning system does not exist to protect the private interests of one person against the activities of another, although private interests may coincide with the public interest in some cases. It can be difficult to distinguish between public and private interests, but this may be necessary on occasion. The basic question is not whether owners and occupiers of neighbouring properties would experience financial or other loss from a particular development, but whether the proposal would unacceptably affect amenities and the existing use of land and buildings which ought to be protected in the public interest. (Office of the Deputy Prime Minister 1997)

In the United States, land-use control through zoning became legally sanctioned by the Supreme Court in the famous case of *Euclid v. Ambler* in 1926 (see Schulz 1989, 59–86; and Wolf 2008 for an excellent account of this case and Haar and Kayden 1989 for an analysis of its twentieth-century legacy). In this case, a private developer, the Ambler Realty Company, wished to develop industry in the Town of Euclid, a suburb of Cleveland, Ohio. The company claimed that the value of its property was diminished because the town had zoned parts of Ambler's 68-acre lot for single-family homes only. The court ruled in favor of the town. *Euclid v. Ambler* has been so important that zoning took its name from the case: for decades the traditional practice has been known as Euclidean zoning.[7] Since that time, municipal land-use control through zoning has been considered a legitimate exercise of the police powers of government. Municipalities are granted the power to regulate the use of their land by enabling state acts.[8] Municipal powers vary, however, depending on the state charter. In the so-called home rule states, local governments can typically invent zoning (and other) tools as they see fit, whereas in states operating under the doctrine of Dillon's rule,[9] local governments need explicit state authorization (typically by the state enabling acts) for the specific zoning (or other) techniques they use (Kayden 2004, 3).[10] Either way, zoning in the United States is not embedded in national legislation—another aspect of U.S. exceptionalism in land-use law. Unlike European national governments, the U.S. government has generally remained silent on matters of urban land-use control. Only one model act on zoning has been authored by a federal body. This is the Standard State Zoning Enabling Act (U.S. Department of Commerce, Advisory Committee on Zoning 1926),[11] which encouraged states to pass their own enabling acts granting zoning power to locales. The act dealt mostly with procedural matters, but it arguably helped shape discourses on the basic zoning taxonomy by mentioning that in addition to regulating things such as "height, number of stories, and size of buildings and other structures, the percentage of lot that may be occupied," zoning can designate land for "trade, industry, residence or other purpose." It also hinted, in a footnote, at the desirability of "one-family residence districts" (4–5). The act paved the way for the basic police-power justifications of zoning by dressing them in the language of "health, safety, morals, or the general welfare of the community." This language can be found on the first pages of many current ordinances in the country. Still, the act had no authority over what states and locales would do. To this day, there is no federal law on urban land use.[12] Zoning thus remains primarily a local matter (Fischel 2010).[13]

As we will see in detail in chapter 4, urban codes including rules that restrict the right of private parties to build a certain way have existed throughout the history of human civilization (Ben-Joseph 2005; Talen 2009b; Marshall 2011). In the United States, a number of large cities such as Boston and New York passed regulations that restricted bulk and shape well before the twentieth century (as we shall see in chapter 5). In an early experiment with land-use separation, some cities and even some states banned specific noxious industries from certain locations (Talen 2009b, 2012a). Private neighborhood rules in the form of neighborhood deed restrictions preceded municipal zoning as well (Garvin 2002).[14] But the way zoning distinguished itself from these other means of controlling the urban fabric was through greatly expanding the extent and scope of municipal control. Furthermore, zoning took an unprecedented interest in regulating the perceived *nature* of human activities on land and in buildings. It introduced a system of land-use categorization under which the activities were placed into the now-conventional land-use (or functional) classes (residential, commercial, industrial, etc.), which was followed by a system of land-use separation (i.e., placing these classes in different parts of town).

The land-use taxonomy system grew much more complex over time, and the number of land-use-based districts greatly proliferated (see Elliott 2008; Talen 2012a). The first comprehensive citywide zoning ordinance in the country, New York City's 1916 ordinance, introduced only three basic land-use categories: residential, business, and unrestricted (the latter encompassed most industries; see Willis 1993). But by the mid-twentieth century, the categories had grown much more intricate. First, the residential category was split into a few basic subtypes: single-family, two-family, and multifamily. The single-family district, which was initially absent in New York because of concerns about its constitutionality, became ubiquitous nationwide. By the late 1920s, it covered nearly 50 percent of land in the typical U.S. city (Bartholomew 1928, 1932)[15] and much larger portions in suburbs. Protecting this district from other uses was often presented by lawyers and scholars as the very purpose of zoning, as in this example:

> The design of our zoning laws has been to restrict the use of certain property, and thus to guarantee to the homeowner that the area in which his home is located shall not be subjected to uses which might have a tendency to destroy the area for home purposes. (Pollard 1931, 15)

In addition, the single-family and the multifamily housing categories were split into multiple subtypes (e.g., single-family homes on various lot sizes and with various numbers of maximum units per lot, two-family homes, multifamily homes of various sizes and maximum number of units per lot).[16] Likewise, subcategorization was applied to the commercial and industrial land-use classes. Add to this the various new types of districts that have become part of the land-use lexicon over time: public districts, institutional districts, agricultural districts, open space districts, historic districts, parking districts (not to be confused with park districts), downtown districts, special-purpose districts, planned unit development districts (more on these later), university districts, urban design districts, public utility districts, and so forth. Eventually, the zoning system created urban and suburban worlds in which everything was not only in its place but was also in its own *separate* place (Perrin 1977; Boyer 1983), as the ordinances began to commonly allow only one land-use class per zoning district to the exclusion of all the others. Tables 2.1 and 2.2 provide two current examples of the intricate land-use taxonomy used in American cities today: one from Jacksonville, Florida, and one from Fort Worth, Texas.

Of course, not all land-use-based districts exclude all else. For example, in the original New York ordinance, as I will discuss in greater depth in the historical chapters, only the residential districts placed restrictions on where other (nonresidential) structures could be located. Business districts allowed residences alongside commerce, and the unrestricted districts permitted more or less all uses. This approach is often referred to as hierarchical zoning. The concept is based on an imaginary pyramid consisting of three basic land-use classes: residential, commercial, and industrial (hence the other commonly used term: pyramidal zoning). Residential, which in the American tradition is deemed the least intense but the most "delicate" land use, occupies the top of the pyramid, and industrial is located at the bottom. Land uses located higher in the pyramid are permissible in areas designated for lower uses, but not vice versa.[17] In other words, under the hierarchical principle, just as in New York in 1916 and in the 1926 Euclid system, an owner can build homes in commercial and industrial areas and commercial facilities in industrial areas. But industrial facilities were banned in residential

TABLE 2.1 Land-use districts in Jacksonville, Florida

LAND-USE NOTATION	LAND-USE DISTRICT	LAND-USE SUB-DISTRICT
RR-Acre	Residential	Rural
RLD-120	Residential	Low density
RLD-100A	Residential	Low density
RLD-100B	Residential	Low density
RLD-90	Residential	Low density
RLD-80	Residential	Low density
RLD-70	Residential	Low density
RLD-60	Residential	Low density
RLD-50	Residential	Low density
RLD-TND	Residential	Low density
RLD-TNH	Residential	Low density
RMD-A	Residential	Medium density
RMD-B	Residential	Medium density
RMD-C	Residential	Medium density
RMD-D	Residential	Medium density
RMD-MH	Residential	Medium density
RHD-A	Residential	High density
RHD-B	Residential	High density
CO	Commercial	Office
CRO	Commercial	Residential office
CN	Commercial	Neighborhood
CCG-1	Commercial	Community/general
CCG-2	Commercial	Community/general
CCBD	Commercial	Central business district
IBP	Industrial	Business park
IL	Industrial	Light
IH	Industrial	Heavy
IW	Industrial	Water related
AGR	Agriculture	
PBF-1	Public buildings and facilities	Governmental use
PBF-2	Public buildings and facilities	Public and private
CSV	Conservation	
ROS	Recreation/open space	
PUD	Planned unit development	
PUD-SC	Planned unit development—satellite development	

Source: City of Jacksonville (2011).

TABLE 2.2 Land-use districts in Fort Worth, Texas

A. Special Purpose Districts
1. Agricultural district (AG)
2. Community facilities district (CF)
3. Historic preservation overlay districts (HSE, HC, DD)
4. Planned development district (PD)
5. Conservation district (CD)
6. Manufactured housing district (MH)
7. Design overlay district (DO)
8. Downtown urban design district (DUDD)

B. Residential Districts
1. One-family[a] district (A-2.5A)
2. One-family district (A-43)
3. One-family district (A-21)
4. One-family district (A-10)
5. One-family district (A-7.5)
6. One-family district (A-5)
7. One-family restricted district (AR)
8. Two-family district (B)
9. Zero lot line/cluster district (R1)
10. Townhouse/cluster district (R2)
11. Low-density multifamily district (CR)
12. Medium-density multifamily district (C)
13. High-density multifamily district (D)
14. Urban residential district (UR)

C. Commercial Districts
1. Neighborhood commercial restricted district (ER)
2. Neighborhood commercial district (E)
3. Low-intensity mixed-use district (MU-1)
4. Low-intensity greenfield mixed-use district (MU-1G)
5. General commercial restricted district (FR)
6. General commercial district (F)
7. Intensive commercial district (G)
8. Central business district (H)
9. Trinity uptown district (TU)
10. Near Southside district (NS)

D. Industrial Districts
1. Light industrial district (LI)
2. High-intensity mixed-use district (MU-2)
3. High-intensity greenfield mixed-use district (MU-2G)
4. Medium industrial district (J)
5. Heavy industrial district (K)

Sources: City of Fort Worth (2011).

[a]The notation used for the residential districts is sometimes confusing. In Fort Worth's case, the A-2.5 notation refers to a one-family district in which the minimum required lot size is 2.5 acres. A-43 means a minimum lot size requirement of one acre (43,560 square feet), etc.

and business areas, and residential areas were destined only for housing. This means that, unlike the residential districts, the business and industrial districts permit a variety of uses (figure 2.1 illustrates the hierarchical method).

During the mid-twentieth century, however, the zoning system was substantially modified, especially in suburban areas. The hierarchical principle was rejected, and flat zoning ordinances became much more common. In these ordinances, each land-use class became exclusive; that is, residential uses in commercial or industrial districts were banned (figure 2.2 illustrates the flat principle).

This approach made the co-location of various activities in American munici-palities increasingly difficult. The issue was further compounded by the fact that individual zones became much larger (Gerckens n.d.; Elliott 2008; Talen 2012a). In fact, initially, even if the land-use districts were mutually exclusive (e.g., even if housing could not be built in commercial areas and businesses could not be built in housing areas), the districts were small enough that people could easily access whatever they needed by simply walking from one city block to another

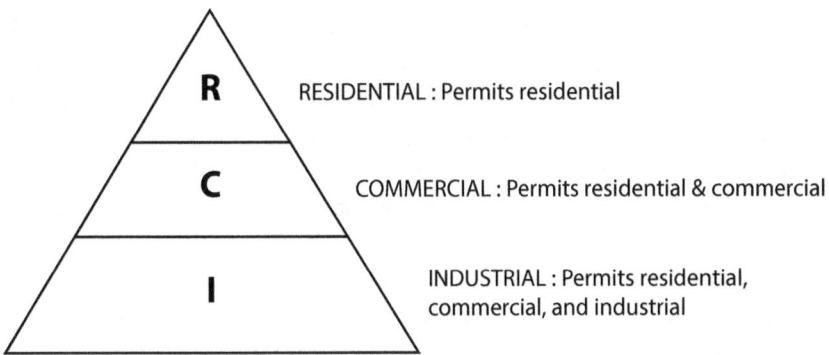

FIGURE 2.1 Hierarchical zoning.
Source: Prepared by Shraddha Nadkarni.

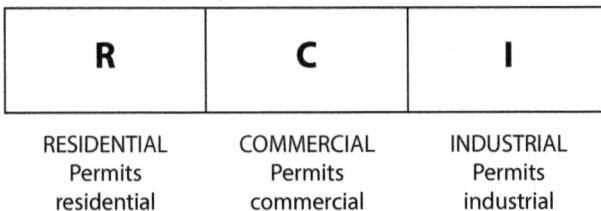

FIGURE 2.2 "Flat" zoning.
Source: Prepared by Shraddha Nadkarni.

(Talen 2012b). But during the mid-twentieth century, in response to Americans' growing reliance on the automobile as their chief means of transportation, the zoning districts became larger and more distant from each other. Also, shape and bulk standards in residential areas were increased to the point that in some districts whole classes of people could not afford to construct large enough homes on large enough lots ; these classes of people were "zoned out" (Levine 2006). This gave rise to the term "exclusionary zoning" (see Davidoff and Brooks 1976), and today, fairly or not, this term is often used interchangeably with the term Euclidean zoning. Much of the contemporary debates on zoning center on the extent to which the exclusionary and segregationist elements of the system have been softened; some authors foresee the "twilight" of traditional zoning (e.g., Ohm and Sitkowski 2003) and others argue that tradition persists (e.g., Levine 2006; Hall 2007).

A zoning ordinance has two basic components: text and map. The rules pertaining to each zone can be properly applied only if the precise areas they cover are clear. The areas are spatially articulated and are usually color-coded on a map. Since zoning districts have multiplied over the course of a century, zoning maps are often wonderfully vibrant creations showing dozens of shades of yellow, green, orange, brown, blue, gray, green, and whatever other hues the human eye can grasp and distinguish in intricate gradations.[18] In a powerful exercise of Euclidean spatial mastery, these maps represent cities as two-dimensional planes composed of geometric boxes, each distinguishable from its neighbors by a specific set of attributes related to use, shape, and bulk. The fact that zoning maps are excellent examples of Euclidian geometric maneuvering and that U.S. zoning is called Euclidean is a pure coincidence. Yet one could hardly wish for a historic accident that would produce a name that more accurately reflects the way zoning principles are articulated on a map. Take, for example, the map of Fort Worth, Texas, in figure 2.3, which spatially defines the city's thirty-seven land-use zoning districts.

Each of the districts shown on a zoning map typically allows land uses under three banners: permitted (principal) uses, accessory (secondary) uses, and conditional uses (special, limited uses or those that are permissible by exception). Permitted uses are those that are considered primary or integral to the basic purpose of a zoning district (e.g., single-family residences in a single-family district). Accessory uses are those that are considered to be closely associated with the principal uses; they could not exist without them (e.g., a garage by a single-family home in a single-family district). Conditional uses include activities that may be beneficial to a district but may also create conflicts and thus are listed separately in the ordinance for potential approval at the discretion of

Fort Worth Zoning 10-31-2011

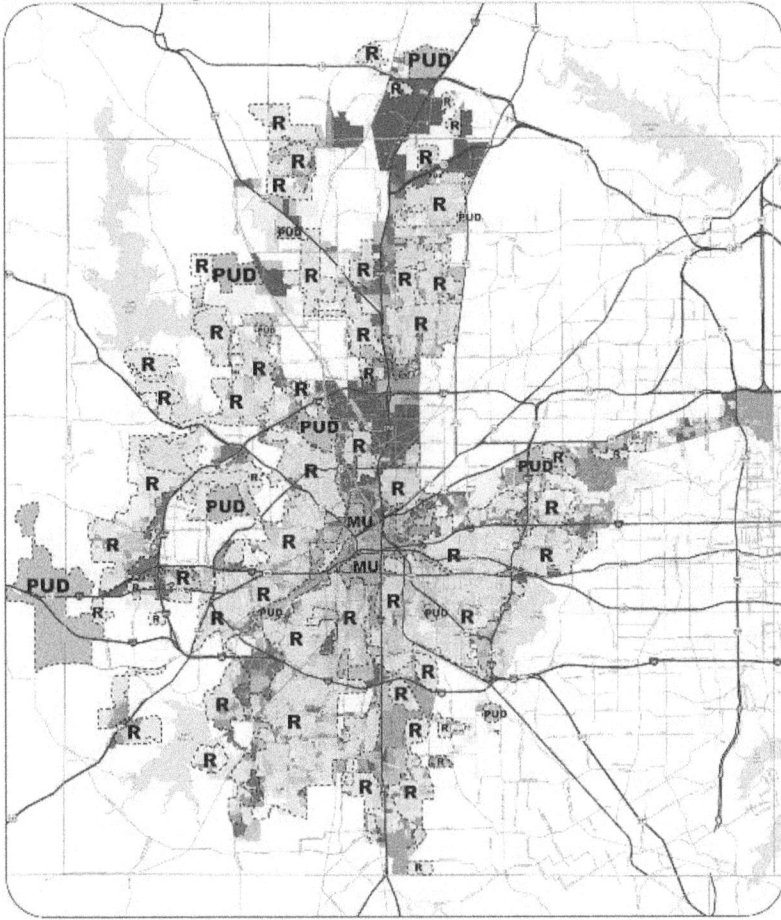

FIGURE 2.3 Zoning map of Fort Worth, Texas. Courtesy of the City of Fort Worth, with additional notation by the author: R designates residential districts, MU designates mixed-use districts, and PUD designates planned unit development districts.

authorities, often under certain conditions (e.g., day-care centers in residential districts).[19] Table 2.3 shows what is permitted today in the medium-density multifamily districts of Jacksonville, Florida: the principal land uses are dwellings, parks, cultural and religious buildings, and certain home-based occupations[20]; the conditional uses are facilities that sell basic convenience goods but *only* to the residents of the multifamily structures; and the uses permitted by

TABLE 2.3 Permitted uses in medium-density residential districts in Jacksonville, Florida

(a) *Permitted uses and structures*

    (1) Single-family dwellings

    (2) Multiple-family dwellings (RMD-B, RMD-C, and RMD-D districts only)

    (3) Townhomes, subject to Section 656.414

    (4) Housing for the elderly

    (5) Family day care homes meeting the performance standards and development criteria set forth in Part 4

    (6) Foster care homes

    (7) Community residential homes of six or fewer residents meeting the performance standards and development criteria set forth in Part 4

    (8) Essential services, including water, sewer, gas, telephone, radio, television and electric, meeting the performance standards and development criteria set forth in Part 4

    (9) Churches, including a rectory or similar use, meeting the performance standards and development criteria set forth in Part 4

    (10) Golf courses meeting the performance standards and development criteria set forth in Part 4

    (11) Parks, playgrounds, and playfields or recreational or community structures meeting the performance standards and development criteria set forth in Part 4

    (12) Country clubs meeting the performance standards and development criteria set forth in Part 4

    (13) Home occupations meeting the performance standards and development criteria set forth in Part 4

(b) *Permitted accessory uses and structures*

    (1) See Section 656.403

    (2) In connection with multiple-family dwellings, including housing for the elderly, coin-operated laundries and other vending machine facilities, day care centers, establishments for sale of convenience goods, personal and professional service establishments; provided, however, that these establishments shall be designed and scaled to meet only the requirements of the occupants of these multiple-family dwellings or housing for the elderly and their guests with no signs or other external evidence of the existence of these establishments.

    (3) In connection with housing for the elderly, in projects with a minimum of 150 bedrooms, facilities for the sale of alcoholic beverages to occupants and their guests in accordance with (i) a Special Restaurant Exception beverage license issued pursuant to F.S. Ch. 561, as may be amended from time to time, and (ii) Part 8 of the City's Zoning Code; provided, that there are no signs or other external evidence of the existence of these facilities.

(c) *Permissible uses by exception*

    (1) Cemeteries and mausoleums but not funeral home or mortuaries

    (2) Schools meeting the performance standards and development criteria set forth in the Part 4

(3)   Borrow pits subject to the regulations contained in Part 9

(4)   Bed and breakfast establishments meeting the performance standards and development criteria set forth in Part 4

(5)   Essential services, including water, sewer, gas, telephone, radio, television and electric, meeting the performance standards and development criteria set forth in Part 4

(6)   Day care centers meeting the performance standards and development criteria set forth in Part 4

(7)   Nursing homes

(8)   Residential treatment facilities

(9)   Private clubs

(10)   Commercial neighborhood retail sales and service or professional office structurally integrated with a multi-family use, not exceeding 25% of the structure which it is a part

(11)   Churches, including a rectory or similar use, meeting the performance standards and development criteria set forth in Part 4

(12)   Home occupations meeting the performance standards and development criteria set forth in Part 4

(13)   Emergency shelter homes (RMD-C and RMD-D Districts only)

(14)   Community residential homes of seven to 14 residents meeting the performance standards and development criteria set forth in Part 4

(15)   Golf driving ranges

(16)   Boarding houses (RMD-D and RMD-E Districts only).

(17)   Group care homes (RMD-B, RMD-C, RMD-D and RMDE Districts)

Source: City of Jacksonville (2011).

Key: RMD-A: Residential medium density-A; RMD-B: Residential medium density-B; RMD-C: Residential medium density-C; RMD-D: Residential medium density-D; and RMD-E: Residential medium density-E.

exception include civic facilities such as schools and "soft" commercial uses such as day-care centers and bed and breakfasts.

No matter how good a zoning code is, it must be modified on occasion to respond to particular circumstances. The basic tools for changing a parcel's zoning designation are variances, amendments, and rezoning (these are often collectively referred to as zoning relief).[21] The first, variances, refers to granting exceptions administratively in cases of hardship affecting an individual property owner (e.g., when he or she has an irregularly shaped lot); these usually relate to bulk and shape rather than land use. Amendments involve legal change: modifying the text of the ordinance (e.g., expanding or restricting the list of permitted uses for all single-family districts). Rezonings are also changes in the law: they involve modifying the zoning map (e.g., changing the zoning designation of a particular lot without changing the textual regulations linked to any of the zoning districts). Unlike amendments, rezonings may be applied to individual parcels and can thus be regarded as unfairly privileging one property owner over another. Thus, they have not been viewed favorably by courts and may be referred to as "spot zoning"—a term with negative undertones. Either way, zoning exceptions are typically given under a relatively narrow set of circumstances and heavy public scrutiny. The list of land uses permitted or prohibited in most zoning districts is meant to be explicit and exhaustive. Rules are strict and allow "as-of-right development": if a private party follows them, his or her ability to build on the private land is, in theory, guaranteed.

The Critique of Traditional Zoning

Traditional zoning as described above has been under fire since the 1950s. Calls for its demise date back at least to the 1960s (Jacobs 1961; Reps 1964). Since then, several broad streams of critique have emerged: libertarian, economic, social, environmental, and aesthetic. Some of the arguments are part of a broader critique of all government policies that contribute to sprawling U.S. landscapes, which I outlined in chapter 1. Other critical arguments pertain specifically to zoning.

To begin with, critics argue that zoning of any type works against the free market. The sway of this argument, embedded in the long-standing U.S. tradition of political individualism and liberty from heavy-handed government intervention, threatened to prevent the very adoption of zoning in the United States and has maintained a strong presence in libertarian circles (see Ellickson 1973). Fedako (2006) recently put this succinctly: "Zoning is theft!"—the theft of individual property rights and freedoms by poorly informed government bureaucrats with questionable social goals, who introduce inefficiencies into the land-market system. On both libertarian and social grounds, standard zoning has been blamed for favoring built forms that are lower-density and are more segregated than those the market would otherwise produce:

> Although the private market may well have sprawling tendencies of its own, it is capable of producing alternatives but is impeded by municipal regulations that lower development densities, separate land uses, specify wide roadways and mandate large parking areas. (Levine 2006, 3)
>
> The evidence is clear that most suburbs are zoned for minimum lot sizes greatly in excess of what the market would generate. . . . It is theoretically possible for communities to become stratified without zoning, but the conditions for doing so seem unlikely. . . . Even under "ideal" conditions for spontaneous income segregation, at least a weak form of

zoning for minimum lot size was necessary to obtain such stratification. (Fischel 1999, 156–157)

According to this line of thought, the discrepancy between conventional zoning and markets grows perpetually because the low-density mandates, which are established when an area is first developed, persist even though the area may be becoming increasingly more attractive to a greater number and variety of residents and builders. (This is the typical process of urban growth, or what would occur if no low-density regulations existed.) This discrepancy is said to be especially pertinent today, when consumers and the building industry are progressively warming up to alternative, more compact, and mixed-use forms of development (Levine 2006; Nelson 2012). Furthermore, this argument goes, the lower-density patterns mandated by traditional zoning inflate housing prices (see Glaeser and Gyorko 2002) and require perpetual extensions of infrastructure, the massive costs of which are passed on to the taxpayers. The critics point out that the potential economic benefits of zoning (e.g., fuller community coffers due to the expected increases in property values) hardly outweigh the costs associated with infrastructure waste, longer commutes, and so forth.

The social arguments against zoning have likely been the most scathing. The classic point here is that by categorizing and separating housing types, by establishing large residential districts that permit only large homes on large lots, zoning segregates people by class and by race; it acts as a gatekeeper that favors insiders (those who already have property in a given place) over outsiders (those who wish to acquire property in this place but cannot). Zoning in this sense serves as a local "immigration law" that protects the rich from the poor (see Davidoff and Brooks 1976; Downs 1973; Haar and Kayden 1989; Choppin 1996; Frug 1996; and Silver 1997). Following decisions of their supreme courts, states such as New Jersey and Pennsylvania have addressed the problem by requiring their locales to zone for low- and moderate-income housing ("inclusionary zoning"; see Haar 1996 and Calavita 1998).But it is unclear to what extent this has eliminated the overarching exclusionary effect of the zoning system. While the traditional anti-exclusionary argument targets class- and race-based residential segregation, it can be extended to include issues of age and gender (e.g., Pollak 1994). For example, much like the poor, the very young and the elderly have limited access to automobiles. By contributing to sprawl and land-use separation, zoning restricts their access to services. Also, since women continue to prefer to travel shorter distances to work than men (Crane 2007) and continue to spend more time and effort in child-rearing and other household-related activities, separating them from the employment and service centers through traditional zoning mechanisms affects them more negatively than it does men (Micklow 2008). In broader social terms, standard zoning has been blamed for limiting possibilities of social interaction—an argument dating back to Jacobs (1961) and Sennett (1970), which has been considerably expanded in recent years by prominent New Urbanists such as Peter Calthorpe (1993), Andre Duany and Elizabeth Plater-Zyberk (et al. 2000).

The main environmental argument has been that by promoting low-density patterns, zoning brings about excessive land consumption, thus harming natural habitats. Furthermore, by shielding housing from all else, it implicitly mandates car travel, thus contributing to pollution. In addition, it may have a negative impact on public health (e.g., by fostering a car-dependent lifestyle and contributing to obesity; see American Public Health Association 2010).

Finally, zoning has been strongly criticized on aesthetic grounds for encouraging cookie-cutter environments and for reducing the complexity of urbanism (Kunstler 1996). The complexity problem was perhaps most succinctly, if sarcastically, summed up by architect Leon Krier (1988): What if we all tried "zoning" our diet by eating vegetables on Monday, potatoes on Tuesday, fats on Wednesday, liquids on Thursday, etc.? Krier's answer, just like Jacobs's several decades ago (1961), is self-evident: reducing a complex organization (in this case, the city) to simple parts (in this case, by using simple physical attributes as a basis for taxonomy and division) suppresses the organization's core vitality, aesthetic and otherwise.

Not everyone agrees with these arguments. Cities would surely not end up better *without* some type of regulation (unregulated cities during the industrial revolution are an obvious example), and there are still legitimate reasons to separate some land uses (e.g., housing from polluting industries). Also, as long as U.S. consumers prefer lower-density and homogeneous environments they will surely get built, with or without government help (although without government help these environments would likely become denser and more varied over time).[22] Yet there is a nearly universal consensus among scholars that traditional U.S. zoning has severe shortcomings. Indeed, regulatory reform intended to promote compact and mixed-use cities and suburbs has become part of the urban planning mantra across North America (Grant 2002, 2005). Given this shift, what alternatives to standard zoning practice have emerged in the United States?

The Alternatives

Over several decades, the U.S. planning and legal professions have developed many modifications to the traditional zoning system. To begin with, the sheer scope of what municipalities can accomplish through zoning has expanded dramatically. Today, it is customary to regulate signs, landscaping, parking, aesthetic characteristics (especially of buildings in historic and other special areas) and many other aspects of built form in ways that the founders of zoning in the United States would probably have failed to see as advancing the health, safety, morals, or general welfare of the community. In addition, the rigidity of the original approach has been partially overcome by significantly strengthening the powers of municipal governments to exercise discretionary judgment (see Weaver and Babcock 1979, 257–278; Kayden 2004).[23]

Among the key inventions is incentive zoning, which was pioneered in the New York City in the early 1960s. This method grants density and other bonuses to developers in exchange for community improvements such as publically accessible open space, thus shifting the focus of zoning from the issuing of prescriptions and prohibitions to the offering of incentives (see Kayden 1986, 2000; Morris 2000). Another crucial innovation is inclusionary zoning, which, as mentioned earlier, was prompted by the decisions of some state supreme courts. In addition, zoning today can transfer "development rights" from one district to another (e.g., in order to concentrate development in chosen locations while preserving intact others that have unique historic or environmental features) and enable builders to purchase them.[24] It can be also used as a growth-control tool that links the issuance of development permits to impact fees or exactions that are calculated on the basis of the expected impact of a proposed project on the existing community.[25]

From this brief initial list, it is clear that many of these zoning reforms have aimed to soften the exclusionary impacts of traditional zoning, curtail sprawl, and reduce the rigidity of the system (i.e., to promote creative design as opposed to cookie-cutter projects such as houses on rectangular one-acre lots).[26] Some local reforms have required state-level enabling legislation (see Salkin 2003). The reforms broadly align with the agendas of the fashionable contemporary planning and design paradigms of Smart Growth and New Urbanism (Grant 2005). But they can also be dated to early critics of zoning such as Jacobs (1961), who especially opposed the separation of urban functions and forcefully advocated zoning for mixed uses. Jacobs's call has been translated into practice: in addition to regular residential, commercial, industrial, and other standard land-use districts, zoning ordinances today often include mixed-use districts, which allow the coexistence of more than one of the standard land-use classes, either by right or at least conditionally.[27]

Another common way that U.S. planners and lawyers have attempted to overcome the rigidity of traditional zoning is via Planned Unit Development (PUD) districts. PUDs are one of the oldest zoning inventions in the United States; they back to the post–World War II years (Burchell 1972). Instead of regulating development through lot- or district-specific standardized rules, the PUD process allows authorities to consider unified development plans for selected areas of town, where some rules are predetermined by the municipal law but others are negotiated by planners and developers.[28] A mixture of uses is commonly required in PUDs, even though it is possible for a PUD to allow just a single land-use class.

Whereas all of these methods are meant to modify traditional zoning, two inventions, performance zoning and form-based zoning, have the potential to serve as wholesale alternatives. Performance (or impact) zoning, an idea first championed in the United States by Lane Kendig (Kendig et al. 1980), entails abandoning regulations that employ the traditional land-use categories (residential, commercial, etc.) and replacing them with regulations based on the expected environmental impact of a proposed project (e.g., noise, vibrations, traffic counts, emissions, impervious surface). From the viewpoint of performance zoning, whether a future building will be multifamily housing, a hotel, or a combination of office and retail is immaterial if its expected impact on its environs is the same (Marwedel 1998). However, performance zoning has been slow to take root, likely because of the complexities of preparing an impact study for each project.

Form-based zoning was first proposed in the 1990s. It has been championed by the New Urbanists (Congress for the New Urbanism 2001; Duany and Talen 2002; Parolek, Parolek, and Crawford 2008) and has attracted the greatest attention in recent years. Like performance zoning, it attempts to do away with traditional land-use categories. But unlike performance zoning, its method of operation is to replace them with categories that pertain to architectural character: the size, style, and shape of buildings and building landscapes.[29]

The empirical question, then, is whether these innovations have become routine practice. Half a century after John Reps's well-known "Requiem for Zoning," has the traditional system entered its twilight years, as some suggest (Ohm and Sitkowski 2003), or is there a "surprising mildness" in zoning reform, as others argue (Levine 2006; Hall 2007)? This is a difficult question to answer, because unlike land-use regulation in European countries (where, as the next chapter explains, there are national, unified land-use codes), zoning in the United States remains a local matter. No database fully covers the variety of municipal zoning regulations. Thus, studies that attempt to answer the question have been often limited to individual metropolitan regions (e.g., Hirt 2007b) or states (e.g., Talen and Knaap 2003). The bulk of attention has focused on the new form-based codes under the banner of New Urbanism. The websites of the Congress of New Urbanism, the Form-Based Institute, and Smart Code Central cite around 300 form-based codes across the country but note that there are nearly 40,000 U.S. locales. And closer scrutiny of the form-based codes shows that a great majority of them are optional and apply only in a piecemeal fashion either to greenfield sites or to small portions of town.[30] Perhaps the most comprehensive nationwide recent study that tried to assess the state of zoning reform was Pendall, Puendes, and Martin (2006). Its authors used a survey distributed among planners in more than 3,000 local jurisdictions that were selected to make a representative sample (about 1,800 jurisdictions responded). The study showed mixed results, pointing to some progress, especially in the area of inclusionary zoning in certain parts of the country. The study's reliance on the answers of local officials, however, presents some problems. Evaluating officials' responses may lead to different results from those reached by analyzing the actual zoning ordinances.[31] Also, the authors did not analyze the spatial distribution of districts. What if form-based or mixed-use districts exist but occupy only miniscule portions of town?

An Empirical Assessment of Zoning Reforms

In order to provide a partial answer to the question of whether traditional U.S. zoning has been reformed, I examine the texts and maps of the current zoning ordinances of twenty-five of the fifty largest cities in America in this section (table 2. 4 and figure 2.4 show these cities; see also Hirt 2013a).[32] My focus is on the extent to which the traditional method of separating land uses and shielding single-family housing from all else has been reformed. I searched specifically for signs of overhaul of the traditional system through the adoption of PUDs, mixed-use districts, and performance- and form-based zoning.

Table 2.5 summarizes the results. To begin with, it shows whether the zoning ordinances are hierarchical (that is, whether the commercial and industrial districts automatically permit a mixture of land uses since they permit residences; column 3). Additionally, it shows whether there is a hierarchy in the residential category (e.g., if single-family homes are allowed in the multifamily districts—a mechanism that permits at least the mixing of housing types; column 4). I also examined residential zones to determine whether they permit nonresidential uses such as retail establishments or offices (column 5). Column 6 notes the presence or absence of districts set up to permit mixture of uses, especially a residential-business mix. Column 7 shows whether there are PUDs permitting a residential-nonresidential mix. Columns 8 and 9 reveal whether the city has a performance or a form-based zoning code. The last few columns show the percentage of land designated under residential zoning (column 10), under low-density residential zoning (typically single-family and two-family detached) (column 11), and under zoning that permits a residential-business mix (column 12). However, only ten cities were able or willing to provide this spatial data.

TABLE 2.4 Largest 50 cities in the United States (25 selected cities shaded in gray)

CITIES	POPULATION	LAND AREA (MI.²)
New York, NY	8,175,133	303
Los Angeles, CA	3,792,621	469
Chicago, IL	2,695,598	228
Houston, TX	2,099,451	600
Philadelphia, PA	1,526,006	134
Phoenix, AZ	1,445,632	517
San Antonio, TX	1,327,407	461
San Diego, CA	1,307,402	325
Dallas, TX	1,197,816	341.
San Jose, CA	945,942	177
Jacksonville, FL	821,784	747
Indianapolis, IN	820,445	361
San Francisco, CA	805,235	47
Austin, TX	790,390	298
Columbus, OH	787,033	217
Fort Worth, TX	741,206	340
Charlotte, NC	731,424	298
Detroit, MI	713,777	139
El Paso, TX	649,121	255
Memphis, TN	646,889	315
Baltimore, MD	620,961	81
Boston, MA	617,594	48
Seattle, WA	608,660	84
Washington DC	601,723	61
Nashville-Davidson, TN	601,222	475
Denver, CO	600,158	153
Louisville-Jefferson County, KY	597,337	325
Milwaukee, WI	594,833	96
Portland, OR	583,776	133
Las Vegas, NV	583,756	136
Oklahoma City, OK	579,999	606
Albuquerque, NM	545,852	188
Tucson, AZ	520,116	227
Fresno, CA	494,665	112
Sacramento, CA	466,488	98
Long Beach, CA	462,257	50
Kansas City, KS	459,787	125
Mesa, AZ	439,041	136
Virginia Beach, VA	437,994	249
Atlanta, GA	420,003	133
Colorado Springs, CO	416,427	195
Omaha, NE	408,958	127
Raleigh, NC	403,892	143
Miami, FL	399,457	36
Cleveland, OH	396,815	78
Tulsa, OK	391,906	197
Oakland, CA	390,724	56
Minneapolis, MN	382,578	54
Wichita, KS	382,368	159
Arlington, TX	365,438	96.50

Sources: U.S. Census Bureau (2010a; b) and U.S. Census Bureau (2012b).

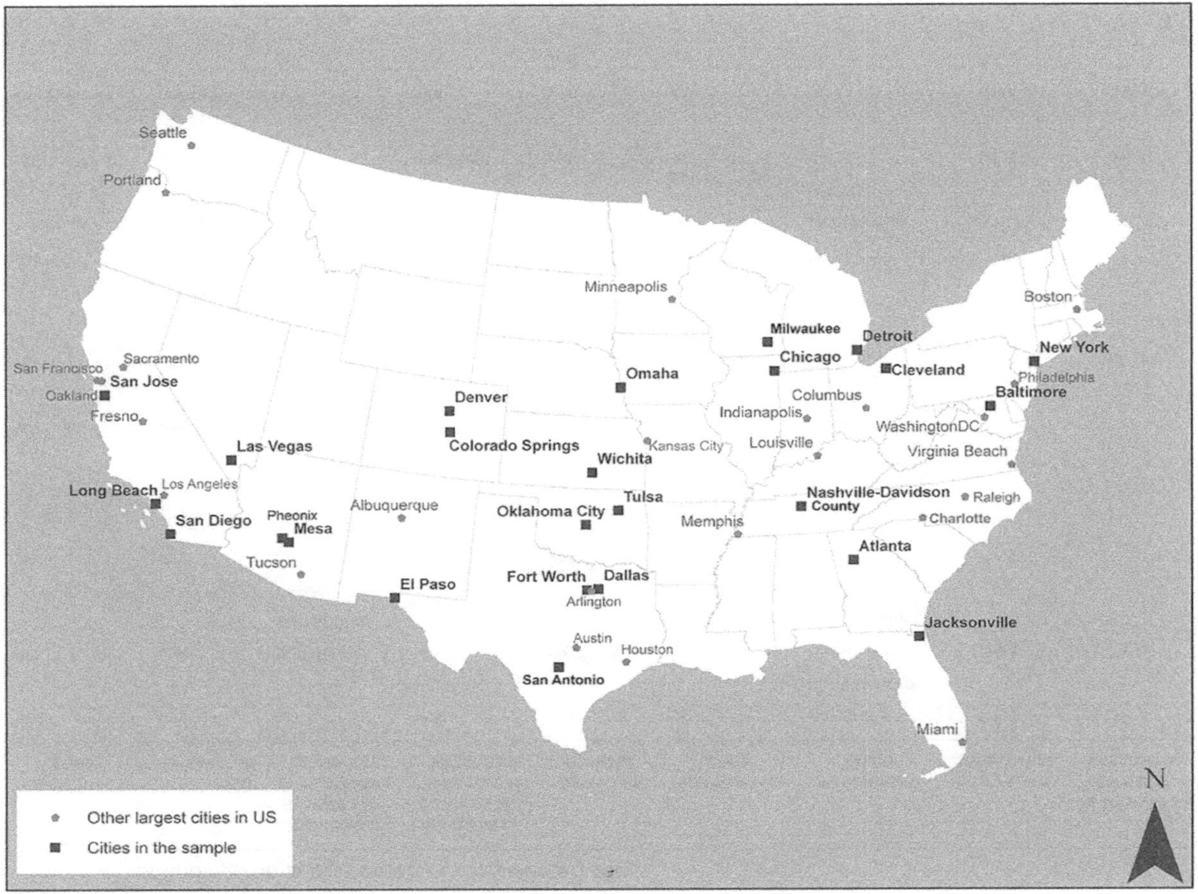

FIGURE 2.4 Select largest cities in the United States, for which zoning data was collected.

Source: Prepared by Cynthia Lintz.

TABLE 2.5 Summary of findings on zoning districts, 25 selected cities

CITY	HIERARCHICAL CODE?	RESIDENTIAL HIERARCHY?	RESIDENCE/BUSINESS MIX IN RESIDENTIAL DISTRICTS?	RESIDENCE/BUSINESS MIX IN MIXED-USE DISTRICTS?	MIXED USE IN PUDS?	PERFORMANCE CODE?	FORM-BASED CODE?	% TOTAL AREA RESIDENTIAL	% TOTAL AREA LOW-DENSITY RESIDENTIAL	% TOTAL AREA MIXED USE
Atlanta	yes	yes	no	yes	yes	no	no (under consideration)	53.2	38.7	0.30
Baltimore	no	yes	limited; conditional use	yes	yes	no	no (under consideration)	45.1	21.4	0.49
Chicago	no	yes	no	yes (with restrictions)	yes	no	no			
Cleveland	yes	yes	no	yes	yes (with restrictions)	no	no	36.8	33.1	2.00
Colorado Springs	partially	yes	no	yes	yes	no	yes (optional)			
Dallas	no	part ally	no	yes	yes	no	yes (partial, optional)	45.16	39.16	2.57
Denver	not applicable	part ally	no	yes	yes	no	yes			
Detroit	partially	yes	no	yes	yes	no	no			
El Paso	partially	part ally	no	yes	yes	no	yes (partial, optional)	31.25	31.23	
Fort Worth	no	yes	no	yes (with restrictions)	yes	no	no	52.64	45.7	2.22
Jacksonville	partially	part ally	no	yes	yes	no	no	38.63	33.63	0.05
Las Vegas	no	yes	no	yes	yes	no	no	38.3		

City									
Long Beach	no	yes	limited; conditional use	yes	yes	no	no			
Mesa	no	yes	limited; special use	yes	yes	no	no (under consideration)			
Milwaukee	partially	yes	limited; special use	yes	yes	no	no			
Nashville-Davidson	yes	yes	no	yes	yes (with restrictions)	no	no			
New York	yes	yes	some	yes	yes	no	no	39.5	27.3	3.00
Oklahoma	partially	yes	no	yes	yes	no	no			
Omaha	yes	yes	limited; conditional use	yes	yes	no	yes (partial)	57.36	55.41	1.26
Phoenix	partially	partially	no	yes (with restrictions)	yes	no	no (under consideration)			
San Antonio	partially	yes	limited	yes	yes	no	yes (optional)			
San Diego	partially	yes	limited	yes	yes	no	no			
San Jose	no	yes	no	yes	yes	no	no			
Tulsa	partially	yes	very limited; accessory use	yes	yes (with restrictions)	no	yes (partial)			
Wichita	yes	yes	very limited; conditional use	yes	yes	no	no			

Source: Zoning ordinances of the 25 cities listed in the table (see the reference list) and e-mail correspondence with individual city planning departments.

The table shows that about a quarter of the reviewed ordinances are hierarchical: specifically, their commercial zones generally permit residential uses.[33] Ten ordinances are partially hierarchical (e.g., only certain residential types are allowed in only some commercial zones). In eight cases, the ordinances are "flat": each zone is dedicated to a single land-use class. The ordinances are consistently more welcoming of mixed housing: all of them allow some single- and/or two-family homes by right or at least conditionally in the multifamily districts. On the other hand, the residential zones are generally closed to nonresidential functions. As a rule, cities do not allow retail establishments, offices, or industries (even light industries) in areas labeled residential, unless the areas are intended specifically for a mix of residential and nonresidential activities.[34] In ten cases, a limited number of nonresidential uses—those considered either halfway residential (e.g., bed and breakfasts) or least intrusive to the residential function (e.g., day-care centers)—are allowed. These are usually listed as conditional uses. However, conditional nonresidential uses generally do not exist in single-family districts.[35]

Districts dedicated to mixed use are very popular; every city in the database has more than one such district. Examples include Neighborhood Mixed Use in Chicago, Traditional Neighborhood Development in Colorado Springs, Residential-Professional-Institutional in Jacksonville, Town Center in Las Vegas, Community Commercial in Long Beach, Downtown Districts in Mesa, and Neighborhood Shopping in Milwaukee. A significant part of New York's 3,400-page ordinance is devoted to Special Purpose Districts, most of which allow a residential-nonresidential mix.

PUDs are an equally popular tool. Although some cities have monofunctional PUDs (e.g., all-residential or all-commercial PUDs), in all cities a PUD that allows or even requires mixed use exists. However, both mixed-use zoning and PUD zoning typically apply to parts (often relatively small parts) of a city, and the rest remains under standard, land-use-based zoning. The only city that uses PUDs broadly is Las Vegas, Nevada.[36] Dallas, Texas, offers an example of a city with mixed-use districts. There, a mixture of uses is permitted by zoning in just 3 percent of the city area, whereas about 45 percent is zoned solely for residential uses, as Table 2.6 shows.

As mentioned above, unlike PUDs or mixed-use districts, performance or form-based zoning can replace the land-use-based principle in its entirety. But there are no such cases in the database. In a nominal sense, all cities have some performance standards related to permissible noise or emissions levels, and so forth, especially for industrial facilities.[37] But none of the codes in the database allow performance criteria to replace land-use-based rules and classifications, even for a part of town. The performance standards only provide requirements in addition to those associated with land use.

TABLE 2.6 Base zoning districts in Dallas, Texas

BASE_ZONING	BASE_ZONING	AREA IN MI.²	PERCENT TOTAL AREA
Agricultural	A(A)	63.07	16.53
Central area	CA-1(A)	1.12	0.29
Central area	CA-2(A)	0.046	0.01
Conservation	CD	2.98	0.78
Clustered retail	CH	0.37	0.10
Commercial retail	CR	7.81	2.05
Commercial service	CS	6.95	1.82
Duplex residential	D(A)	1.97	0.52
General office	GO(A)	0.43	0.11
General retail	GR	0.002	0.00
Industrial manufacturing	IM	11.55	3.03
Industrial research	IR	35.58	9.33
Light industry	LI	4.74	1.24
Limited office	LO-1	0.44	0.12
Limited office	LO-2	0.04	0.01
Limited office	LO-3	0.20	0.05
Multiple commercial	MC-1	0.43	0.11
Multiple commercial	MC-2	0.007	0.00
Multiple commercial	MC-3	0.16	0.04
Multiple commercial	MC-4	0.09	0.03
Multi residential	MF-1(A)	6.65	1.74
Multi residential	MF-1(A)(SAH)	0.13	0.03
Multi residential	MF-2	0.002	0.00
Multi residential	MF-2(A)	9.17	2.40
Multi residential	MF-2(A)(SAH)	0.09	0.02
Multi residential	MF-3(A)	0.28	0.07
Multi residential	MF-4(A)	0.06	0.02
Manufactured residential	MH(A)	0.93	0.25
Midrange office	MO-1	0.01	0.00
Midrange office	MO-2	0.008	0.00
Mixed use	MU-1	1.12	0.30
Mixed use	MU-1(SAH)	0.01	0.00
Mixed use	MU-2	1.43	0.38
Mixed use	MU-2(SAH)	0.07	0.02
Mixed use	MU-3	5.78	1.52
Mixed use	MU-3(SAH)	0.19	0.05
Neighborhood office	NO(A)	0.82	0.21
Neighborhood service	NS(A)	0.47	0.12
Office	O-2	0.001	0.00
Parking	P(A)	0.09	0.02
PUD	PD	57.8	15.14
Single-family residential	R-1/2ac(A)	2.99	0.78
Single-family residential	R-10(A)	17.27	4.53
Single-family residential	R-13(A)	0.55	0.14

(Continued)

TABLE 2.6   (Continued)

BASE_ZONING	BASE_ZONING	AREA IN MI.²	PERCENT TOTAL AREA
Single-family residential	R-16(A)	8.60	2.26
Single-family residential	R-1ac(A)	7.66	2.01
Single-family residential	R-5(A)	11.1	2.91
Single-family residential	R-7.5(A)	99.2	26.01
Regional retail	RR	5.66	1.49
Townhouse residential	TH-1(A)	0.92	0.24
Townhouse residential	TH-2(A)	1.99	0.52
Townhouse residential	TH-3(A)	2.32	0.61
Walkable mixed use	WMU-5	0.01	0.00
Walkable urban residential	WR-5	0.002	0.00
Total		381.47	99.96

Source: Correspondence with city of Dallas (2011).

Note: The districts zoned for residential and nonresidential mixed use, which are shaded in light gray, occupy less than 3% of the city area. The districts designated solely for residential development, which are shaded in dark gray, occupy over 45% of the city area.

Form-based zoning, on the other hand, has attained greater popularity. In several cities (Atlanta, Baltimore, Mesa, and Phoenix), a form-based code is in some stage of preparation. In a few others (Colorado Springs, El Paso, and San Antonio), a form-based code exists on the books: it *may* be used instead of traditional use zoning.[38] All other cities have some regulations that address the shape and style of buildings and building landscapes, most commonly in historic or other special areas. However, just as with performance criteria, these form-based rules or guidelines are not intended to reduce the significance of rules and classifications based on land use; rather, they impose an additional layer of regulation.

The only zoning ordinance in the database that calls itself fully form-based is Denver's. But Denver's ordinance (City of Denver 2010) is in essence a hybrid. It explicitly follows the principles advocated by the New Urbanists and establishes several "neighborhood contexts" that are distinguishable from one another based not on functions alone but on neighborhoods' "overall physical and functional characteristics including but not limited to: street, alley, and block patterns; building placement and height; diversity, distribution and intensity of land uses; and diversity of mobility options." These contexts are Suburban (S), Urban Edge (E), Urban (U), General Urban (G), and Urban Center (C). Within each context, the code states that it uses a form-based method to distinguish between additional categories based on "dominant building form and character." These include Single Unit (SU), Two Unit (TU), Town House (TH), Row House (RH), Multi Unit (MU), Residential Office (RO), Residential Mixed Use (RX), Commercial Corridor (CC), Mixed Use (MX), and Main Street (MS). Zone Districts are then created based on the combination of "context" and "dominant building

TABLE 2.7   Land-use zoning districts in some of Denver's neighborhood contexts,"
which feature single-family units.

SUBURBAN NEIGHBORHOOD CONTEXT		URBAN EDGE NEIGHBORHOOD CONTEXT		URBAN NEIGHBORHOOD CONTEXT	
S-SU-A	Single Unit A	E-SU-A	Single Unit A	U-SU-A	Single Unit A
S-SU-D	Single Unit D	E-SU-B	Single Unit B	U-SU-A1	Single Unit A1
S-SU-Fx	Single Unit Fx	E-SU-D	Single Unit D	U-SU-A2	Single Unit A2
S-SU-F	Single Unit F	E-SU-Dx	Single Unit Dx	U-SU-B	Single Unit B
S-SU-F1	Single Unit F1	E-SU-D1	Single Unit D1	U-SU-B1	Single Unit B1
S-SU-Ix	Single Unit Ix	E-SU-D1x	Single Unit D1x	U-SU-B2	Single Unit B2
S-SU-I	Single Unit I	E-SU-G	Single Unit G	U-SU-C	Single Unit C
S-TH-2.5	Town House 2.5	E-SU-G1	Single Unit G1	U-SU-C1	Single Unit C1
S-MU-3	Multi Unit 3	E-TU-B	Two Unit B	U-SU-C2	Single Unit C2
S-MU-5	Multi Unit 5	E-TU-C	Two Unit C	U-SU-E	Single Unit E
S-MU-8	Multi Unit 8	E-TH-2.5	Town House 2.5	U-SU-E1	Single Unit E1
S-MU-12	Multi Unit 12	E-MU-2.5	Multi Unit 2.5	U-SU-H	Single Unit H
S-MU-20	Multi Unit 20	E-RX-5	Residential Mixed Use 5	U-SU-H1	Single Unit H1

Source: City of Denver (2010).

form and character" (e.g., S-SU for Suburban Single Unit and G-MU for General Urban Mixed Use; Table 2.7 lists some of these districts).[39]

Closer scrutiny, however, reveals that Denver's approach softens but does not seek to eliminate dependence on functional categories, nor does it allow residential-business mix in a particularly liberal manner. In the Suburban Neighborhood Context, for instance, there are twenty-five districts, twelve of which only for housing. True, the code promotes relatively dense patterns (there are minimum lot requirements, as opposed to the traditional maximum ones), but mixed-use districts are generally confined to major intersections, and the Single Unit category allows only single-family homes in all three contexts in which it exists.

Finally, Table 2.5 illustrates the prevalence of the residential function in U.S. cities. In the ten cities that provided spatial data, between 31 percent and 57 percent of land is locked in a residential category and between 21 percent and 55 percent is locked in low-density (single- and two-family) housing.[40] The percentage of land marked for high-density (multifamily) housing is limited to the single digits. These numbers are quite similar to the numbers from the 1920s and 1930s mentioned earlier (Bartholomew 1928, 1932).[41]

In all cities I studied, the residential category generally prohibits nonresidential uses. This means that significant percentages of land are destined for a single human activity. And in all cities for which data could be collected, much like in Dallas, the percentage of land allowing a residential-commercial mix is in the low single digits. A single-family category is omnipresent. In all cities, this category targets a particular family type and tends to exclude everything but basic accessories (e.g., garages and swimming pools) and some civic (religious, cultural, and educational) buildings. Current definitions for the single-family category emphasize the same benefits of the serene "family-friendly" lifestyle that have accompanied the history of U.S. zoning. Textbox 2.1 includes examples from the current zoning ordinances of some cities included in the sample of twenty-five. The definitions are highly uniform: the single-family districts permit only what is in their titles (i.e., single-family homes and their accessories).

TEXTBOX 2.1   The Single-Family Zoning District as Defined in Select Cities

Detroit

61-8-11 R-1 Single-family residential district. This district is designed to protect and preserve quiet, low-density residential areas now primarily developed and those areas which will be developed with single-family dwellings and characterized by a high ratio of homeownership. The regulations for the district are designed to stabilize and protect the essential characteristics of the district and to promote and encourage a suitable environment for activities associated with family life. . . . Uses permitted by right are limited to single-family detached dwellings which provide homes to the residents of the area.

Chicago

17-2-0102 RS, Residential Single-Unit (Detached House) Districts. The primary purpose of the RS districts is to accommodate the development of detached houses on individual lots. It is intended that RS zoning be applied in areas where the land-use pattern is characterized predominately by detached houses on individual lots or where such a land use pattern is desired in the future. The Zoning Ordinance includes three RS districts—RS1, RS2 and RS3—which are differentiated primarily on the basis of minimum lot area requirements and floor area ratios.

Cleveland

337.01 Limited One-Family Districts
(a)   Permitted Buildings and Uses. In a Limited One-Family District the following buildings and uses are permitted:

(1)   One-family dwelling houses and their accessory buildings and uses. Except as otherwise provided in this Zoning Code, no main building or premises in a Limited One-Family District shall hereafter be erected, altered, used, arranged or designed to be used, in whole or in part for other than a dwelling house occupied by not more than one family.

Milwaukee

1. SINGLE-FAMILY RESIDENTIAL DISTRICTS. a. RS1-RS5 Districts. The purpose of the RS1-RS5 districts is to promote, preserve and protect neighborhoods intended for single-family dwellings. . . .

Oklahoma City

RA2 Single-Family Two-Acre Rural Residential District.
The RA District provides single-family residential housing with rural amenities in the rural development areas of the City at densities from 0.35 to 0.45 dwelling units per acre. Special attention should be given to overall design and location of lots within this district to assure adequate provision of light, air and open space, and to protect the area from being subject to intensified zoning once the district has been established and developed.

Source: City of Detroit 2011; City of Chicago 2011; City of Cleveland 2011; City of Milwaukee 2008; City of Oklahoma City 2007.

It seems then, based on a review of the zoning ordinances from twenty-five of the largest cities in the United States, that the obituaries for the traditional approach are premature. Although changes have certainly occurred over time and we see a proliferation of innovative tools such as mixed-use, form-based, and PUD districts, land-use classification and separation remain core premises. Single-family residential-only zoning districts continue to be widespread. How unusual U.S. exclusively residential zoning is becomes clearer in the next chapter, in which I contrast the American system with the land-use regulation systems of select other industrialized countries.

HOW OTHERS DO IT

To unequivocally claim that U.S. land-use control is exceptional in the world would require a very broad, multinational comparison. This is a nearly impossible task since a comprehensive, worldwide database of urban land-use control systems has yet to be put together. Even the best scholarly accounts that have tried to place aspects of U.S. land-use regulation in international perspective have relied on investigations of a just a few European countries; in many cases, primarily England (e.g., Delafons 1969; Haar 1984; Cullingworth 1993). Comparisons with European nations have been most common for three reasons: the significant historic, economic, and institutional similarities between Europe, especially western Europe, and the United States (at least relative to other world regions); the fact that land-use planning in the European countries has been fairly well studied; and the fact that U.S. urbanists often consider European cities to be examples of "good urbanism" in terms of vibrancy, sustainability, and levels of social and functional integration (e.g., Nivola 1999; Beatley 2000; Siy 2004). But even comparisons with (and between) European nations are challenging. Land-use planning and control are unique to each European country and continue to be under national jurisdiction, even since the formation of the European Union. The European Commission has attempted to provide a basis for comparative studies in its compendium of planning policies of the EU countries (1999), but even this document pays only limited attention to urban land-use control (which is, at any rate, just one type of urban policy) and emphasizes the difficulties of making international comparisons when each EU member state has its own complicated legal framework and terminology.

In this chapter, I review how urban land-use control is exercised in five European countries, especially how governments restrict the land development actions of the private building sector. For each country, I first outline the fundamentals of the urban land-use planning and control system. However, since my aim is to emphasize the specificity of American residential zoning, I focus on the ways public regulation uses land-use taxonomies to govern the relationship of the residential function to all others. The five European countries are England, France, Germany, Sweden, and Russia (see also Hirt 2012). I chose these countries because each of them represents one the five European urban planning families shown in figure 3.1 according to the well-known typology used by Newman and Thornley (1996, 27–75), which in turn builds on earlier work on the world's legal and administrative families (Zweigert,

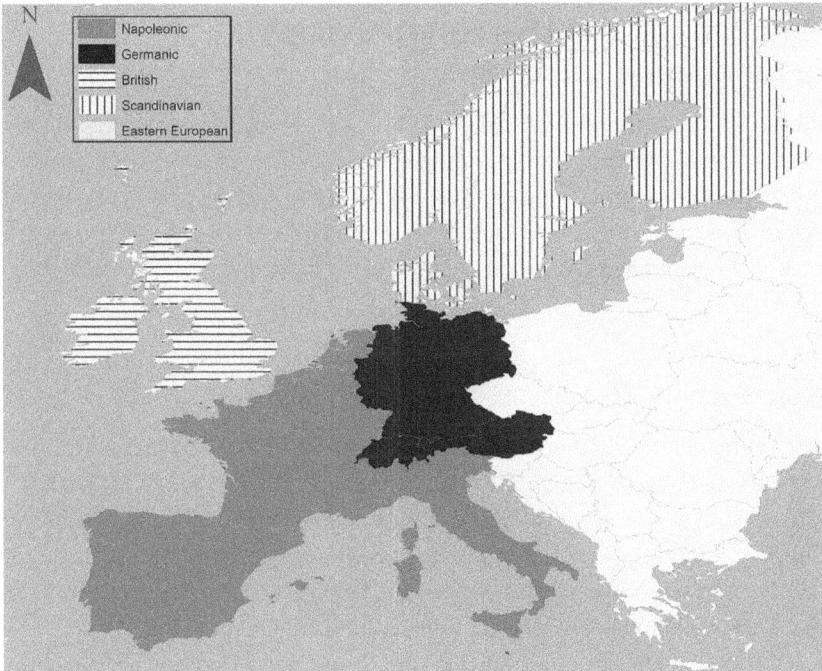

FIGURE 3.1 The five European planning families according to Newman and Thornley (1996).

Source: Prepared by Cynthia Lintz.

Köte, and Weir 1998; see also Nadin and Stead 2008).[1] In fact, each of the five selected countries is the largest in its family. In analyzing the urban land-use control system of the five countries, I hope to come as close as possible to a pan-European representation. This would enable me to build a case for the particularity of U.S. land-use regulation, with special emphasis on the treatment of single-family housing. After the European cases, I will follow up with a brief discussion of three other industrialized countries, Japan, Australia, and Canada. I examine contemporary national and state (territorial/provincial) laws and land-use regulations in individual cities as examples. For now, I pay attention to the historic storyline only insofar as some context for contemporary developments is required. The more in-depth historical comparison between the United States and the other nations, primarily Germany (the country that ostensibly invented zoning) and England (the country whose land-use control system also influenced early twentieth-century U.S. planners), is located in chapters 5 and 6.

Regulating Land-Use Relationships in European Countries

England, France, Germany, Sweden, and Russia—the European countries that represent the five European planning schools—all practice land-use control differently. But together they also stand apart from what we find in the United States: in none of them is local-level land-use control as strong as it is in the United States and in none does the single-family home hold such a legally privileged position.

England

The contemporary British (or, more precisely, English-Welsh) urban land-use control system[2] is so unique in Europe (and probably in the world) that it constitutes its own family (Newman and Thornley 1996). This has not always been the case. The English system changed to its present form abruptly right after World War II, but traces of the old way of doing business can be found in countries such as Australia and Canada, as we will see later in this chapter.

How do the English control urban land development and how do they treat the residential function? England was the first country in the world to industrialize; its cities experienced the congestion, pollution, and public health risks brought about by the industrial revolution early on and in an acute form. As in other parts of industrializing Europe at the time, the problems were initially addressed through urban nuisance and building laws. In London, such laws date back to all the way to the twelfth century. As we will see in later chapters, the laws proliferated and became stricter during the nineteenth century, when industries became more noxious and urban population densities skyrocketed. Simultaneously, private deed restrictions were used to inhibit the influx of lower-income residents into upper-class enclaves, much as they were in the United States (McKenzie 1994, Platt 2004).

As mentioned above, the Germans are usually credited with being the first to fully divide their cities into zoning districts. However, English municipal officials followed suit soon thereafter by designating districts for different uses in their "planning schemes," which were formalized under the Housing and Town Planning Act of 1909. These served as de facto zoning instruments (Delafons 1969; Cherry 1994; Duxbury 2009).[3] The practice of zoning, or districting, was eventually adopted throughout Europe, so by the early to mid-twentieth century, England was a "typical" European country in terms of land-use development control.

The English planning system radically departed from tradition in 1947, with the adoption of a new Town and Country Planning Act. This act mandated that all development—both physical construction and change of land use—be subject to planning control (only minor alterations were excepted). At first, this hardly seems surprising: isn't development always subject to public control, at least in the modern era? But here is what was radical about this step: the act did away with the presumption that if a person who wishes to develop private land complies with the rules postulated in a "planning scheme," his or her right to construct is a given. The right to develop private land was separated from the right to possess it. Ownership no longer guaranteed at least some development. One could say that development rights were "nationalized" (Cullingworth 1993): all were assumed to belong to the nation, and planning permissions were granted at the discretion of local authorities (hence, the English system is often called discretionary; see Booth 2003).[4] Of course, some discretion is also embedded in all regulatory systems, including that of the United States, where rezoning, amendments, and planned unit developments are all done at the discretion of local authorities (Kayden 2004). Yet the English system goes much further in this respect.

Despite some modifications, the English system has remained stable since 1947. Today, planning authorities make decisions on a case-by-case basis following precedent. Permissions are granted after the authorities take into account the policies of generalized urban plans and other pertinent "material considerations" (see Cullingworth and Nadin 2006). According to the law, the material considerations that could be taken into account include previous cases, the set of policy documents written by the central government called planning policy statements (PPS)[5], and various concerns related to loss of trees/green space, landscaping needs, design, appearance, and materials. Perceived incompatibility between residential and other uses of land does not occupy a prominent place (although there is a reference to noise and disturbance from noise in neighborhoods). The law specifically excludes loss of private property value as a basis for making decisions; thus, it provides no direct legal basis for compensation to private owners if planning permission is denied.

This is obviously not the place for a full discussion of the origins, merits, or drawbacks of the English discretionary system (for excellent reviews, see Booth 2003). For my purpose, the point is as follows: England does not zone.[6] It lacks a system of regulation plans that, if followed, in theory guarantee in advance the right of private parties to develop their land. Decisions to allow or prohibit private development proposals are made without a set of predetermined, strict rules that apply to large chunks of uniformly zoned land, as is common in the United States. Instead, decisions for what is appropriate (and therefore permissible) are reached at the discretion of public officials, after debates and negotiations with the private owners, the developers, and the larger community. The primary question that English authorities address is not whether a proposed development is legal but whether it is appropriate (Cullingworth and Nadin 2006).[7]

Current national law (Planning Policy Statement 12) requires locales to prepare local development frameworks (LDFs), portfolios of planning documents (Cullingworth and Nadin 2006). Following procedure, if a private party wishes to initiate development on a particular private lot, the starting point is to consult the LDF's site-specific allocations, which outline the development options for various parts of town. These allocations are accompanied by proposals maps, which do not serve the same purpose as U.S. zoning maps. The only areas shown in color are existing major public, infrastructure, conservation, industrial, and retail sites, and the sites where major new development or land-use changes are expected (e.g., new housing, retail cores). Most of the area on these maps is left white, showing only streets and the footprints of existing buildings. In these white areas, land uses are assumed to stay as they are. How then does a private party change a building's use? The applicable document is the national-level Use Classes Order (UCO), which exempts some changes in land and building use from full planning review. It divides uses into four classes and several subclasses, as Table 3.1 shows (ODPM 2005; on the evolution of the UCO, see Home 1992). The general rule is that changing a building's use to a different use within the same class does not require

TABLE 3.1 Summary of the English use classes

TOWN AND COUNTRY PLANNING USE CLASSES ORDER	USE/DESCRIPTION OF DEVELOPMENT	PERMITTED CHANGE
A1: Shops	Retail sale of goods to the public: shops, post offices, travel agencies and ticket agencies, hairdressers, funeral directors and undertakers, domestic hire shops, dry cleaners, internet cafes, sandwich bars (where sandwiches and other cold food are to be consumed off the premises).	None
A2: Financial and professional services	Financial services, including banks, building societies and bureaux de change; professional services (other than health or medical services); estate agencies and employment agencies; other services that are appropriate to provide in a shopping area, betting shops (where the services are provided principally to visiting members of the public).	A1 (where there is a ground-floor display window)
A3: Restaurants and cafes	Restaurants and cafes (i.e., places where the primary purpose is the sale and consumption of food and light refreshment on the premises). This excludes internet cafes, which are now A1.	A1 or A2
A4: Drinking establishments	Public houses, wine bars, or other drinking establishment (i.e., premises where the primary purpose is the sale and consumption of alcoholic drinks on the premises)	A1, A2, or A3
A5: Hot food take-away	Takeaways (i.e., premises where the primary purpose is the sale of hot food to take away)	A1, A2, or A3
B1: Business	a) Offices other than a use within Class A2 (financial services) b) Research and development of products or processes c) Light industry	B8 (if no more than 235 m²)
B2 General industrial	General industry: structures used to carry out an industrial process other than those that fall in class B1	B1 or B8 (if no more than 235 m²)
B8: Storage and distribution	Structures used for storage or distribution	B1 (if no more than 235 m²)
C1: Hotels	Hotels, boarding houses, or guesthouses where no significant element of care is provided.	None
C2: Residential institutions	Hospitals, nursing homes, residential schools, colleges, or training centers that provide residential accommodation and care to people in need of care (other than those in C3 dwelling houses).	None

(Continued)

TABLE 3.1   (Continued)

TOWN AND COUNTRY PLANNING USE CLASSES ORDER	USE/DESCRIPTION OF DEVELOPMENT	PERMITTED CHANGE
C2A: Secure residential institutions	Institutions that provide secure residential accommodation, including uses as prisons, young offenders institutions, detention centers, secure training centers, custody centers, short-term holding centers, secure hospitals, secure local authority accommodations, and military barracks.	None
C3: Dwelling houses	Dwelling house (whether or not as a sole or main residence) used by a) a single person or people living together as a family or b) not more than six residents living together as a single household (including a household where care is provided for residents).	None
D1: Nonresidential institutions	Clinics and health centers, creches, day nurseries and day centers, museums, public libraries, art galleries and exhibition halls, law courts, nonresidential education and training centers, places of worship and religious instruction, church halls.	None
D2: Assembly and leisure	Cinema, concert hall, bingo hall, dance hall, swimming bath, skating rink, gymnasium, or area for indoor or outdoor sports or recreations not involving vehicles or firearms.	None
Sui-generis	A use on its own, for which any change of class will require planning permission. Includes theatres, nightclubs, retail warehouse clubs, amusement arcades, launderettes, petrol filling stations, and motor car showrooms.	None
	Casinos—following declassification, planning permission is needed for any premises, including D2 premises, to undergo a material change of use to a casino.	D2

Source: "Change of Use Planning Permission," Planning Portal, http://www.planningportal.gov.uk/permission/commonprojects/changeofuse/, accessed April 12, 2012. Prepared by Cynthia Lintz.

Note: Where uses do not fall within the four main classes they are classified as sui-generis. Provided are examples of sui-generis, but this list is not exhaustive.

planning permission. Only switching between use classes requires permission, which can be granted after the planning authorities evaluate the strength of the specific proposal in relationship to policy documents at the local, regional, and national levels and take into account the various types of material considerations outlined in the law.

The UCO classifications come very close to what we usually find in U.S. zoning codes: A (shops and services), B (business and industrial), C (residential), and D (social). But unlike in U.S. practice, the English use categories are defined at the state rather than the local level (for the precise definitions, see OPDM 2005). For my purposes, it is important to note that Class C3, Dwelling Homes, does not explicitly exclude multifamily homes. The line between single-family and multifamily homes—a hallmark of traditional U.S. zoning practice—is vague: "The term dwelling house is not defined in the UCO. Nor is its definition limited . . . so as to exclude flats" (ODMP 2005, 11). The subdivision of a single-family home into several dwellings requires planning permission (ODMP 2005, 3), but such requests are typically not too difficult to obtain. Furthermore, the entire idea of "residential" appears to be broader than what is customary in the United States: hotels are deemed a residential (rather than commercial) use, and live-work units are assumed to be permissible as long as a home-based business "does not change the overall character" of a residential building (ODMP 2005, 12).

The UCO applies only to existing buildings. Local planning authorities use their discretion when they grant permissions related to new construction, taking into account the policies stated in the LDFs and the regional and state policy documents. And although it is customary for LDFs to designate areas, say, for housing (thus implicitly restricting nonresidential uses), it is unusual to designate areas as limited to single-family homes (or detached housing, in British terminology). Rather, the LDFs would normally list permissible housing types by maximum number of units per land area rather than by family type. In short, although some separation between the various uses of land is embedded in the English land-use system, the legal boundaries around residential uses (especially single-family homes) seem more porous than they are in the United States.

Readers accustomed to the U.S. system will likely be struck by how authoritarian the English example appears to be. Although it stops short of bluntly nationalizing all urban land, it places a significant burden on private property owners, who must prove that their proposed projects are congruent with public priorities and who must live with the uncertainty that comes from not having a set of clear rules to abide by.[8] But here comes the intriguing part. From the perspective of die-hard private property enthusiasts, the elimination of zoning was the less draconian part of the 1947 Town and Country Planning Act. Another radical component was that all major cities in England were to be surrounded by large greenbelts.[9] Development in the greenbelts has been strictly prohibited, which has generally preserved the English countryside from conversion to private subdivisions; that is, from urban sprawl. Any urban planning student knows that adopting a greenbelt system at the national level would be politically and legally unacceptable in the United States, where land-use planning issues have remained largely outside the authority of the federal government (Kayden 1999) and the legal-political environment is sensitive to the issue of government appropriation of land. Some U.S. cities such as Portland, Oregon, and Denver and Boulder, Colorado, have experimented with limiting sprawl in their peripheries by using a greenbelt-like tool (by imposing urban growth boundaries) or negotiating conservation easements.[10] However, the English method of eliminating the right to develop private land in the vicinity of large cities and thus prohibiting private owners *around the country* from deriving profit from their land (and precisely where profit may well be greatest, at the urban edge) is not likely to gain traction in the United States. Another strong contrast between England and the United States pertains to the balance of power between state and local authorities. Through its policy guidelines and through various other institutional mechanisms,[11] the English central government exerts extraordinary power over local land-use planning and regulation. In this sense, English municipalities may well be the weakest in Europe, whereas their U.S. counterparts will likely occupy the other extreme of the spectrum (Newman and Thornley 1996).

In summary, despite some shared traditions, today England and the United States do urban land-use control in very different ways. The American way, as we shall see next, is technically closer to the urban land-use regulation systems of the continental European countries in the sense that the U.S. regulatory system envisions as-of-right development (Booth 1996). The English are obviously more comfortable with an open-ended and flexible approach, which gives greater freedom of judgment to municipal planners and higher-level administrators to make land-use decisions while using written documents only as guidelines. They are also much more willing than both Americans and continental Europeans to accept greater national government control over the rights of private parties; they perceive these rights to be secondary to a shared national interest in having planned urban development patterns and a countryside that is conserved. Americans require a much greater degree of certainty in the form of detailed regulations that are agreed upon well in advance of any specific development proposal. The English predisposition to go on without extensive written rules that come in a single document (like a U.S.-style zoning code) may have to do with the fact that England, unlike most other countries of the world, does not have a single core constitutional document. And a strong English tradition in land stewardship and preservation of the countryside may have contributed to the ease with which the rights of parties to develop private land was constrained after World War II (Booth 2000, a, b; 2003).[12]

France

In the nineteenth century, French cities, like their English counterparts, had serious public health, sanitation, and overcrowding problems that were addressed through nuisance and building laws. In Paris, these date back to the 1600s. As in England and the United States, private rules guarding the exclusivity of upper-class enclaves existed in the early 1800s (Le Goix and Callen 2010).[13]

In the world of contemporary planning systems, France can be credited with giving name to the Napoleonic family, which includes Belgium, Holland, Greece, Italy, Spain, Portugal, along with France itself. The Napoleonic mode of planning has been influential throughout Europe: all continental European families can be seen as its offshoots (Newman and Thornley 1996). Following the spirit of the 1804 Civil Code, public life in France has been highly codified, and development in French cities is much more bound by detailed rules than in England. Still, as in England, all private development (aside from minor alterations) requires permission, but whereas in England permission is given at the discretion of authorities, in France it is granted as long as the private party follows detailed, legally binding, area-based regulations prepared in advance. In other words, in contrast to England where development rights belong to the nation and control is discretionary, in France private development rights are (at least in theory) guaranteed if one complies with the law. (This is the case throughout continental Europe.) In this respect, French control of urban development is technically more similar to the U.S. than to the English system. In fact, we could say that France and the United States zone, while England does not. Unlike the United States, however, France has important national documents related to planning, of which the five-year indicative economic plan is the best known. Planning is also practiced regionally. However, French locales (communes) have greater autonomy in land-use matters than their English counterparts (Newman and Thornley 1996; Booth et al. 2007). In addition, the local government system is relatively fragmented: there are over 36,000 local governments in France, a number similar to that in the United States, a country five times France's size.

Today, French planning and development control are organized as follows. The overarching national-level law is the Code of Urbanism (Code de l'Urbanisme; Legifrance 2011), which dates back to the 1950s but has been continuously revised (Kopf 1996; Loew 1998). The current code guides regional and local planning and outlines the procedures for obtaining permits (*permis de construire*). It explains that communes shall prepare local plans with a land-use component. These local plans are called Plans Local d'Urbanisme (PLUs; Legifrance 2011, Articles L 123-1 à L123-20). (These replace the earlier Plans d'Occupations des Sols, or POS.) The PLUs are not required, but they afford communes control over local land-use matters; thus, all large cities have a PLU. For our purposes, a key point is that the code denotes four very broad types of zones: U (urban, already built out), AU (urbanizing, suitable for future urbanization), A (agricultural), and N (natural areas and forests). This nomenclature must be used across the country, although communes are not all obliged to use all four zones if they are not deemed pertinent.

Paris's PLU provides an example of how the zones are applied (Mairie de Paris 2011). It follows up on earlier municipal land-use legislation from 1967 (Plan d'Urbanisme Directeur). In 400 years of intense planning activity in Paris, this 1967 ordinance was the first to split the city into functional areas (e.g., business, residential, university, and government zones; Hall 2007). A 1977 law slightly redefined the districts but it never fully barred one land-use class from zones dominated by another. For example, commercial uses were barred in heavily residential areas only if they would lead to "significant job creation" and therefore to excessive noise, traffic, and so forth (Hall 2007, 940).

Today, under the classifications scheme in the current Code of Urbanism, the French capital is of course labeled as "urban" (U); that is, built out. Paris's zoning map (Plan de Zonage) shows four districts: General Urban (Zone Urbaine Générale), Urban Zone, Large Public Services (Zone Urbaine de Grands Services),[14] Urban Green Areas (Zone Urbaine Verte), and Natural and Forest Areas (Zone Naturelle et Forestière). These are shown in figure 3.2. The General Urban zone is split further into "Residential protection sector," "Sector where mixing housing and employment is encouraged," which includes a subsector especially favorable for employment, "Sector for mansions and villas without a FAR requirement," and "Sector without a FAR requirement." These zones resemble those common in the United States only nominally. As figure 4.2 shows, the General Urban zone covers almost all of the French capital. Building or changing the use of a building in this zone—that is, in almost all of Paris—allows for a startling variety of establishments, including houses, apartment buildings, shops, restaurants, cafes, and offices (see also Hall 2007). This is because the key determinant of what one can and cannot build (or refurbish) in Paris is not based on land or building use but on the Coefficient d'Occupation du Sol, or COS, the French equivalent of floor-to-area ratio (FAR). The two largest subzones of the General Urban zone, the "Residential protection sector" and the "Sector where mixing housing and employment is encouraged," both allow mixed land uses;

the difference is that the latter permits a higher percentage of the allowable FAR to be occupied by nonresidential uses, except for uses that create nuisances. (In this sense, from a U.S. standpoint, the very term "Residential protection sector" is a misnomer.) The FAR is certainly not the only requirement outlined in the PLU; all sorts of additional stipulations are attached to the various city blocks. These have to do with building height, color, setbacks, parking, landscaping, roof shapes, and even in some cases the number of windows (regulations are especially detailed and stringent in the historic parts of Paris). As a French colleague put it, "The municipal council is anxious to keep the built envelope of Paris as it is, or rather keep its character, while allowing the maximum flexibility in land use so that building[s] get renovated and economic activities take place to pay the taxes to maintain a high level of services." Instead of splitting Paris into dozens of monofunctional zones—the typical U.S. zoning approach—the French generally allow the mixture of various urban functions all over the city. Thus dozens of zones based on land use are not even necessary (see Hall 2007). Most of Paris is, simply, General Urban. Even the sector for mansions and villas is not quite what one might expect. It occupies a small portion of the city and exists to protect the exceptional architectural character of the old aristocratic mansions and estates rather than to keep the area where they are located solely for residential land use.

Germany

The German urban planning and regulation tradition has long been a source of inspiration to other Europeans and Americans. In the early 1900s, Germany was widely considered to be the world's most advanced society in terms of municipal administration (Horsfall 1904; Williams 1922; Cherry 1996) and it took two world wars for this reputation to fade.[15] German cities had experimented with urban building codes and with rules restricting the location of certain activities to certain areas of town for a very long time (Logan 1976), and these efforts strongly intensified after the industrial revolution (Düwell and Gutschow 2001). The invention of zoning, a municipal instrument that classified and organized urban land uses, partially to mitigate urban pollution, strongly contributed to Germany's standing as the world leader in the "scientific" management of cities at the dawn of the twentieth century (Mullen 1976; Cherry 1996).

Today Germany, Austria, and Switzerland make up the Germanic planning family. Like the Napoleonic countries, the Germanic ones are characterized by a high degree of codification. The Napoleonic planning family consists of unified

A - PLAN DE ZONAGE

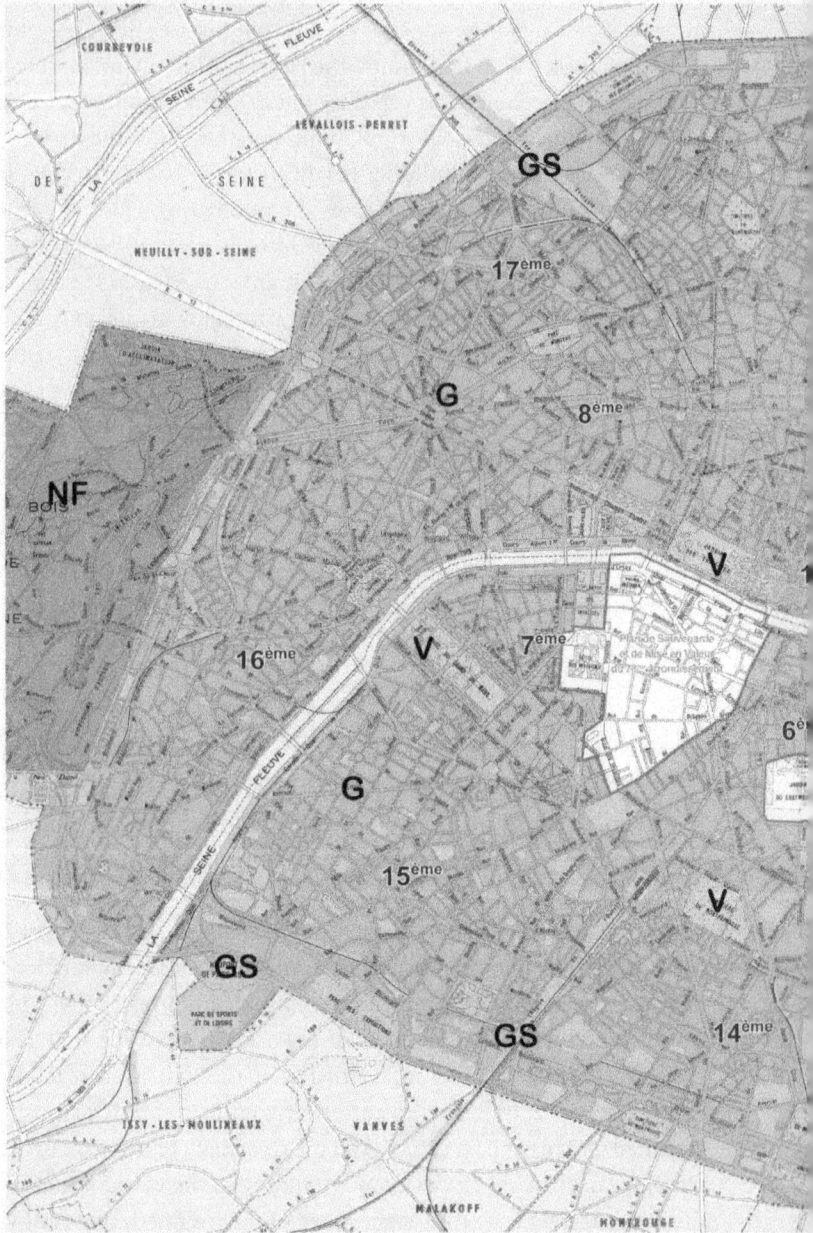

FIGURE 3.2 Zoning map of Paris, showing four broad zones. Of those, the General Urban zone—which permits mixed use—is clearly the largest. Courtesy of the City of Paris. Additional notation by the author: G (General Urban) GS (Grand Services), V (Urban Green Areas), and NF (Natural and Forest Areas).

Zone Urbaine
Générale

Zone Urbaine de
Grands Services
Urbains

Zone Urbaine
Verte

Zone Naturelle
et Forestière

GS

V

19ème

10ème

G

3ème

20ème

11ème

V

4ème

G

GS

GS

12ème

NF

13ème

Révision simplifiée
des 8, 9 et 10 juillet 2013

Echelle : 1/25 000ème

73

nation-states, whereas the Germanic planning family includes Europe's federa-tions, whose state and local governments enjoy a greater autonomy in all mat-ters, including land-use planning (Newman and Thornley 1996), although this autonomy is much more limited than what we find in the United States (Schmidt and Buehler 2007).[16]

In Germany, planning occurs at the federal, state, regional, and local level, guided by federal planning legislation (see European Commission 1999; Schmidt-Eichstaedt 2001). The power to develop in nonurbanized areas is highly prescribed by higher levels of government (a very un-American approach), and the development process is generally limited to areas adjacent to existing urban areas. Local municipalities have the greatest say in the control of development control in the built-out areas located in their jurisdiction and their immediate vicinity. In addition, locales exercise control by owning or acquiring land at the edge of built-out areas. Once detailed plans have been drawn up, they could sell the land to private developers with specific conditions attached, thus ensuring a high degree of government involvement in the development process (Beatley 2000; Schmidt and Buehler 2007).

Unlike in the United States, in Germany several federal laws are related to plan-ning. The federal Land-Use Ordinance (*Baunutzungsverordnung*, or BauNVO) is the most pertinent for my purposes. This law outlines four general land-use classes: residential, mixed, commercial, and special (quite like the English UCO and like a traditional U.S. zoning code). These general classes are then divided into eleven subclasses: small-scale residential, exclusively residential, general residential, special residential, village-type, mixed-use, town-center, commercial, recreational, industrial, and special, as shown in table 3.2.

The intriguing thing about these subclasses is that despite their nominal similarity to the categories in "typical" U.S. zoning ordinances, they appear to segregate land uses much more softly. There is no exclusively single-family category. The "small-scale residential" areas (*Kleinsiedlungsgebiete*) may include single- and two-family homes, farms, small shops, restaurants, crafts, and nondisruptive industries. The "exclusively residential" areas (*Reine Wohngebiete*) permit all dwellings and, under some conditions, small shops, crafts, hotels, and civic buildings. The "general residential" areas (*Allgemeine Wohngebiete*) allow by right all dwellings, small shops, restaurants, and civic buildings; in some cases, they may include hotels, gas stations, and non-disruptive industries (BauNVO 1993; see also Hirt 2007a, 2013b; Cable 2009).[17] The German labels for "exclusively residential" are as misleading to U.S. plan-ners as the French label "residential protection sector." Both the German and the French terms refer to something that, from a U.S. perspective, is mixed-use urban fabric.

TABLE 3.2 Land-use categories in the BauNVO

CATEGORY	ACRONYM	USES PERMITTED BY RIGHT	CONDITIONAL USES
Small-scale residential	WS	Small-scale residential (one- and two-family); retail and restaurants that serve the daily needs of the residents; nondisturbing crafts	Multifamily housing; religious, cultural, social, public, health, and sports facilities; gas stations; nondisturbing industries
Exclusively residential	WR	Residential buildings	Retail and restaurants that serve the daily needs of the residents; nondisturbing crafts; small hotels; religious, cultural, social, public, health, and sports facilities
General residential	WA	Residential buildings; retail establishments and restaurants that serve the daily needs of the residents; nondisturbing crafts; religious, cultural, social, public, health, and sports facilities	Hotels; nondisturbing industries; gas stations; office buildings; horticulture enterprises
Special residential	WB	Residential buildings; retail establishments, hotels, restaurants, and other related commercial establishments; business and administrative facilities; religious, cultural, social, public, health, and sports facilities; nondisturbing crafts	Large office headquarters; entertainment facilities; gas stations
Village type	MD	Agriculture and forestry enterprises; small-scale residential buildings associated with agriculture and forestry enterprises; other residential buildings; retail establishments; hotels; nondisturbing industries; religious, cultural, social, public, health, and sports facilities; horticultural enterprises; gas stations	Entertainment facilities
Mixed use	MI	Residential buildings; office buildings; retail establishments, restaurants, and hotels; nondisturbing industries; religious, cultural, social, public, health, and sports facilities; horticultural enterprises; gas stations	

(Continued)

TABLE 3.2   (Continued)

CATEGORY	ACRONYM	USES PERMITTED BY RIGHT	CONDITIONAL USES
Town or city center	MK	Office facilities (including large ones); retail establishments, hotels, restaurants, and other related commercial establishments; religious, cultural, social, public, health, and sports facilities; nondisturbing industries; parking garages; housing for owners, managers, and workers in all above-listed facilities; gas stations	Other housing
Commercial		Commercial and office buildings of all types; offices, warehouses, and industrial enterprises; gas stations; sports facilities	Other housing; religious, cultural, social, public, and health facilities; entertainment facilities
Industrial	GE	Industry; retail establishments and offices; gas stations	Housing for owners, managers, workers in all above-listed facilities; religious, cultural, social, public, health, and sports facilities
Recreational	GI	Weekend and vacation housing; related services; camping grounds	
Special	SO	Tourist complexes; large retail complexes; convention centers; college campuses; hospital complexes; energy facilities	

In Germany, local planning is mandatory.[18] There are two basic instruments of local land-use planning and control: the general or preparatory plan (*Flächen-nutzungsplan*) and the detailed development plan (*Bebauungsplan*, or B-plan) (Wiegandt 2000; Schmidt and Buehler 2007; Hirt 2007a; Cable 2009). The former is the near equivalent of the land-use component of a U.S. master plan. It designates broad areas for various purposes (e.g., growth, conservation) and serves as the basis for the preparation of the latter. The B-plans are legally binding documents that determine the rules of building. The "typical" large German city is covered by hundreds of B-plans, each representing an area that may be as small as an individual city block—an unusual approach from an American point of view. The plans must use the federal BauNVO land-use classifications—small-scale residential, exclusively residential, and so forth—none of which is purely residential in the sense commonly used in the United States. The B-plans, which include a map and a text component, regulate not only land use but also many other aspects of the built environment related to bulk, density, design, landscaping, and so forth. The municipality typically prepares the plans, but a developer may propose a new B-plan or request an amendment to an existing B-plan; in fact, this is how most new development is done. The B-plans are not exactly zoning (the term zoning, *Zoneneinteilung*, is not commonly used in Germany). One cannot see, for example, all of Leipzig or all of Stuttgart in a single zoning map, as one can see all of Paris (or all of Fort Worth or other U.S. cities). But the B-plans provide the same legal near-certainty that private developers generally expect from French or U.S. zoning: they give detailed area-based rules, and compliance with these rules in theory guarantees the right to develop. Municipalities are not required to use all BauNVO functional categories and may choose to change their definitions to some extent. It is possible for a particular B-plan to label a city block as "exclusive residential" and indeed allocate it only for residences. The BauNVO itself gives flexibility by listing some uses by right and some uses conditionally (e.g., in the exclusively residential areas, all retail falls in the conditional category). Still, truly exclusive residential areas remain a relative rarity in German cities. The largest part of the urban fabric is typically designated as "general residential"—a category in which mixed uses are permitted by right (the exception is industries, which must meet federal performance standards in order to locate in residential areas). In Stuttgart, for example, about 25 percent of the urban area is "general residential," whereas only about 1 percent is "exclusively residential" (Hirt 2007a). This is not to say that anything can move in among residences. The extensive form-based and density regulations would prohibit the location of a large commercial facility (say, an IKEA) in a quiet neighborhood, but they would not prevent the location of a local bank, a small store, or a medical office (Hirt 2007a), types of uses that are commonly intermingled with housing in residential neighborhoods (Figures 3.3 and 3.4 are images from Stuttgart). Another general rule of thumb is that in a residential neighborhood, German planners allow nonresidential services that serve the everyday needs of the neighborhood residents (activities that meet the so-called daily-needs test), but they prohibit those that are expected to attract a regional crowd. As in France (Hall 2007), the German regulations do not aim to achieve functional purity in residential areas. They do not prohibit the full spectrum of activities in a particular land-use class, say, by forbidding all industries in residential areas. But they achieve the effect of outlawing large-scale and noxious facilities that urban planners may deem incompatible with residential character.

FIGURE 3.3 A Stuttgart residence that also serves as a doctor's office in the Stuttgart Hills neighborhood, the most expensive in the city, which is zoned general residential. Stuttgart has fewer regulatory obstacles to the co-location of small retail establishments, offices, and residences than one finds in typical upscale housing areas in America. Photo by Sonia Hirt.

FIGURE 3.4 A mixture of offices and residences in Stuttgart Hills, as permitted in the general residential category. Photo by Sonia Hirt.

Sweden

Despite its distance from the industrial core of Europe, Sweden too began to industrialize in the early 1800s. Swedish municipal administrators adopted zoning rules at nearly the same time as their German colleagues. In Stockholm, such rules dated back at least to the city's master plan from 1866. As in Germany, the regulations mostly dealt with buildings, sites, and streets. The National Building Act of 1874 required towns to pass physical plans and set forth detailed building rules. Reportedly, it was the first national law of its kind in the world (Swan 1913, 157). The Swedish government has maintained a say in physical land-use matters over time. Since the 1960s, it has produced national land-use plans that designate areas for urban development, agriculture, major industries, and recreation (Magnusson 2000; COMMIN: The Baltic Spatial Conceptshare 2007). These plans, however, are advisory. The central government requires regional planning in select areas, such as the Stockholm metropolis.

Today Sweden, Denmark, Norway, and Finland make up the Scandinavian planning family. Like other continental European planning families, the Scandinavian family does not significantly deviate from the Napoleonic planning model. What warrants its relative autonomy is the fact that local self-government in Scandinavia is stronger than in the Napoleonic and the Germanic planning families. This is the outcome of a long tradition of local self-governance in countries whose population has always been concentrated in just a few cities located far apart from each other (Newman and Thornley 1996). In Sweden, despite the state's physical planning efforts (*fysisk riksplanering*), locales have stronger control over land use and other issues in their territory than locales in the remainder of continental Europe, including the rest of Scandinavia (Nordregio 2004),[19] although their autonomy is weaker than that of U.S. locales. The Swedish term for local autonomy in land-use matters is "planning monopoly"—a concept introduced by the National Building Act of 1947 (Ceginskas 2000). Swedish locales also exercise strong control over development because of the high percentage of urban land and housing that they formally own—percentages that are generally higher than elsewhere in continental Europe and certainly much higher than in the United States. In Sweden, like other parts of Europe, local control is mediated by regional planning (Sweden has twenty-one *län*, or regions or counties) and is framed by national planning legislation.

Current planning in Sweden is organized under the auspices of the 1987 Planning and Building Law (Plan och Bygglag), which has been subject to minor amendments since its adoption. As in Germany, municipalities are required to prepare general but nonbinding land-use plans covering their entire territory (*översiktplaner*) and legally binding, detailed development plans (*detaljplaner*) that prescribe specific area-based regulations. Compliance with these regulations guarantees the issuance of a permit (*bygglov*) and thus the private party's right to develop (City of Stockholm 1999; City Planning Administration 2009; Ducas 2000; European Commission 2000; National Board of Housing, Building and Planning 2006). The detailed development plans, like the German B-plans, include graphic and text components that outline and illustrate various rules related to land use, bulk, and density and designate areas for public space and infrastructure. They may include detailed specifications about vegetation or building design, color, or materials (especially in historic or other sensitive areas). Since an individual *detajlplan* may cover an area as small as a city block, Swedish cities, like their German counterparts, are covered by hundreds of detailed plans. Stockholm has more than 1,000 such plans. The plans designate urban functions using notations such as residential (B, for *Böstader*), commercial (H, for *Handel*), offices and hotels (K, for *Kontor*), and so forth (see Boverket 2002). Introducing a new commercial function (in a new or existing building) in an area labeled for residential uses requires an amendment to the detailed plan and an application for a permit. Such amendments are quite common, and neighborhood-scale retail is routinely permitted on ground floors, at street corners and elsewhere. The general policy, according to an official of the city of Stockholm I interviewed, is to "make it very easy for shop-owners to open businesses everywhere appropriate." And whereas a detailed development plan could allocate land for single-family housing alone, an all-encompassing housing category is a far more common category. Subdividing an existing single-family home into multiple flats would also require a permit but is not normally questioned, either by urban planners or the public at large.

Russia

Russia's largest cities began to industrialize in earnest in the mid-nineteenth century. However, systematic planning and building control efforts preceded the industrial period. St. Petersburg is well known for its phenomenal rise from the ground in the first decade of the eighteenth century. Most of the city's fabric was erected under direct royal supervision, but private buildings were also subject to various royal decrees (*ukazi*). In Moscow, royal decrees imposing rules on private construction (e.g., related to building materials and street setbacks) existed as early as the late 1500s (Gutkind 1972). Until the Bolshevik Revolution, private building continued to be regulated through urban plans that were stipulated in a national building law (*Rosiiskoya Imperiya* 1900).

In 1918, a Soviet decree titled "O zemle" (On land) eliminated private ownership of urban land. In the new socialist context, regulations about how, what, and where the private sector could build became meaningless and ceased to exist (Trutnev and Bandorin 2010). The state acquired a near-monopoly on urban development through its ownership of land, large real estate, and the means of production (French and Hamilton 1979). Municipalities produced general plans that served as virtual blueprints of future development, since the public sector served as both planner and developer. That is not to say that all went according to plan (the flaws of the Soviet top-down planning system are well known); the point is simply that land uses could be designated with a precision that would be impossible under capitalist conditions (e.g., plans designated locations for specific types of retail: bakery, restaurant, etc.). Some private building did occur, however. There were recreational zones where the urban citizenry could build single-family secondary homes (the famous dachas) and own garden plots. Such building was tightly controlled. After the collapse of communism, most urban land was restituted or privatized (e.g., Hirt and Stanilov 2009), and the country needed to adopt new regulations that could govern private construction. Since these regulations were an overt acknowledgment of the return of the private real-estate market to Russia and the necessity of governing urban development through municipal laws, they were seen as a hallmark of the return of democratic municipal self-rule to the country (Trutnev and Bandorin 2010).

Newman and Thornley (1996) categorize postcommunist Russia as part of the East European planning family. But this family exists solely based on its members' common communist heritage; it could be debated whether the terminology still applies more than two decades after the end of the Soviet Union (Tosics 2010). As we shall see in the next paragraphs, the technical side of urban land-use control in today's Russia is not too different from what we find elsewhere in continental Europe.[20]

The overarching current federal law is the Urban Development Code of 1998. This came after the adoption of several regional and municipal ordinances, starting in Veliky Novgorod (a fact with important symbolic undertones, since this city is often considered the historic seat of Russia's democratic traditions).[21] The latest version of the federal code was passed in 2011 (Rossiiskoya Federatsiya 2011). It dictates various planning hierarchies and the documents builders need and the procedures they must follow, including regulations related to land-use control and the issuance of building permits. The general plan (*generalnyi plan*) remains the key planning document in Russia's municipalities.[22] Unlike in Soviet times, however, this plan is now linked to rules for private development: legally binding zoning plans (Golubchikov 2004).

The code requires all cities to adopt general plans with "functional territorial zoning," but, as elsewhere in Europe (and in the United States), these general plans do not provide rules that legally bind the private sector. The legally binding rules come in the form of Land Use and Development Rules (Pravila zemlepol-zvaniya i zastroiki). In Article 35, the federal code defines the land-use classes to be applied at the municipal level: residential, public and business, infrastructure, industrial, agricultural, recreational, and special. These definitions (like those in the German BauNVO) are quite general, allowing locales great flexibility in application. Furthermore, as elsewhere in Europe, the concept of zones occupied solely by a single land-use class seems absent. For example, in residential zones (*zhilye zony*) a municipality may include single-family and multifamily dwellings as well as social, cultural, and communal buildings; schools; hospitals; and retail establishments that serve the residents' daily needs without harming the overall residential character of the area. Although municipalities have the discretion to limit the types of land uses in any portion of their territory, the regulations of individual Russian cities leaves one with the impression that monofunctionality is out of the ordinary. Take, for instance, St. Petersburg (Pravitelstvo Sankt-Peter-burga 2011). The territory of the city is divided into many small zones, each of which has permitted uses (listed as primary, special, and conditional—a classifi-cation system similar to that used in American zoning). Yet all residential zones allow social and commercial uses if they are not detrimental to the residential environment. The single-family zones, which occupy a small part of the city, are no exception. In these zones, the category "single-family" includes both attached and detached houses (something that is common in Europe but uncommon in the United States). Height, bulk, and design rules (especially in historic areas) seem to take precedence over rules restricting land use, and no large zoning dis-tricts are dedicated solely to detached single-family housing.

Regulating Land-Use Relationships in Other Industrialized Countries

The three countries covered below are very different from each other in terms of control of land use. But, as is the case in European countries, in each of them the land-use actions of local governments follow national legislation. None of them surrounds the single-family home with firmly defined legal borders to the extent we find in the United States.

Japan

In Japan, planned urban patterns date back at least to the eighth century (Kostof 1991, 175). One could argue, however, that modern-day urban planning and coding in Japan originated during the Meiji era (1868–1912), a time when the nation was urbanizing rapidly and its imperial regime was aggressively embracing policies that favored modernization (Sorensen 2002). Since then, the Japanese central government has maintained a very strong role in guiding urbanization patterns. In the mid-nineteenth century, Japan's rapidly growing cities, especially the national capital, were beneficiaries of various improvement schemes by the central government that included major industrial infrastructure projects and the beautification of public spaces in central areas. However, private building in cities remained unregulated. The first attempt at comprehensive regulation was Tokyo's City Improvement Ordinance (Tokyo shiku kaisei jōrei) of 1888 (Fiévé and Waley 2013),[23] which included provisions related to the location of public buildings and spaces, main transportation corridors, and major industrial areas. It also introduced various city-wide standards for fire prevention and building control that paid specific attention to twenty-two fire-prevention districts in downtown Tokyo. This ordinance was the predecessor of regulatory planning in Japan. Although attempts to pass a nationwide planning act and a nationwide building code date back to the late nineteenth century, partially inspired by German legislation from the same time period, Tokyo's City Planning Act and Urban Building Standard Act were not adopted until 1919 (Sorensen 2002; Shibata 2008). The acts defined three basic types of land-use districts—residential, commercial, and industrial—the same ones we find at the time in European and American contexts.[24] The newly adopted system, however, never completely excluded one land-use class from areas designated under the other land-use categories. The restrictions confined the heaviest manufacturing facilities to industrial zones and the noisiest commercial uses to commercial zones. It also mandated stringent building regulations in the residential zones. Aside from that, however, land-use mix continued to define the Japanese city (e.g., housing could still be located in both commercial and industrial zones, and light, small-scale industries could still locate anywhere in the city; Sorensen 2002, 115–118).[25]

Japan's contemporary planning system is built on the 1968 City Planning Law (Shin toshi keikaku hō).[26] This law stipulated the procedures for obtaining planning permissions and set up the basic planning procedures and hierarchies at the national, regional, and local levels. Local governments were to employ three basic planning instruments: fundamental (strategic) plans, master plans, and implementation regulations (Oshugi 2010).[27] These instruments are not too different from what we find in Europe. The urban regulatory system was slightly revised in 1980 to follow the German Bebauungsplan system even more closely (Sorensen 2002, 264).

The 1968 law provided a national land-use system that had eight zoning classifications. It also included three residential types. The Exclusive Residential I zone was restricted to low-rise dwellings (including both detached and attached family houses and multifamily buildings) and small-scale shops and offices that are part of a residential structure. The Exclusive Residential II zone allowed medium- and high-rise residences and some larger retail establishments (e.g., restaurants, offices, hospitals, and department stores). The broader "Residential" district was defined to include a wide variety of land uses (Sorensen 2002, 221).[28] Once again, as in Europe, the central idea was to control what land use can be located where through various requirements related to form, bulk, and density instead of barring an entire land-use class from parts of a municipal territory. This land-use tradition continues today. Current national legislation includes the following residential zones: Category I Exclusive Low Rise Residential, Category II Exclusive Low Rise Residential, Category II Exclusive Medium and High Rise Residential, Category II Medium and High Rise Residential, Category I Residential, Category II Residential, and Semi Residential (German 2010). From a U.S. perspective, the use of the term "residential" in Japan's legislation, much like the use of the term in German, French, and Russian laws, is a misnomer: all residential districts allow additional land uses. And no zoning classifications legally designate large areas solely for single-family housing.

Australia

Planning law in Australia has been heavily shaped by British law. Of the nations I surveyed, Australia is the only one that still uses the term "planning schemes," the term the English used for their early twentieth-century equivalent of zoning.[29] Plans for the layout of individual towns began in the early to-mid-nineteenth century (e.g., the 1837 plan for Adelaide), just a bit before the first attempts to regulate private building activity in cities (e.g., Sydney had a Streets Alignment Act in 1834 and a Building Act in 1837, the latter modeled after nineteenth-century English building acts). Industrial growth in the late nineteenth century in Australia produced rapid urbanization and, the attendant serious housing, sanitation, and public health problems. These issues led to the first debates about controlling urban expansion and separating urban territory with functional zoning, including zoning that establishes residential areas (Proudfoot 2000). These debates were heavily influenced by planning theories from the United Kingdom. After England adopted its Housing and Town Planning Act in 1909, Australian states began to pass legislation that underscored the need for local land-use regulation, including planning schemes and urban districting (e.g., the Local Government Act of 1919 in New South Wales and the Town Planning and Development Act of 1928 in Western Australia). However, the regulatory practice spread slowly and did not truly take off until the mid-twentieth century (Fogg 1974; Hamnett and Freestone 2000; Ashton and Freestone 2008).

Today planning is conducted at all levels of government in Australia. States and territories (rather than the national government) play a primary role in establishing the legislative framework of land-use planning and regulation. This is typically done by state planning and development acts. Municipalities[30] prepare both generalized, strategic plans and statutory plans (planning schemes or territory plans). In fact, regulatory schemes are prepared at both town and regional levels and must conform to each other, a requirement that is typical in Europe but not in the United States. (Unlike England after World War II, Australia did not embrace discretionary planning fully, although some discretionary elements have been added over time.) For example, the Planning and Development Act of Western Australia (Government of Western Australia 2005) outlines the purpose and the procedures related to the production of local planning schemes. The law permits zoning in planning schemes that designates land for residential, commercial, industrial, public, recreational, institutional, religious, etc., uses, while trying to minimize land-use conflicts (Government of Western Australia 2014). We can see the application of this general idea in the city of Perth (2013), Western Australia's capital and largest city, for example. Aside from lands set aside as city and metropolitan reserves, Perth defines several "scheme use areas" (city center, residential, commercial, residential/commercial, official/residential, commercial, etc.) and several use groups (business services, civic, community and cultural, residential, office, etc.). In each scheme use area, uses may be preferred, additional, contemplated, prohibited, nonconforming, and so forth.[31] In addition, there are detailed rules pertain to design, site layout, bulk, and so forth (such as building or plot ratios, heights, and setbacks outlined in residential design regulations). Most of the terms are broadly equivalent to standard terms found in U.S. zoning codes. Notably, the residential use category includes both single and multifamily housing (or "single house" and "multiple dwelling," in Australian terminology).[32] Land-use tables summarize the land-use mix that is "favoured" or "contemplated" in the city's precincts. Regarding residential scheme use areas, the text states: "The emphasis in these areas is very much on permanent residential accommodation of various types . . . with associated home business also favoured. Preferred use groups are therefore Residential and Home Occupation[s]. A limited range of complementary uses may also be considered appropriate use groups including Special Residential, Recreation and Leisure, Retail (Local), Community and Cultural, Education 1, and Health Care 1, as well as nursing homes in the Healthcare 2 category, are classified as contemplated uses" (City of Perth 2013, SI-I). Hence, Perth's scheme opens the door for nonresidential land uses in residential areas, even if tentatively (as contemplated uses), in ways that are not typical in American cities of comparable size.

Canada

Canada has the regulatory system most similar to that of the United States in its treatment of land-use relationships. Primary land-use authority in Canada rests with provinces, which provide the major legislative framework for planning, and localities. The latter prepare general community plans and detailed land-use control plans (Cullingworth 1993).[33] Thus, as in Australia, in Canada one needs to look at the planning acts of individual provinces and territories and the ordinances of individual cities to get an impression of how the system works. This is because of the significant autonomy of Canadian provinces and the absence of a national-level land-use ordinance of the type of the German BauNVO. Arguably, the Canadian system is harder to characterize definitively than the Australian one. Both systems have been heavily impacted by foreign planning models, but whereas in Australia the source of influence has been single (the United Kingdom), in Canada there are three major sources—England, continental Europe, and the United States. This has led to a complex hybrid. For example, there is significant variation between the planning systems in the provinces,[34] and land-use tools vary from U.S.-style zoning bylaws to English-style discretionary controls. Although some land-use categories are quite similar to those in the United States, Europe's influence on Canada is likely reflected in the fact that the balance of power in land-use matters is skewed toward a higher-tier government, the province, rather than toward local municipalities, as is the case in the United States.

The planning of settlements took off in nineteenth century Canada, especially after the 1872 Dominion Land Act.[35] Since urbanization and industrialization pressures were significantly lower in Canada than in the United States, there was a weaker impetus for passing building and zoning controls. Nevertheless, enthusiasm for planning well-ordered cities dates back to the late nineteenth and early twentieth centuries, when most provinces passed legislation that empowered municipalities to operate zoning controls. Some cities adopted quasi-zoning bylaws in the early twentieth century (e.g., Toronto in 1904) that were based on rudimentary rules from the mid-nineteenth century related to buildings and land use (Fischler 2007).[36] Debates on the necessity of early zoning focused on mitigating nuisances, improving public health, and preserving property values (Van Nus 1979; Cullingworth 1993). The creation of exclusively residential districts was seen as a possible partial solution to urban problems.[37] In Canada, however, zoning spread much more slowly than in the United States, even though the first comprehensive municipal zoning codes were passed just a few years after New York's zoning law; both Point Grey, British Columbia (later part of Vancouver), and Kitchener, Ontario, passed zoning laws in 1924 (Huron 2014, 204).

Furthermore, following the passage of England's Town and Country Planning Act in 1947, some Canadian provinces and municipalities shifted from a purely zoning approach to one that combines zoning with discretionary controls.

Regardless of the historical and procedural differences between the two neighboring North American countries, there is an obvious similarity in the way their planning regimes treat the residential function. In British Columbia, for example, locales are authorized (but not required) to produce community plans and bylaws that include designations for commercial, industrial, institutional, agricultural, recreational, and public utility uses (Government of British Columbia 1996). The City of Vancouver (2012) has seventy-six zoning districts[38] (quite similar to what we find in U.S. cities of similar size). Of those, about half are residential, including ten one-family districts and seventeen two-family ones. As is common in the United States, the one-family districts are quite restrictive (no retail or industry is allowed). Notably, though, "secondary suites" are permitted conditionally (in the United States, the term is "accessory dwellings," which are not often allowed in single-family districts), as are daycare centers and bed-and-breakfasts (which too are rarely permitted in U.S. single-family zones). As in U.S. ordinances, a hierarchical principle is at play in Vancouver's residential districts (two-family districts permit one-family homes; multifamily districts permit all types of housing). The commercial zones permit certain residential buildings—an approach that is perhaps only slightly more liberal than what we routinely find in the United States. However, there is one notable difference. Even the lowest-density one-family districts in Vancouver mandate a minimum lot size of 334 square meters (0.08 acre), thus requiring residential densities that are much higher than what we typically find in the United States.[39]

A Nation of Homezoners?

This brief review of urban land-use regulation internationally cannot fully convey the complexity of the issue. A number of fundamental contrasts between the surveyed countries and the United States in the way the public sector controls private building activity were only implied here. For example, whereas in the United States the focus has traditionally been on regulating the private sector, in Japan—likely the most centralized of the surveyed countries—the national government exerts a much heavier influence on city-building through aggressive investment, construction, and industrial policies (Sorensen 2002). Russia maintains a "state-led" model of development by allowing municipal and regional governments to exercise broad discretion in selecting which private development firms (some of which have links to the public officials making the choices) are permitted to undertake large projects and framing the conditions under which they operate. This is an approach that is not feasible legally or politically in the United States and most other western democracies to the same extent (Pagonis and Thornley 1999).

One of the most distinctive feature of the American land-use regulatory model, as compared to the others covered in its chapter, is its high degree of decentralization. Land-use matters in the United States remain an intensely local matter (Fischel 2010), more so than in other countries, despite the decades-long incursions of states into local land-use practices (the "quiet revolution" that entailed some transfer of power from locales to states in the field of environmental regulation; Bosselman and Callies 1971). The U.S. model is likely closest to the models used in Canada and Australia, but the role of state or provincial governments in both of these countries is significantly stronger than in the United States.

Among the countries I have considered, England is exceptional. Its planning system is unusually centralized, hierarchical, and tilted heavily toward goals set by the public sector. It is also the system permitting the greatest level of government discretion. However, some aspects of the English system are not too far removed from what we find in continental Europe. Continental European governments, which favor the protection of farmland, compact cities, and urban densification, have at their disposal very powerful, English-like control mechanisms that are absent in the United States (Siy 2004), likely because the U.S. federal government has little authority on land-use matters (Kayden 1999) and the U.S. constitution has strong protections against government taking of private land (Alterman 1997; 2010). The Netherlands, whose land-use control system was not covered here, is the classic example of aggressive urban containment policy (Lefcoe 1979; Van der Krabben and Jacobs 2013): Dutch locales can purchase land at the edges of cities at below-market values, thus controlling urban futures through high public landownership or through attaching conditions that private developers must comply with if they were to purchase the public land. (This is also the case in Scandinavia, including Sweden.) Authorities in the other European countries employ similar techniques. France and Germany, for example, have long designated large green sectors where private building cannot occur, and their higher-tier governments control what occurs on greenfields in ways we do not see in the United States (The greenbelt practice and other similar arrangements also exist in Canada and Australia, albeit in a form less advanced than in England and the Netherlands; e.g., see Ali 2008; Amati 2012.)

The European countries also have a number of national-level policies in the realms of taxation, housing, and transportation that favor compact and denser cities (e.g., Light 1999; Nivola 1999; Beatley 2000, Buehler and Pucher 2009). U.S. national policies generally push in the opposite direction as noted in chapter 1.

The United States is also unique among all countries covered here because it lacks national-level land-use legislation. Zoning as a form of land-use control plays a uniquely important role in the United States likely because other tools of public intervention in the making of urban space are relatively weak: there is less public planning, less public building, and less public ownership in the United States than in western Europe (and in most other capitalist democracies). In the United States, the primary purpose of zoning is to regulate the private sector, which remains the main actor in city-building. Finally, the U.S. land-use control system is also unique in the elevated status it grants to one particular housing type, the detached single-family home, which it protects vigorously from inter- action with other uses. Canada seems to be the only place where comparable, but weaker, favoritism exists. It appears then that Americans are different from others not so much in being a "nation of homeowners" but in being a "nation of homezoners."[40] In the next chapters, I put the basic principles of the U.S. land-use control model in historical context, starting with the oldest building and land- use-related regulations in the world.

ROOTS

Urban regulations, of which zoning is a part, span centuries. The first written record of regulating private building activities goes back to Babylon. The
Code of Hammurabi from about 4,000 years ago said that builders who failed
to provide safe construction conditions would be severely penalized (potentially with death). Since then, all major civilizations have aimed to regulate
land use and construction in cities in some way. Regulations have been put in
place by both governments and private groups (the latter for at least as long
as real property has been subject to deeds).[1] In the western world, the rise of the
Enlightenment philosophy, which emphasized the need for rational order and
the scientific administration of society, and the advent of the industrial revolution, which placed new and intense pressures on cities, contributed to adopting stricter and much more comprehensive regulations. This chapter briefly
reviews the development of several city-planning ideas and approaches that
were predecessors of present-day zoning: the idea of urban regulation itself,
the idea that public and private spaces are so different that they require different regulations, the idea that certain potentially harmful activities should
be subject to control wherever they may occur, the idea of districting a city
(adopting different rules for different parts of town), the idea of dividing
a city based on the type of activities performed, and the idea of separating
residential quarters from quarters where other activities occur. It discusses
regulations related to land use in select ancient civilizations; in medieval,

Renaissance, and Baroque Europe; and in early modern times. The chapter periodization ends about 1875.

The Old World

Human settlements are often categorized as either organic or planned (Kostof 1991), but since their growth and change always require some level of deliberate human foresight, they are all planned in a sense, at least at the individual level. On the other hand, even settlements that may have initially been the outcome of highly orchestrated planning (e.g., where land was cleared, carved into spaces, owned and built upon by some government authority, or subdivided by government and transferred to individuals) eventually allow individual building choices. Many cities in history, from Roman military camps to Soviet new towns, that have popped up on the map entirely because of the actions of authorities eventually included built forms created by the relatively free actions of individuals in order to become larger, living, multifunctional cities (rather than remaining, say, solely seats of a princely court or a religious order) (Kostof 1991). But since individual choices often clash with one another or with those of some power above, authorities and collective bodies of all shapes and forms, from kings and mayors to neighborhood associations, have found it necessary to intervene in individual building actions through regulation. Rules about building are only a subset of the regulatory apparatus the state and other powers use. The first building regulations we have a written record of, those of Hammurabi, consist of a few lines in a long legal treatise that sought to govern all sorts of behaviors (theft, dark spells, infidelity). When Peter the Great erected St. Petersburg—a classic case of a centrally planned city—in the early eighteenth century, he too had to regulate (which means that he too could not build all of his new capital through direct state action alone). He did so by passing rules about uniform street frontages and housing types alongside rules requiring the shaving of beards and the wearing of western dress, thus providing one of many proofs that far from being technical exercises, land-use and building regulations implicitly or explicitly pursue the imposition of social order[2] (Kostof 1991, 256; see also Ben-Joseph 2005; Talen 2009b).

Throughout history, urban regulations have typically pertained to overall city layout (e.g., banning growth beyond a certain limit or requiring public spaces); street layout; and the bulk (most often the height), materials, and orientation of buildings (in rarer cases, also decoration). Most regulations also dealt with cities as a whole (sometimes all cities nationwide) without carving them into sections with different rules for each and without referring to particular human activities (Talen 2009b, 2012a). But there were exceptions, as we shall see.

To begin with, relatively sophisticated city-building rules can be found in the ancient Indus and Egyptian civilizations. Mohenjo-Daro and Harappa in present-day Pakistan had rectangular city blocks in which most houses were located in a uniform manner along broad streets and around courtyards. Uniformity *can* happen by social custom, but probably not to the extent found in Mohenjo-Daro and Harappa. Hence, it is likely that some city-building rules existed at the time.

Other examples of ancient planning standards, including standards based on rudimentary residential classification systems were cited in the Vedic treatises.[3] These treatises reported rules such as "the houses of the Brahmans [the priests] . . . must occupy four sides of the quadrangle which is an open space in the center" and "the houses of the Kshatriyas [the soldier class] must occupy the three sides of the rectangular plot" (quoted in LeGates [1935] 2004, 42). They also included what may be the first height regulations for different classes of residential buildings: "The imperial palaces should be raised to eleven stories, the buildings for Brahmans to nine stories, those of the ordinary kings to seven stories, the buildings of the provincial satraps to five stories" (quoted in LeGates [1935] 2004, 42; see also Dutt 1925, 248–257; Ben-Joseph 2005, 6).[4]

In China, city rules likely date back to the Zhou dynasty (1100–200 BCE) and the *Zhou Li Kao Gong Ji* (Record of the Rites of the Artificiers of the Zhou Dynasty), which contained detailed prescriptions on matters ranging from the overall layout of cities to the width of roads and the form and color of buildings (Miao 1990; Cai 2011). The Chinese authorities used a land-use dichotomy of public and private spaces: for example, cities were divided into nine identical squares, one of which was designated for public use (Guo 2011). In addition, cities were commonly laid out in a master plan that showed the locations and sizes of the public buildings and the main markets (Guo 2011).

In Greece, formal town planning was initiated in the fifth century BCE, for example, in the grid system of Piraeus designed by Hippodamus. According to Plato and Aristotle, by the fourth century BCE, city laws mandated that a public square (agora) be constructed in every town. In addition, there were laws pertaining to the dimensions of streets and city blocks; laws mandating the central location of temples, markets, and the houses of the city officials; and laws pertaining to the quality and upkeep of private dwellings (Haverfield 1913, Ben-Joseph 2005, Talen 2009b). The Romans took formal planning and regulation to new heights. The writings of Vitruvius provide a

glimpse not only into what were considered important city-planning principles at the time (e.g., how a city should be laid out from a defense and a
climate point of view, how to position the important civic buildings, how to
orient the streets), but also what standards for public and private construction existed. From Vitruvius and other sources, we know that the standards
pertained to issues such as wall thickness, building materials, spaces to be left
open around buildings, relationship of buildings to other buildings and to
public streets, layout of streets, and building height (Robinson [1922] 1994;
LeGates [1935] 2004; Ben-Joseph 2005; Lahanas n.d.).[5] Formal planning and
regulation declined in post-Roman Europe but revived again in Byzantine
times. The fifth-century Treatise of Julian of Ascalon is a good example. The
Byzantines added rules related to drainage, planting, and the preservation
of views to the sea to the earlier Roman rules about building and city layout
(Hakim 2001, Ben-Joseph 2005).

Planning in the ancient societies briefly mentioned above, much like planning
today, inevitably involved the mental and material division of space into various
components: land was subdivided into blocks, a conceptual and legal distinction
was established between public and private buildings, and spaces were designated
for pathways, squares, markets, civic and religious buildings. The mere act of
walling off cities and surrounding them with other defensive devices, which was
practiced by most civilizations until the advent of modern weaponry, already
established a division between urban and nonurban land, between urban insiders
and urban outsiders. In this sense, walling off was a predecessor of present-day
zoning, something that early twentieth-century U.S. zoning advocates well recognized (e.g., Williams 1914a, Bassett 1922b).

Ancient authorities divided urban space using a variety of approaches.
Some divisions were established through social custom and without formal
planning or regulation. Typically, there were principal differences between
which activities took place and which people lived outside and inside the city
walls: poor people and the most objectionable (i.e., the noisiest, the smelli-
est, the most unsightly) activities were almost always relegated to the outside.
In addition, there was some separation of activities within the space bound
by city walls because people sensed that certain activities such as butchering,
the boiling of blood, the disposal of waste, and the firing of bricks should be
done away from living quarters because they might be unhealthy or dangerous (e.g., Kolnik 2008). Social groups also sometimes separated themselves
in different quarters of town, typically along ethnic and occupational lines
(e.g., Vance 1990). These divisions reflected the social stratification and labor
specialization that intensified over time (Marshall 2009).[6] In many ancient

societies, however, rulers attempted not just to continue de facto social separa-
tions but to impose them or reinforce them de jure, following various theories
on how this should be done. One early way of dividing cities was based on
caste. This was the model used in some ancient Indian cities, where different
classes of people may have been expected to live in separate housing wards
(Ben-Joseph 2005). Hippodamus, whom Aristotle erroneously credited with
being the inventor of "the art of planning cities" and "the divisioning of cities" (quoted in Marshall 2009, 24), proposed a caste-based, three-part division
consisting of sacred, public, and private urban areas, each corresponding to
one of three classes he believed existed in Greek society. Aristotle said that
Hippodamus "cut up Piraeus"; he "planned a state, consisting of ten thousand
persons, divided into three parts, one consisting of artisans, another of hus-
bandmen, and the third of soldiers; he also divided the lands into three parts,
and allotted one to sacred purposes, another to the public, and the third to
individuals. The first of these was to supply what was necessary for the established worship of the gods; the second was to be allotted to the support of the
soldiery; and the third was to be the property of the husbandman." The division was meant to be not only symbolic but also physical: the inscriptions on
boundary stones from the fifth century BCE attest that the various districts
of Piraeus were intended to serve the three different purposes as Hippodamus
envisioned them (Gates 2010).

Caste-based divisions were accompanied by and partially overlapped with
some rudimentary divisions based on land-use specialization, which some rulers
also attempted to dictate. In planned cities, a citadel housing the upper caste and
the large civic buildings was almost always located in the center. The important
ceremonial areas were recognized for their distinct function, and warehouses and
granaries were also grouped together, forming functional nodes. The largest part
of town was typically reserved for dwelling quarters.

According to Hugo-Brunt (1972, 48–50), some Vedic-era planning manu-
als provide examples of layouts reminiscent of contemporary land-use zoning
maps: land was reserved for palaces, temples, open public areas, storage areas,
and residential areas. The latter were subdivided in detail by caste and by profession: from elites such as priests and architects to commoners such as bas-
ket-weavers and blacksmiths; status clearly declined from the city center to the
periphery.[7] We can infer from the fact that these plans did not foresee separate
places for production and professional practice that most of the basket weavers
and blacksmiths conducted their work where they also resided. Zhou Li plans
in China assigned spaces for palaces, temples, and various other civic spaces
and buildings and for the main markets and the dwellings of the common folk
(Kostof 1991, 175–176), but again, they did not seem to foresee areas where only

household-related activities would be conducted. Roman military camps, many of which later became full-fledged cities, were also organized with basic land-use divisions in mind. There were separate areas for the *principia* (the military headquarters) adjacent to the hospital and the commander's villa, the *fabrica* (workshops), the *horreia* (granaries), and the *striga* (barracks) (Hugo-Brunt 1972, 70–71).

The planned land-use divisions were likely hard to carry out in real life, how-ever (e.g., in the many cases where an original military camp became a large, fully functioning city). In Greece, for example, most cities other than Priene and Olynthos, which were strictly planned, had a rather messy spatial organization that suggests that little central control over land-use distribution was exercised over time. Spaces and activities were highly intermixed. Only the most impor-tant sacred spaces and the major civic structures (council chambers, gymna-sia) were carefully planned and positioned in clearly demarcated spaces (Gates 2010). Areas that fell under the public category, if we are to use Hippodamus's taxonomy, blurred what today we would refer to as civic and commercial. The agora is a primary example of a space used for many purposes, from trade to debate, from games to theater (Marshall 2011, 222). Furthermore, Greek private quarters, which occupied the largest part of town, were not necessarily resi-dential in the contemporary sense: on the contrary, rooms in houses were used for trade and for production activities such as weaving textiles, making tools, making pottery, healing, and extracting olive oil. Most craftsmen worked alone and at home. Factories employing more than twenty workers existed only in the very few industries where large spaces and specialized production processes were required (e.g., in ship-building). This may explain why although literature and inscriptions refer to workshops, very few specialized structures for indus-tries have been found by archeological excavation in ancient Greek cities. It follows that "the [Greek] house ... was not isolated from work" (Jameson 1990, 102–103). Hatzfeld and Aymard describe the spatial distribution of work in the Greek city as follows:

> Production was distributed over a number of small workshops, each with a master employing a limited number of workers. Only towards the end of the fifth century [BCE] do we find workshops employ-ing more than a handful of workers. The "industrial" quarters in large towns of the Hellenic world should be pictured as looking very like the streets in the bazaars of modern Turkey or even present-day Greece with their wide-open shop-fronts of coppersmiths, shoemak-ers, weavers, and wood-turners. Two industries, however, required both a rather more ambitious establishment and more numerous

personnel—the shipyards and the mines. Yet fifty-nine small shipyards existed in the single town of Piraeus in the course of the fifth
century [BCE]. . . . Industrial conditions affected commercial methods. To begin with the manufacturer was often also the salesman,
and retailed the products of his labour himself. The same reasons
that favoured the small work-place also favoured the small shop.
(Hatzfeld and Aymard 1996, 122)

Dividing cities into separate districts was not the only way land-use activities
in cities could be controlled. Another way was to prohibit activities in certain
parts of town while allowing them everywhere else. Imperial Rome, for example,
had rules that aimed to keep brickyards and cemeteries out of the central populated areas, although it is not clear that these were strictly observed (Haverfield
1913). In addition, Roman laws placed restrictions on the operation of some
presumably harmful productive activities (e.g., in tanneries and cheese smoker-
ies) and sought to avert harm inflicted on one individual by his or her neighbors.
The latter goal was accomplished through private contracts between neighbors
about the use of their properties[8] (Robinson [1922] 1994; Hakim 2001; Talen
2009b, 2012a).

In the sixth century, Julian of Ascalon's treatise discussed detailed rules about
land use that were based on performance for Byzantium. The treatise suggested
the prohibition of activities that could damage adjacent buildings through fire,
sparks, smoke, unpleasant odors, and strong vibrations unless precautionary measures were taken. Julian went so far as to restrict the location of taverns, brothels, and baths in the immediate proximity of residential quarters (Hakim 2001),
thus showing that the idea of keeping dwellings away from uses deemed harmful or immoral has a history of nearly 2,000 years, if not longer. However, it is
not clear whether and how rules of this type were applied in either Byzantium
or in Rome (Robinson [1922] 1994). Regardless of some broad spatial divisions,
mostly between the public and ceremonial places on one side and the residential quarters on the other, Roman cities (like Greek ones) were scenes of highly
intermixed human activity; rich and poor mingled freely in public spaces. This
was partially a function of density (by today's standards, ancient cities were very
compact and distances were very short, and thus everything and everybody had
to be close together)[9] and partially because rules for full-scale land-use separation
did not exist. Such separation was, in all likelihood, something the ancients could
neither conceive of nor appreciate. Only the largest and most important ceremonial buildings—baths, gymnasiums, government headquarters—were grouped
together to form specialized public nodes. Aside from that, the customary
modern-day dichotomies of residential versus other urban functions, of home

versus not home, of public versus private are, in fact, inapplicable to premodern societies, whose spaces were highly multifunctional (e.g., Bowes 2010; Nevett 2010).[10] The main streets of the best-preserved Roman city, Pompeii, illustrate this: fancy villas were located nearby shops, taverns, and brothels.[11] Furthermore, the core interaction between wealthy Roman patrons and their clients was conducted at no other place but the home, the patrician *domus*, making it as much a place of residence as a place of business and politics, from today's point of view. The first floors of the *insulae*, the cramped multistoried buildings where most citizens of Rome lived,[12] were typically occupied by shops (*tabernae*) (Benevolo 1981). The same was true for individual houses, which often included shops facing the street. And although some quarters of Rome were dominated by patrician *domus* or plebian *insulae*, overall its population was distributed in an intermixed fashion. According to Morris:

> With the exception of the emperors' palaces on the Palatine Hill and possibly separate working-class districts on the downstream banks of the Tiber and the slopes of the Aventine, "high and low, patricians and plebeian, everywhere rubbed shoulders without coming into conflict." On the subject of workers' housing Carcopino states that "they did not live congregated in dense, compact, exclusive masses; their living quarters were scattered almost in every corner of the city but nowhere did they form a town within the town." (Morris 1979, 46)

Mixture of this sort may have been standard feature of ancient and medieval cities internationally. Here is how 1,000 years later, in 1147 AD, the writer Meng Yuanlao saw the "residential" areas of the Chinese city of Keifeng, capital of the Song dynasty:

> On the east side, there is the mansion of the official Zhen's family, the Gild of the Fish Market, and the Eastern Jing-Lin palace. . . . To the south, there is Gold and Silversmith of the Tang family, the Wenzhou paint and hardware shop, the Da Xiang temple, the thirteen lofty buildings, and the old Song gate (quoted in Xie 2012b, 33).

> The Imperial Way continues towards the south across the Zhou Bridge, thrust into the residential areas. There is a coal shop of the Che family and a tavern of the Zhang family on the eastern side of street. Next to these premises, there is a food shop selling stuffed buns, a perfume shop of the Li family, a meat pancake shop of the grandmother Chao, and a teahouse of the Lee family (quoted in Xie 2012a, 154).

This mixture of spaces and structures was possible because although medieval Chinese rulers on occasion tried to control the distribution of commerce (e.g., by limiting stores to only a few preplanned market wards), more commonly their plans showed "only the rigid layout of the city core and the encircling walls.... The areas in-between were totally ignored.... [This] perhaps indicated the authorities' acquiescent attitude toward individual developments (domestic and commercial) in the city. The possibilities of land use in the remaining areas were quite diverse. Any individual plot could be developed into residential, commercial, or religious premises" (Xie 2012b, 33). Modern-day land-use taxonomy was thus meaningless in medieval China (perhaps just as elsewhere), since most families combined production, marketing, and living within the same spaces (Xie 2012a, 2012b).

Seeds of Modernity

Europe of the late first and early second millenniums produced several important developments that relate to modern-day urban regulation. Several legal constructs from this time period came to form the conceptual basis of contemporary land-use control in the western world (Platt 2004, 61–92). The first is the feudal manor and commons, the unit of basic institutional division in medieval England, whose origins can be traced to the eighth century. The manor consisted of a core village and the surrounding farmland, both of which were in the domain of a feudal master. In Platt's interpretation (2004), the manor is important because it established the principle that since land is used collectively, individuals must practice some degree of self-restraint in order to keep resources usable in the long term.[13] The second invention is the medieval commune (city). Communes began to acquire substantial powers of self-governance as reflected in municipal charters during the eleventh century and attained a significant level of self-governance through the medieval era. The charters established the principle that many aspects of urban life are subject to municipal supervision. Medieval municipal statutes gave towns the right to build a wall, control entry, hold courts, and have a central market, for example. They also included building regulations on the relationship between public and private spaces (e.g., colonnades, external staircases, and the parts of private buildings that projected over the streets or compromised the spaces around the defensive walls [Benevolo 1981, Ben-Joseph 2005]).[14] Over time, municipal statutes in European cities expanded the scope of building control. The best-known example is probably London's Assize of Buildings issued in 1189 by London's first Lord Mayor, Henry Fitz-Aylewin (Manco 2009; Green 2011). It dealt with construction materials and, to a lesser extent, the relationship of buildings to their neighbors and the street (mostly to prevent fire). The third important legal development was the application of the trespass and nuisance doctrine in twelfth-century England (Fifoot 1949, Platt 2004). Initially, the concept was employed only by the Crown against perceived encroachments upon royal lands and public roadways. But in the subsequent centuries, the principle became widely used by private individuals who could sue other private individuals to recover damages. Simultaneously, the number of activities covered under the principle expanded greatly. They included issues related to public health and safety and on occasion acquired modern-day exclusionary undertones: e.g., when offenders were accused of having subdivided their houses to the point that they had become "overpestered" with the poor (Spencer 1989, Abrams and Washington 1989).

The Renaissance (approximately, 1400–1600) and Baroque (approximately, 1600–1800) periods in Europe marked the dawn of western modernity and brought about a new attitude toward city-building that centered on formal, precalculated notions of order and standardization of space. These principles followed from the widely held belief of Renaissance and Baroque artists and scientists in universal verities that underlie both good social organization and good city form (Benevolo 1981). They were manifested in the design of the grandest and best-known public spaces and structures constructed during the period (e.g., London's St. Paul and Rome's St. Peter), and in the substantial reshaping of the street network and city-block structure that took place in many of Europe's major cities. They were also reflected in an increased level of urban regulation that was grounded as much in cultural change as it was in practical matters. Many European cities grew immensely during the fifteenth and sixteenth centuries, leading to health and congestion problems of proportions that had not been seen before. The population of London, for instance, grew exponentially, construction spilled well beyond the city walls, and living conditions worsened significantly. Elizabeth I responded by passing a decree that made it an offense to construct any new buildings within the cities of London and Westminster or within three miles of their gates. Another decree mandated that new buildings be constructed using existing foundations. The subdivision and subletting of existing houses was also banned (Green 2011).

Later decrees regulated building methods and materials in much greater detail. London's great fire of 1666 led to the Rebuilding Act of 1667, which took urban regulations to a new level, technically in the name of fire safety but ultimately transforming the overall city structure. Narrow alleys were prohibited and new streets had to conform to new standards. Notably for our purposes, buildings were divided into four categories based on both the type of streets they faced and on class. Each type was subject to specific rules about building materials, wall thickness, and height:

> There shall be only four sorts of buildings: the first and least sort front-
> ing by-lanes, the second sort fronting streets and lanes of note, the
> third sort fronting high and principal streets. The roofs of each shall
> be uniform. The fourth and largest sort of mansion houses for citizens
> or other persons of extraordinary quality not fronting the three former
> ways. (Charles II 1666)

The rules became more detailed in a sequence of building acts through the next century, when many other English cities, such as Bristol and Liverpool, passed their own building acts (Manco 2009; Green 2011). The proliferation of private deeds was another important English development from the same period that underpins contemporary land-use control. As growth pressures in London increased, aristocratic owners of land in the city's vicinity began to subdivide it and make it available for development in order to further enrich themselves. What eventually became the fashionable West End of London, for example, was not subject to the Act for Rebuilding London but was built on the basis of private contracts between landowners, builders, and occupants (Platt 2004, 85–87). London's seventeenth- and eighteenth-century landowners had a "vested interest in minimizing uncertainty" (Green 2011, 28), and the contracts they made covered many issues, from site layout to aesthetics, that sought to ensure that the class makeup of new residents remained stable and desirable.[15]

The interest of Renaissance and Baroque elites in universal ideals of beauty also translated into the proliferation of aesthetic regulations. German regulations were especially advanced, some dating before the Renaissance (Arntz 2002, Talen 2009b). By the seventeenth century, some German locales (e.g., Dresden) issued permits only after they felt that a building's design fit well with that of its neighbors; in the outskirts of Berlin during the same time period, "everything was prescribed," from house number to street color (Kostof 1991, 258).

Artistic interest in both aesthetics and utopian social orders was reflected in various fancy schemes for ideal cities during the fifteenth and sixteenth centuries that typically focused on establishing a well-defined framework of civic spaces and a neat geometric street layout. But artistic concerns with what types of buildings and people would fill the city blocks remained limited (Morris 1979). Renaissance planners of ideal towns seem to have abandoned the ancients' interest in dividing cities by caste. On occasion, however, they proposed divisions based on land use. Leon Battista Alberti, for example, proposed a proto-zoning idea by advocating that the most disturbing industries be banned from town altogether and that the remaining crafts be grouped only in select urban quarters (Reps 1965). Some version of this idea was practiced in German cities, where select industrial activities could be located only on the outskirts of town; even more specifically, only in parts of the outskirts where the prevailing winds would not drive smoke toward the town center. In London, fairly strict regulations on the activities of some industries such as brick manufacturing were passed as early as the 1600s (Green 2011). In addition, private deed restrictions in the upscale neighborhoods of London and other English cities continued to guard upscale residential areas from infiltration by industries. In the early seventeenth century, Amsterdam set in motion a much more aggressive approach based on proactive public policies rather than on mere regulation: its city council began to acquire land at the urban edge. If the city later sold this land to private parties, the buyers had to sign covenants stating that they would not use it for purposes other than those stipulated. In addition, in 1607, Amsterdam designated an area on its outskirts specifically for industries (Morris 1979, 185–188).

The principles of Renaissance- and Baroque-period urbanism were superimposed on parts of the fabric of medieval European cities, producing an environment that was not only more orderly (at least if we think of geometry as order) but also more segmented: the grand public spaces were more clearly demarcated and there were discrete groupings of wealthy residents whose enclaves were protected by invisible boundaries (e.g., through private deed restrictions). However, it does not seem that the European city of the sixteenth through the eighteenth centuries was rigidly divided by either class or function. According to Morris (1979, 158), in sixteenth-century Paris, palatial residences nestled between ordinary homes with "poultry yards, rabbit hutches, stables and fields." According to Dursteler (2006, 27), in Constantinople of the same era, although there was some ethnic segmentation, merchants of various faiths lived in houses in many areas of the city and typically had their shops, ovens, baths, and warehouses on the first floor of the structure they lived in. At the beginning of the eighteenth century, Peter the Great attempted a caste-based zoning system in newly built St. Petersburg. But he failed: "The population was divided in three gilds consisting of merchants and the professional specialists, shopkeepers and craftsmen, and the commoners, but although the authorities sought to separate them into special areas, they were unsuccessful" (Hugo-Brunt 1972, 135). Even private covenants in England were not entirely successful in what they attempted to do: "As new squares and streets were created further out, pockets of working-class housing developed around, and eventually in a number of the original [upper-class] squares" (Morris 1979, 224). Central London continued to be mixed as well; in fact, the idea of single-use areas remained thoroughly inconceivable at the time: "The physical separation of conflicting elements was impossible, for industry and working-class housing usually edged perilously close to the heart of the town" (Tarn 1980, 73). Work and home continued to coexist seamlessly, if on occasion dangerously, in the same spaces:

The basic principle of a city like London before 1750 was that work and residence were combined within each house. Almost all middle-class work enterprises were extensions of the family, so that it was not only the Spitalfields weaver who lived with his loom or the grocer who lived above his shop. The banker conducted business in his parlor, the merchants stored goods in his cellar, and both housed and fed their apprentices along with their families. (Fishman 1987, 7)[16]

This is how an anonymous writer described London of 1748, at the onset of the Industrial Revolution:

Here lives a personage of high distinction; next door a butcher with his stinking shambles! A Tallow-chandler shall be seen from my Lord's nice Venetian window; and two or three brawny naked Curriers in their Pits shall face a fine Lady in her back Closet, and disturb her spiritual Thoughts. (Quoted in Fishman 1987, 8)

City of Dreadful Night

The industrial revolution (1750–1850) fundamentally changed urban life in European cities. The first machine-based manufacturing facilities were built in the English countryside, since access to natural resources such as coal and water was initially a requirement for factory operation. However, by the early nineteenth century, the factories had moved into England's major cities, transforming them into places of pollution, overcrowding, and misery that had likely never before been seen in human history. London was poignantly dubbed by one Victorian poet the "city of dreadful night" (Hall 1996).[17] Friedrich Engels's description of Manchester, the country's leading industrial city at the time, remains one of the most compelling:

Such is the Old Town of Manchester, and on re-reading my description, I am forced to admit that instead of being exaggerated, it is far from black enough to convey a true impression of the filth, ruin, and uninhabitableness, the defiance of all considerations of cleanliness, ventilation, and health which characterise the construction of this single district, containing at least twenty to thirty thousand inhabitants.

And such a district exists in the heart of the second city of England, the first manufacturing city of the world. If any one wishes to see in how little space a human being can move, how little air—and such air!—he can breathe, how little of civilisation he may share and yet live, it is only necessary to travel hither.

True, this is the Old Town, and the people of Manchester emphasize the fact whenever anyone mentions to them the frightful condition of this Hell upon Earth; but what does that prove? Everything which here arouses horror and indignation is of recent origin, belongs to the industrial epoch. (Engels 1942 [1845]: 53–54)

Between 1800 and 1890, the urban population of England grew from 17 to 72 percent (Fishman 1987, 10). In London, which became Europe's fastest-growing nineteenth-century city, the population increased by 23 percent between 1800 and 1810 and by 21 percent between 1840 and 1850. During no decade between 1800 and 1850 was growth lower than 17 percent (Brown 2004). Most of London's population, which by 1900 had reached six million, lived in the type of squalor Engels depicted. In the average housing arrangement, a family, which often numbered eight to ten wretched souls, lived in a single room. Many families shared a single cooking and sanitary facility (Hall 1996). Housing congestion, lack of sanitation and ventilation, and contaminated drinking water led to the spread of typhoid, cholera, and other diseases that brought about an alarming death rate. Dangerous working conditions also contributed to the high mortality rate.[18] Conditions were slightly better in England's small cities and in the rest of the continent because they were less industrialized. But as industrialization spread, large cities in Germany, France, and other areas of Europe did not fare much better. Arguably, conditions in Berlin and Paris were actually worse than in London because these cities were much more compact and dense. By the late nineteenth century, the average number of inhabitants per building in 1890s London was only 7.6; in Berlin, it was 52.6 (Horsfall 1905, Hall 1996, 33). In the United States, the trend was slightly delayed, but severe problems erupted by the end of the nineteenth century as the population exploded in prime industrial cities such as Chicago and Detroit.

The nineteenth century marked the beginning of greater functional specialization in cities than ever before. Because of the logistics of the processes of mass production and mass consumption, it became increasingly beneficial for businesses engaged in similar activities to locate their activities and buildings next to each other. This allowed them to take advantage of common supply and transport facilities and compete with each other for the same consumers. By the mid-1800s, the leading industrial cities had already acquired well-defined and highly specialized urban quarters: high-end retail establishments and banking and other service providers in the central business districts and manufacturing establishments and warehouses in the immediate vicinity of those central districts (Knox and McCarthy 2005). Simultaneously, dwelling spaces became more separated from other spaces in the city as more and more working activities were conducted in highly specialized structures (offices, banks, department stores, etc.). As historian

Peter Stearns notes, the biggest jolt that the industrial revolution administered to western lifestyles was the removal of work from the home (Stearns 1993).

The reasons for this increasing separation are perhaps obvious yet nonetheless important to highlight. To begin with, it became impossible to conduct either complex manufacturing or mass-oriented commerce in small spaces, since their success depended on economies of scale, large numbers of workers, and specialized equipment. Furthermore, with the advent of new transportation technologies, from the horse-drawn omnibus to steam and electric trams, it became feasible for upper- and upper-middle-class industrialists, managers, and merchants to withdraw from urban chaos and overcrowding into class-homogeneous, purely residential environments at the urban edge; that is, in suburbs. Indeed, the upper class no longer needed to combine home and work. The population of London's center, once home to the cream of English society, began to dwindle, from 129,000 people in 1851 to only 50,000 in 1881 (Best 1971, 80). It was the poor who still had to live close to work, in the dark alleys between the factories, because they had to be at work for over sixty hours a week, and walking long distances was not an option. Many of the urban poor carried on additional production activities in their cramped dwellings in order to survive. British royal commissions that studied urban health and housing in the nineteenth century reported that practices such as rag-picking, sack-making, and matchbox-making were widespread in the huts and tenements of the poor, noting that these traditional activities posed a great danger to health and lives when they were performed in buildings where mind-boggling population density existed (Hall 1996, 22). However, over time, the separation of home and work increasingly affected the lower classes as well. By the end of the nineteenth century, factory workers were earning a better living than "homeworkers" (those who earned their living by doing piecework for manufacturers at home; Xie 2012b) and the ratio of London workers employed in factories and workshops to those who worked at home grew to 10 to 1 (White 2007, 174; Xie 2012b, 195).

But the processes of land-use separation and, specifically, the process of the separation of work from home among the upper classes that accompanied the industrial revolution did not proceed uniformly in different international settings. In his classic study of the origins of suburbanization, Robert Fishman (1987) makes a case for the emergence of culture-based differences between Anglo-Saxon and continental European contexts. Whereas the Anglo-Saxon bourgeoisie, first in eighteenth-century England and later in nineteenth-century United States, chose to respond to the horrors of urbanization by escaping from the city into quaint residential suburbs, the French bourgeoisie embraced a radically different vision. This vision was implemented in the grand restructuring of Paris under the leadership of Baron Georges-Eugéne Haussmann between 1853 and 1870. Haussmann cleared the slums of central Paris and relocated their inhabitants to the urban fringe. The French elite then reclaimed the city center and reshaped it to their liking, with broad boulevards flanked by elegant shops and apartment buildings (see Barnett 1987). And even though continental European cities such as Paris became more segregated by class, their density remained higher and their uses more mixed than they were in their Anglo-Saxon counterparts throughout the industrial age (Fishman 1987), much as Ernst Freund, the "two-culture" man, observed at the dawn of the twentieth century.

The New Zeitgeist

The "city of dreadful night" was a problem too severe to be long ignored by governments. Not only was it noisy, ugly, smelly, and unhealthy, it was also perceived as posing a serious danger to the morals of the masses (because of widespread crime and prostitution) and because of the related and equally serious danger to the well-being and mere survival of elites (i.e., because of the constant threat of riots). Wealthy industrialists in England, France, Germany, the United States, and elsewhere had begun to experiment with the construction of "model" industrial towns dating back to the late 1700s, when the improvement of urban life first became the focus of charity work (e.g., Hugo-Brunt 1972, 149–167). The involvement of national governments began with attempts to exclude the most polluting industries from the predominantly residential parts of cities. In this, the pioneer was likely Napoleon. In 1810, he issued a royal decree that created protected districts in French cities (Reynard 2002). The decree required a large number of polluting industries to obtain state licenses, without which they could not locate in the protected (i.e., predominantly residential) areas of cities (Morag-Levine 2011). Prussian and German imperial laws followed suit soon thereafter: noxious industries had to obtain state licenses that were subject to conditions related to their environmental performance. Without a license, the industries could not locate in most parts of the city (Williams 1922; Logan 1976).[19] Such laws took to the national level the earlier restrictions on industries that had been practiced in some individual German cities.

If the French and Germans led the way in trying to separate polluting industries from residential areas through proto-zoning regulation, the British excelled in comprehensive study of urban conditions that led to the further proliferation of city-building regulations across Europe in the latter part of the century. A series of government surveys beginning in the mid-1800s systematically documented the appalling state of British cities in order to provide the knowledge base necessary for broad urban reform (Hall 1996). These surveys could be regarded as ground-breaking because they established the principles that cities were subject to comprehensive analysis, that cities could be improved through systematic intervention, and that such intervention was, in fact, the task of a national government. As commonsensical as these notions may seem to us today, they were very much inventions of the European age of reason. The Enlightenment had not only paved the way for the industrial revolution by spurring progress in the natural sciences, it had also made social behavior, morals, and all human artifacts (cities included) the subjects of scientific exploration. The scientific method was to be applied to all spheres of life: from forest management to taxation, from government bureaucracy to factory production. Society as a whole and its government were to be reorganized along rational principles (Scott 1998). As French philosopher and political scientist Nicolas de Condorcet posited, the social world could be explored on the same terms, with the same scientific certainty, as the natural world:

> Those sciences, created almost in our own days, the object of which is man himself, the direct goals of which is the happiness of man, will enjoy a progress no less sure than that of the physical sciences. . . . In mediating on the nature of the moral sciences, one cannot help seeing that, as they are based like physical sciences on the observation of fact, they must follow the same method, acquire a language equally exact and precise, attaining the same degree of certainty. (quoted in Scott 1998, 91)

The world of the Enlightenment and the post-Enlightenment, social and otherwise, ceased to be a matter of mystery guided by hard-to-comprehend divine wishes. Not only could it be studied and fully understood through the application of rational human reason, it could also be transformed to better ends.[20] Human beings could both comprehend and control their destiny (their cities included), especially when led by an enlightened technocratic government elite (Scott 1998).[21] The new Zeitgeist was well reflected in the work of mid-century British surveyors. They met the key challenge of their time, which, if we were to believe Lamartine, was "to classify things and men" (quoted in Perrin 1977, 5). And so they did; they counted people—their rooms, their children, their incomes, their occupations, their deaths—and put them in Linnaeus-like taxonomies. In an 1887 survey, for example, London's lower classes were "scientifically" categorized in four classes, from Class A (the real problem group with no constant source of earnings: the "labourers, loafers, criminals, a proportion of the street sellers, street performers and others") to Class D (the group of the deserving poor who "live hard lives very patiently"; Hall 1996, 28–30), each demanding, ostensibly, a different government approach.[22]

Land and buildings and the activities conducted within buildings also became the subject of much more intense government scrutiny, categorization, standardization, and control. Detailed building rules, which in earlier ages had been created only sporadically by pioneering monarchs or city authorities, became the standard practice in European cities by the nineteenth century (Kostof 1991; Hall 2009; Talen 2012a). Regulations proliferated on the topics of overcrowding, public health, sanitation, street lighting, drainage, and aesthetics (see Tarn 1980). For example, whereas seventeenth-century Paris had only basic building design rules that placed restrictions on architectural details that posed a structural threat (Talen 2009b), by Haussmann's era, the city had rules requiring that new boulevards be flanked with buildings with standardized roof lines, floor lines, main façade lines, and building materials (quarry stone). A Parisian law of 1883 left nothing to chance: it prescribed dimensions for "every decorative element, including columns and pilasters, friezes, cornices, consoles and capitals" (Evenson 1979, 149; see also Talen 2009b, 152). The city also had comprehensive rules that classified streets depending on their location, width, and primary function (Talen 2009b). In the nineteenth century, London's regulations also became much more refined than those that were passed in the aftermath of the Great Fire (Ben-Joseph 2005). Street and building dimensions became a major focus of regulation partially because of public health issues. (These were related to the "miasma theory," widely believed at the time, which posited that disease was caused by stagnant air trapped in narrow alleys between overcrowded buildings.) In addition to strict rules about the layout and dimensions of streets, the nineteenth-century codes regulated buildings by classifying them based on the type and age of the street they were flanking and by the primary type of function conducted within them; for example, either domestic or nondomestic buildings (Talen 2009b). The functional division between domestic and nondomestic was a departure from earlier building laws such as the Rebuilding Act of 1667, which classified buildings primarily based on their relationship to a street. The division reflected the ongoing process of separating home from work in English cities.

In 1844, London passed a Metropolitan Buildings Act, which further standardized the building rules and extended them to the greater city region (Great Britain 1844; Manco 2009). The act created an intricate building taxonomy system that far surpassed Napoleon's, for example, implicit simple division of polluting industries and everything else and began to resemble what we have today. It categorized buildings as first class (dwelling house), second class (warehouse, storehouse, granary, brewery, distillery, manufactory, workshop, or stable), and third class (public building class: church, chapel, other place of public worship, college, hall, hospital, theater, public concert room, public ball room, public lecture room, etc.). The act issued detailed building rules for each class and granted vast powers to government surveyors to enforce them. It did not seek to place buildings in different parts of town, however, as modern zoning ordinances do (i.e., land-use categorization did not translate into land-use separation). Still, it paved the way for modern-day zoning taxonomies: residential, industrial, commercial, and civic. At the same time, the authors of the act did not think of urban functions in our modern-day terms precisely: they did not think of industrial activities as separable from commercial ones (both were included in the second building class). And they banned only certain types of activities that were very noxious or were likely to cause fires (e.g., boiling blood or bones or making soap) from dwelling houses and their immediate vicinity, thus leaving room for all sorts of other businesses to locate in and around dwellings (Great Britain 1844). The building rules were supplemented and expanded by other legislation that had a significant impact on urban form. These include the 1848 and the 1875 Public Health Acts and the 1891 Factory and Workshop Act, which led to the adoption of building by-laws, and the Local Government Act of 1858, which gave cities greater authority to regulate the structure of buildings through such by-laws, again with public health issues in mind (Tarn 1980, Manco 2009). The London Building Act of 1894 preserved the three basic classes of buildings defined in the 1844 Building Act: domestic, warehouse, and public. "Domestic" buildings included dwelling houses and buildings not included in the other two classes (warehouse and public). Thus, like its 1844 predecessor, the 1894 act left the door open for various businesses to count as "domestic" activities if they were not on the list of "dangerous and noxious" activities (London City Council 1894).

As urban conditions worsened and the extent of government control over society increased, city-building rules proliferated in the other rapidly industrializing countries of Europe. In Germany, lawmakers surpassed their counterparts in Britain by passing strikingly intricate systems that classified buildings and plots and the landscaping and use of streets, all devised with great precision (Hugo-Brent 1972). The Prussian Building Land Act of 1875 gave local authorities power to regulate multiple aspects of the layout of the city, including the right to prohibit private development in urban peripheries that lacked public infrastructure (Talen 2009b).[25] In Russia, imperial laws required cities to prepare regulatory plans and provided rules for laying out streets and erecting several classes of buildings: public, religious, trade and manufacturing, and private residential buildings (Rossiskaya Imperiya 1900). Russian laws also banned factories that polluted air or discharged waste into rivers, with exceptions granted at the discretion of municipal authorities (Rossiskaya Imperiya 1900, 37–38).

National laws of this type, however, created only rudimentary land-use divisions, primarily between noxious industries and the rest of the city. It was not until the end of the nineteenth century that the Germans invented a much more sophisticated mechanism for building control and for land-use separation: municipal zoning. They were the first ones to fully divide the territory of cities into districts based on land use. The Germans were followed by the English, other Europeans, and, eventually, the Americans. Yet the American experience with land-use control evolved very differently from that of the Germans and the other Europeans (Logan 1976; Light 1999; Talen 2012a, 2012b). We will see how in the next chapters.

AMERICAN BEGINNINGS IN A COMPARATIVE CONTEXT

Since the colonial era, American urban patterns developed under conditions radically different from those in Europe—no surprise here. The Native American civilizations had built impressive urban centers similar in size to those in Europe,[1] but their subjugation by the Europeans put an end to their great urban traditions. From a European perspective, colonial-era American towns were new and tiny. The rules that governed them were initially European-made, but they could have an effect on physical form that was hard to achieve in the countries where they originated. The rules could be more powerful because it was much easier to impose them on new settlements than on existing living cities.

Industrialization was delayed in the United States by several decades, but the urban explosion that occurred during the second half of the nineteenth century created nightmarish conditions similar to those in large European cities. As in Europe, this led to a proliferation of city-building rules, some of which pursued land-use separation. But nineteenth-century American city-building rules were more limited in scope than those in Europe. As the United States embraced laissez-faire capitalism wholeheartedly, the individuals who ran its public institutions were less able and willing than their European counterparts to intervene in the actions of private businesses. This ideological position played a major role in zoning debates later on, at the turn of the twentieth century. However, Americans relied on a strong tradition of private rule-making that sought to protect the housing enclaves of the elite from invasion by working-class and poor people, including racial and ethnic minorities. This motivation was often explicitly cited as a reason for municipal zoning in the early 1900s. Despite its many European influences, the emerging American zoning tradition acquired a distinct profile over time: for example, it focused more heavily on the preservation of property values, it segregated land uses more strictly, and it favored the creation of "pure" residential areas. In this chapter, I try to ground the originality of the U.S. zoning approach in mainstream American views of home, city, and society that developed in the eighteenth and nineteenth centuries.

Colonial Rules

The first settlements in colonial America were established by the Spanish. Between the sixteenth and eighteen centuries, the Spanish built a string of enduring urban communities such as Santa Fe, San Antonio, San Diego, San Francisco, and Los Angeles. Starting a bit later, but quickly catching up, came the English (with the establishment of Jamestown, Boston, Williamsburg), the Dutch (New Amsterdam, later New York), and the French (New Orleans and St. Louis). The first rules governing urban form were also of Spanish origin: the Laws of the Indies. Consistent with the spirit of the late Renaissance, these laws sought the orderly development of society and regulated many aspects of social and economic behavior. This included town planning. The laws dictated street size and arrangement and the location of important public buildings. They also required the allocation of land for commons (King Phillip II of Spain 1573; see also Talen 2009b). In these laws we find the first differential treatment of land uses in colonial America: the laws mandated that slaughterhouses, fisheries, tanneries, and other noxious businesses be placed in locations where their production waste could be easily disposed of. The other colonial powers also passed laws related to the planning of new towns, which in some cases were explicit about the need for order and uniformity in design (Ben-Joseph 2005, 27–28). In 1625, the Dutch colony prescribed what type of houses could be built and where in New Amsterdam (Hason 1977). Some of New England's colonies adopted laws that mapped future street locations (Talen 2009b, 2012a). In 1672, after a great fire, Boston adopted relatively sophisticated regulations pertaining to building materials (e.g., requiring that new structures be built of brick and stone and roofs be built of slate or tile; Garvin 2002, 356–359). Throughout the colonial era, debates on the issue of diminished private property value by government regulations that played such a pivotal role in U.S. debates later on were nearly absent (Cullingworth 1993, 21).

Rules regarding specific land uses, especially noxious ones, emerged during the colonial period in the form of nuisance laws. Some colonial governments passed statutes relegating noxious industries to the periphery of towns (Rosen 2003, 569). In 1692, Massachusetts passed a law confining certain nuisance uses such as slaughterhouses, stills, and tallow rendering factories to special areas of cities (LeGates [1935] 2004, 120; Delafons 1969; Nelson 1977). In 1703, a New York law stipulated that noxious activities such as distilling liquor and making limestone had to be practiced at least half a mile away from a city hall. During the later eighteenth century, some cities passed additional sanitation laws that emphasized the need to protect both public health and private investments (Talen 2009b, 2012a).

Many of the early American urban settlements, of Spanish or other origin, were strictly planned. This is because under the typical colonial model of development, land was cleared and developed after a monarch gave a grant to an individual, who then had immense powers to shape the new settlement according to his wishes. These wishes were often expressed in delightful Renaissance-inspired diagrams. Some of the best-known examples include the plan of Philadelphia, Pennsylvania, by William Penn; the plan of Savannah, Georgia, by James Oglethorpe; and the famous and much more sophisticated Baroque plan of Washington, D.C., by Pierre L'Enfant, which was commissioned by President George Washington. Typically, these early plans envisioned only basic land-use divisions: public and private spaces, built and green areas.[2]

But land-use specialization was already happening in American towns, in part "naturally" and in part following early town rules such as those of Massachusetts from 1692. Although America's small settlements were compact and pedestrian and everything had to be close together, there were still areas where particular land uses were heavily concentrated. The most intense economic activities were grouped by seaports or river ports, whereas industrial establishments that required larger spaces and access to natural resources (e.g., textile mills or breweries) or were noxious by nature (e.g., slaughterhouses) were clustered closer to the periphery of towns. As in Europe, the homes and workshops of well-to-do households were invariably concentrated in town centers (Knox and McCarthy 2005). Overall, however, in American colonial-era towns, just as in European cities prior to the industrial age,

> There was little separation between home and workplace. Factory owners often built their homes right next to factories; artisans and storekeepers lived above or behind their workshop or store; laborers and service workers lived off alleyways and in lofts; servants lived in the upper floors of their masters' houses; and, in Southern cities, slaves lived in compounds behind the main house. (Knox and McCarthy 2005, 116)

Land and Law in Early America

In colonial America, rules targeting spatial form heavily influenced individual towns but arguably played only a limited role in shaping the overall human-made landscape, for the simple reason that very few people lived in towns. America was a colony of farms. In 1700, the entire population of settlers amounted to some 275,000 people, the overwhelming majority of whom lived in rural settings. The largest colonial city, Boston, had just 7,000 people. London during this time already had 600,000. By the time of the American Revolution, the colonial population had increased to over two million. Some cities had grown dramatically (e.g., Boston to 16,000 people, Philadelphia to nearly 30,000), but the country that proudly proclaimed independence in 1776 was definitely an agrarian republic: about 2 percent of the population lived in cities. And even though much of the inspiration that brought about the Revolution came from intellectuals residing in cities, few Americans saw their destiny as urban. With few exceptions, America's new leaders cherished the rural character of their nation and feared European-like cities and population densities (Coppa 1976; Beauregard 2009). George Washington warned that the "tumultuous populace of large cities are ever to be dreaded." Benjamin Franklin asserted that "the great Business of the continent is Agriculture" (quoted in Bender 1975, 3–4). Thomas Jefferson declared, most famously, that "the mobs of great cities add just so much to support of pure government as sores do to the strength of the human body" and that "our governments will remain virtuous for many centuries as long as they are chiefly agricultural; and this will be as long as there shall be vacant lands in any part of America. When they get plied upon one another in large cities, as in Europe, they will become corrupt as in Europe" (quoted in ibid.). Where towns had to exist, Jefferson envisioned them in terms similar to those of William Penn a century earlier. Specifically, Jefferson wanted them to follow a "chequer-board" pattern of built and nonbuilt spaces; he wanted their atmosphere to be "like that of the country" (Jefferson [1805] 1884, 5720).[3]

The ideals of agrarianism and pastoralism came to dominate eighteenth-century and early nineteenth-century intellectual circles in the United States (Coppa 1976). The adjective "agrarian" was a term of high praise, not just a value-neutral descriptor of America as a country of farmers. Agrarianism became a philosophy, a quintessential aspiration that defined what was most virtuous in the American character and what distinguished the new republic from the European autocracies. A society of yeoman farmers living nobly off their land in far-apart settings became synonymous with a free society made of strong, autonomous individuals who were unconstrained by authority, a society "most favorable to the freedom and independence of the human mind (Hamilton 1791). Indeed, the success of

American republican institutions was seen as dependent upon "the independent and virtuous yeoman" (Bender 1975, 25). In the words of John Adams, as long as people lived in dispersed settings "sprinkled over large tracts of land," cultivating land they owned, they were immune from the "contagions of madness and folly, which are seen in countries where large numbers live in small places," and they could live "without any government at all" (Adams 1851, 587). Many yeomen farmers and their families led lives that must have conformed to the expectations of the likes of Jefferson and Adams. Sociologist Claude Fischer describes them as "secluded":

> Seventeenth- and eighteenth-century Americans rarely entered public spaces, that is, places with strangers. More than nine in ten lived outside of cities until well into the nineteenth century, and while the country-side and villages had many social moments, these happened in parochial spaces.... American communities were too sparsely settled ... to sustain really public spaces. Churches, where they existed, welcomed all who sought fellowship in prayer, but in practice they grew from and served small, parochial groups. Most men of the era glimpsed the public world only occasionally, perhaps at open markets, more often at the open mar-ket or "pub"—a term derived from "public house," a place open to all. The history of taverns shows us how limited the public realm of early America was. (Fischer 2010, 163–164)

Tocqueville recognized the uniqueness of U.S. pastoral privatism: the ability and predisposition of individual households to detach from wider communities and associate closely only with extended family and friends (Tocqueville [1838] 1966; see also Archer 2005, 177). He did not see a clear European parallel. Writ-ing at a time when industrialization and urbanization were already taking root in the United States, he still believed that this was a benefit: the absence of great cities, he wrote, was a key reason for the success of the U.S. system of government (Tocqueville [1838] 1966).

The pastoral, anti-urban streak in U.S. culture should not be overstated, however.[4] Powerful intellectual voices have cherished urban life since the early republic (Bender 1975). Furthermore, anti-urbanism is not a uniquely American phenomenon. We find it in many cultures and at many times (see Thompson 2009). The Rousseau-type European Romantics were certainly no fans of cities, for example. What may distinguish the U.S. story from others is the extent to which anti-urban individualism—the heroic image of the lone yeoman farmer standing in proud opposition to the moral corruption of cities and governments—was an integral part of the birth story of the nation (Zelinsky 1973, Marx 1991). After all, America came to nationhood just about the time when Romanticism came to dominate Europe (Coppa 1976, Beauregard 2009). But unlike Europe, America lacked scores of great old cities and a long line of great intellectuals celebrating urbanism as an offset to the pastoral mindset—a mindset reflected in the writings of many of the new nation's iconic authors, including Thoreau, Melville, Emerson, and Poe (Talen 2012a).

The opposite of the city crowd that such intellectuals loathed was open land and lots of it. In that, America was always perceived as exceptionally rich. And while other countries may be rich in land, in none has the narrative of "free" land and its conquest for the purposes of "civilization" been so important as to deserve a name as grandiose as "Manifest Destiny" (Marx 1991). At the onset of it all, in a congressional debate in 1796, Abraham Gallatin, who later became secretary of the treasury and founded New York University, equated the importance of open land in America to that of the wisdom of the country's government: "If the cause of happiness of this country was examined into, it would be found to arise as much from the great plenty of land in proportion to its inhabitants, which their citizens enjoyed, as from the wisdom of their political institutions" (quoted in Delafons 1969, 1). The issue was not the mere physical presence of land, but the *perception* of land as a limitless natural resource that was physically and culturally vacant (since in the minds of most whites, Native Americans did not count for more than "savages"), a resource that could and should be divided and mastered by individuals who were exercising their "natural" rights in order to improve their material situation. This Lochean view ran contrary to Native American traditions that regarded land as a shared asset.[5] But the Lochean view was the winning ideology of the day, an ideology of individual autonomy, restless mobility, the turning of nature into property, and private spatial conquests.[6] Frederick Jackson Turner celebrated it as egalitarian because landownership was available to all "free men." Later commentators have been less kind: in the critical eyes of Leo Marx (1991), this ideology underpins the desire of Americans to "obey centrifugal forces" and prey on nature by urbanizing it.

The legislative act that best expressed and solidified this attitude toward land was the Land Ordinance of 1785. Envisioned before the Constitution and championed by Thomas Jefferson, this ordinance governed the subdivision and selling of all government-owned lands west of the Appalachian Mountains (Gates 1996). It worked somewhat like municipal subdivision ordinance works, except that it targeted a vast continent. America's fields and forests were cut into six-mile-wide square boxes by surveyors.

> The Surveyors, as they are respectively qualified, shall proceed to divide the said territory into townships of six miles square, by lines running due north and south, and others crossing these at right angles, as near

as may be, unless where the boundaries of the late Indian purchases may render the same impracticable, and then they shall depart from this rule no farther than such particular circumstances may require. (Continental Congress 1785)

The six-mile-wide square sections were then to be partitioned into one-mile-wide parcels most of which were made available for purchase to potential settlers—a system of land division that discouraged urban concentration but eventually shaped the grid pattern of many American cities. According to one estimate, some two-thirds of America's twentieth-century built fabric still carries the imprint of the 1785 Land Ordinance; Marschner 1958). How to fit cities with complex topographies into such a simple pattern must have "slipped the minds" of the grid designers (Stilgoe quoted in Talen 2012a, 41). Still, the ordinance laid the foundation of principles that continue to shape contemporary U.S. land practices, including the subdivision of land into discrete parcels in order to transfer them to private development and the use of Euclidean geometry to impose order on an unruly landscape. The simplicity of the grid approach has made it attractive to land conquerors and land administrators for millennia (e.g., the Romans). But Jefferson's vision of a perfectly laid out quilt of farms run by self-sufficient yeomen was likely the boldest, most ambitious attempt to impose the "orderly grid of the enlightenment" on space of such magnificent, continent-wide proportions (McDonough quoted in Wasik 2009, 30). The vision also held a promise that no civilization had extended before: the promise of a society in which land and property would be given in an orderly and systematic manner not just to the very few but to the many (in this case, to all white males). Several decades later, the Homestead Act of 1862 expanded the list of persons eligible for land to include single women, new immigrants, and former slaves and led to the establishment of 1,400,000 homesteads on 247 million acres of formerly public land (Delafons 1969, 17). These homesteads, modeled in the Jeffersonian tradition, were productive landscapes; the separation of home and work that defined latter-day suburbia would have been thoroughly unimaginable to the yeomen famers who made their living off the land they owned.

The Urban Explosion

Industrial expansion began in earnest in North America in the mid-nineteenth century after the importation of technologies from northwestern Europe. Agriculture became more mechanized, forcing thousands of farm workers to look for work in cities.[7] As the possibility of America as an agrarian republican faded, the quaint early plans for cities such as Philadelphia became irrelevant in the face of growth and chaos. Builders of factories and tenements aggressively competed for even the smallest spaces in cities. Even the plan for Washington, D.C., had to be rescued in the early twentieth century by the McMillan Commission, as the nation's capital was growing in a way that was anything but orderly.

America's urban development was occurring at a breathtaking speed. Small towns turned into megacities in a few short decades: Chicago, for example, grew from 30,000 people in 1850 to over a million by 1890. In one century, from 1800 to 1900, America's urban population increased from 6 to 40 percent of the country's total population (Levy 2006). Urban growth was further fueled by the arrival of masses of immigrants in the 1840s and 50s, almost all of whom settled in cities. Initially, most immigrants came from northern and western Europe (England, Germany, Ireland, France, Sweden, the Netherlands, Norway); later on, in the 1880s and 90s, increasing numbers came from central, eastern, and southern Europe and Asia (especially in California). The new immigrants were not kindly regarded by those whose ancestors had settled in America in earlier times.[8] Many of the older ethnic immigrant groups also had deep resentment toward other older immigrant groups. These prejudices contributed to conflicts in a society already marred by the legacy of slavery and sharply divided by race and led to the formation of distinct ethnic and racial quarters in cities. They were also an important factor in the decision of members of upper-class households, mostly of Anglo origin, to trade urban residences for suburban ones, join neighborhood associations with rules that aimed to exclude racial and ethnic minorities, and later on push for the adoption of exclusionary public regulations (Knox and McCarthy 2005).

By the late nineteenth century, some 60 percent of New York City's population lived in overcrowded substandard tenement buildings (Hall 1996, 35), which were the main workplace for many immigrants (e.g., in the garment industry).[9] In late nineteenth-century Manhattan, there were 100,000 people per square mile; in its most populated wards, density was even higher (Levy 2006, 10). These districts were likely more crowded than the districts in any European city at the time (Hall 1996, 36). Industrial emissions and lack of ventilation and sanitation made them not only dirty and smelly but also deadly. Cholera and tuberculosis were among the main causes of death, and the infant mortality rate was staggering. In 1895, the *American Magazine* stated that the death rate in the worst tenements was "something over fifty-seven percent." Although this was an exaggeration, the magazine was so appalled by both tenement conditions and the kind of "species" who resided in them as to consider the figure "almost a matter for congratulation" (quoted in Hall 1996, 34). In the 1890s, the New York State Tenement House Commission produced reports as graphic as those written by the members of the British Royal Commission during the previous decades (and not any more cheerful than Engels's earlier account of Manchester):

> The tenement districts of New York are places in which thousands of people are living in the smallest place in which it is possible for a human being to live—crowded together in dark, ill-ventilated rooms, in many of which the sunlight never enters and in most of which fresh air is unknown. They are centres of disease, poverty, vice, and crime, where it is a marvel, not that some children grow up to be thieves, drunkards and prostitutes, but that so many should ever grow up to be decent and self-respecting. (Quoted in Hall 1996, 37)

Indeed, the cities of the day seemed to be living proofs of Jefferson's worst premonitions of urban squalor and corruption. Henry James declared that New York was a giant "swarming" of various human "species" and that the city should be "fled rather than enjoyed" (quoted in Hall 1996, 34). This was, in fact, a fairly mild proposition compared to what would come from other authors.[10]

Slow to start but quick to catch up with industrialization, how did the United States of the nineteenth century deal with its urban crisis? The short answer is that two broad types of solutions emerged: public and private. Both had parallels in Europe but also developed their own, particularly American profiles. The first solution was public regulations that dealt with a set of issues that were broader than ever before (e.g., nuisances, housing, sanitation, and water supply). The second solution included rules by private citizens, developers and neighborhood groups, who followed the solution proposed by Henry James: fleeing the city to country homes. Ultimately, both came to inform the American zoning tradition, which began in earnest in the twentieth century.

Expanding Public Rule-Making

Until the end of the nineteenth century, the primary means of land-use control in American cities were the nuisance ordinances like the one Boston adopted in the late 1600s (Hason 1977, Talen 2009b, 2012a). Although some individual cities had additional rules (e.g., pertaining to sanitation, building height, street layout), nuisance ordinances were the only ones that had become universally present in large American cities by the late 1800s. These ordinances are premised on the idea that owners cannot use their land in ways that are harmful to the ways their neighbors use and enjoy their land: *Sic utere tuo, ut alienum non laedas* (So use your own not to harm another) (Pollard 1931; Schulz 1989). Some of the early laws of this type were very broad, leading some scholars to conclude that the nineteenth-century United States was already a "well-regulated society" (Novak 1996). An 1837 act of the Illinois legislature, for example, granted to the new city of Chicago a long list of powers, including the power to restrain "disorderly houses," to require the owners many businesses (e.g., grocery stores, soap factories, tanneries) to maintain clean premises, and to direct the location of slaughter-houses, markets, and gunpowder storage facilities (Novak 1996, 3–6). Under such laws, American cities could either prohibit certain noxious activities altogether or, more often, prohibit them in certain areas of town. In some cases, the courts—the ultimate arbiters of American land-use disputes—did not shy away from sup-porting municipal actions against perceived noxious uses, even though these actions deprived a private owner of all intended use of his land (for an excellent legal history, see Schulz 1989, 35–57). For instance, in an 1826 case, the New York Court of Appeals upheld New York City's ban of a church-sponsored cemetery in a central area for health reasons (cemeteries were believed to emit unhealthy vapors; Cullingworth 1993, 22). In the last decades of the nineteenth century, the popular nuisance laws led to some rudimentary "districting" approaches to land-use arrangement, as I discuss later.

In comparison with European laws, however, American nuisance-based ordi-nances were limited. There was no obvious U.S. equivalent of French or German laws that imposed industrial performance standards and created special protected areas in cities across the land. Also generally absent were aesthetic and other regu-lations related to built forms. These had existed in some colonial-era American towns and had become standard fare in large European cities during the second half of the nineteenth century. Comprehensive and detailed building regulations such as those in London's Metropolitan Buildings Act of 1844 did not appear in the United States until after the Civil War. New York State's First Tenement House Act, which was passed in 1867, addressed only rudimentary health and safety concerns (e.g., it merely required fire escapes and one window per room; the requirements were slightly modified in the Second Tenement House Act of 1879). The nuisance laws were generally interpreted as a means of protecting citizens only against indisputable material harm (stemming from excessive pollution and health hazards. They did not aim to address the more ephemeral aspects of urban life (e.g., protection of views, light and beauty, or preservation of the countryside; Rosen 2003). In rare cases, the laws addressed perceived moral hazards (e.g., they prohibited gambling and lotteries in certain areas; Pollard 1931). Preservation of the countryside, specifically, was never a stated goal of early American laws in ways we find in Germany, for instance, with the Prussian Building Land Act of 1875—the act that banned private development in the outskirts of cities when there was no sufficient public infrastructure to support it. In the United States, land continued to be viewed as a resource without limits.

These contrasts should not be surprising. Europeans were ruled by auto-cratic regimes that allowed little opportunity for private challenges to their decisions. But in the United States, the political climate was less receptive to government action and more conducive to individual entrepreneurialism and competitiveness and therefore more sympathetic to an undeterred, free-for-all pattern of urban development (Knox and McCarthy 2005, 118).[11] The Constitution guaranteed the sovereignty of the individual and his property in no uncertain terms. The municipality—an entity that was not mentioned in the Constitution—had limited powers, only those granted to it explicitly by the state. Despite the promise of equality that the land policies of the late eighteenth and early nineteenth centuries held, most land ended up in the hands of a few wealthy land speculators who had no intention of yielding to government authority that would restrict their actions, "men who saw the duty of government to be the defense of private property in every town" (Warner [1972] 1995, 20). The courts were thus inclined to prohibit only land uses that were believed to pose direct harm to their neighbors or a clear threat to public health and safety (cemeteries, brick and gunpowder factories, liquor-manufacturing establishments, etc.; see Cullingworth 1993, 20–24). Otherwise, they tended to affirm the rights of private property owners to develop land as they wished. The attitude is well illustrated in an 1839 case from upstate New York dealing with building heights. In this case, *Parker v. Foote*, the court sided with a property owner whose proposed new store would prevent nearly all light from entering the adjacent buildings. The court believed that European traditions restricting such developments under the "ancient lights" doctrine were not appropriate in the United States on the grounds that they would limit the best and most efficient use of land in a nation proud to embrace private-led growth: "There is, I think, no principle upon which the modern English doctrine on the subject of lights can be supported. . . . It may do well enough in England . . . but it cannot be applied in the growing cities and villages of this country." Restriction of this type, the Georgia Supreme Court stated in 1877 in *Turner v. Thompson*, "does not suit a young and growing country, such as ours is" (quoted in Unger 2005, 540).[12]

This attitude began to change, albeit slowly, during the last decades of the nineteenth century (Abeles 1989). The change came about partly because of European advances in urban planning and partly because of the fast-deteriorating conditions in U.S. cities. In 1892, Congress passed a bill authorizing comprehensive investigation into the conditions of urban slums. By 1900, some 3,000 ostensibly scientific surveys had been conducted (Ben-Joseph 2005, 47). Their findings were no more encouraging than those of New York State's Tenement House Commission had been half a dozen years earlier.

In the 1880s and 1890s, in addition to federal and state interest in housing conditions, the growing awareness of America's urban crisis led to a proliferation of municipal acts that sought to improve the state of American cities. The first debates on the necessity of municipal zoning regulations date approximately to this historic moment. Height laws were adopted in Chicago in 1892, in Washington, D.C., in 1899, and in Boston in 1903. In 1901, New York City passed a Tenement House Act that finally regulated construction practices in the city in a relatively detailed and comprehensive manner.

Simultaneously, in the late nineteenth century, large-scale public improvements began in American cities that included public parks and municipal sewers. But it is worth noting that many of the efforts to study and improve the urban environment in the United States were championed by private organizations. Several of the key housing reformers, such as Jane Addams and Lawrence Veiller, led private charities. Many of the late nineteenth-century scientific surveys of urban conditions that lead to the adoption of health and housing acts were conducted by private philanthropies (Ben-Joseph 2005, 47).[13]

In short, a difference was emerging between the Americans and the western Europeans. Whereas urban reforms in Europe were pursued by an interventionist bureaucracy, in the United States, voluntary and private movements played the leading role. In fact, European reformers traveling in the United States at the time were puzzled by the "evident lack" of government attempts to improve urban life (Hall 1996, 40–41). In 1888, renowned British jurist James Bryce wrote: "There is no denying that the government of cities is the one conspicuous failure of the United States" (quoted in Toll 1969, 119).

Constructing Exclusive Domesticity

As cities grew in size (and in squalor) and the yeoman's America faded, advances in mass-transit technologies facilitated an urban escape strategy for those who could afford it. Horse-drawn omnibuses that could carry up to fifty people appeared in New York in 1829 and quickly spread to other cities. They enabled passengers to make a three- to four-mile commute for 15–25 cents at a time when most workers received just over a dollar a day (Knox and McCarthy 2005, 119–120). But the service became more affordable over time, and the commutes became faster and easier with the invention of the cable car in the 1870s. America's first suburbs, around cities such as Chicago, New York, Philadelphia, St. Louis, and Boston date roughly to this time period.

The formation of these suburbs may have been made possible by new technologies, but it was also grounded in a cultural shift: the emergence of a new notion of the proper relationship between home and work, family and community, individual and city. Starting in the 1830s, American intellectuals coalesced around the idea that healthful living was still possible, even in an urban world consumed by industry. The solution lay in the countryside surrounding cities. In a statement typical of his time, Horace Greeley, a utopian reformer and editor of the *New York Tribune*, saw the relocation of the American middle classes from the city to the countryside as a moral imperative, the major task of moral education to be done in his time:

> Secure to the family the inducements of home, surrounded by fruits and flowers, rational village movements and sports, the means of education and independence. Get them out of the cities and would-be cities into scenes like those, and the work is done. (Quoted in Schwartz 1976, 4)

According to this view, middle-class families could (and should) seek refuge from the squalor and corruption of urban life in single-family "cottages" on the outskirts of cities that would ideally become permanent residences or at least serve as weekend homes for those who kept an urban apartment. In fact, choosing to live year-round in multifamily structures in the city was viewed as a sign of social inferiority or personal immaturity (von Hoffman 1998). This attitude was loosely related to the traditional American ideal of the yeoman farmer-landowner, but with a major twist. Whereas both notions valued individual and household autonomy, the suburban/countryside ideal accepted the inevitable (for the nineteenth century) centrality of cities. Indeed, suburbs dominated by residential spaces could exist only as long as they were connected to urban centers, the economic engines of society (Fishman 1987). And whereas the freeholder's farm was a self-sufficient, productive, and income-generating operation, the single-family home was a purely domestic place, a "personal bastion against society" (Jackson 1985, 47), a place where a small, nuclear family would be protected from the physical and moral filth bred by industries and businesses. Yet inevitably, the family's sustenance depended on keeping a business in the city. According to prominent intellectuals such as landscape architect Andrew Jackson Downing, a society of dwellers in single-family homes—neither miserable city "hovels" nor lowly rural log huts—located in the suburban "middle landscape" (Rowe 1991) was the very pinnacle of civilization. He argued that there were "three excellent reasons" why America should become a country of family "cottages" (see textbox 5.1).

TEXTBOX 5.1   Andrew Jackson Downing's Views on the Virtues of Country Homes

There are three excellent reasons why my countrymen should have good houses. The first, is because a good House (and by this I mean a fitting, tasteful, and significant dwelling) is a powerful means of civilization. A nation, whose rural population is content to live in mean huts and miserable hovels, is certain to be behind its neighbors in education, the arts, and all that makes up the external signs of progress. With the perception of proportion, symmetry, order and beauty, awakens the desire for possession, and with them comes that refinement of manners which distinguishes a civilized from a coarse and brutal people. . . . But, when smiling lawns and tasteful cottages begin to embellish a country, we know that order and culture are established . . .

The second reason is, because the individual home has a great social value for a people. Whatever new systems may be needed for the regeneration of an old and enfeebled nation, we are persuaded that, in America, not only is the distinct family the best social form, but those elementary forces which gave rise to the highest genius and the finest character may, for the most part, be traced back to the farm-house and the rural cottage. It is the solitude and freedom of the family home in the country which constantly preserves the purity of the nation, and invigorates its intellectual powers. The battle of life, carried on in cities, gives a sharper edge to the weapon of character, but its temper is, for the most part, fixed amid those communings with nature and the family, where individuality takes its most natural and strongest development.

The third reason is, because there is a moral influence in a country home—when, among an educated, truthful, and refined people, it is an echo of their character—which is more powerful than any mere oral teachings of virtue and morality . . .

The mere sentiment of home, with its thousand associations, has, like a strong anchor, saved many a man from shipwreck in the storms of life. How much the moral influence of that sentiment may be increased, by making the home all that it should be, and how much an attachment is strengthened by every external sign of beauty that awakens love in the young, are so well understood, that they need no demonstration here. All to which the heart can attach itself in youth, and the memory linger fondly over in riper years, contributes largely to our stock of happiness, and to the elevation of the moral character. For this reason, the condition of the family home, in this country where every man may have a home, should be raised, till it shall symbolize the best character and pursuits, and the dearest affections and enjoyments of social life.

Source: Downing [1850] 2006, 5–6.

The idea that the basic unit of society is the nuclear family and that such families would thrive in autonomous spatial settings originated in England. Victorian-era discourses redefined the traditional balance between public and private, household and city (von Hoffman 1998). Prior to this time, the idea of what constituted a household was nebulous enough to include not only relatives but also co-workers, apprentices, and servants. But in the nineteenth century, England gradually embraced an alternative, the "closed domesticated nuclear family" (Fishman 1987). Empowered by the new transportation technologies, which made it possible to live in suburbs and commute to the city, and by rising living standards, which made it possible for bourgeois women and children to withdraw from income-generating activities, families of this type became the first suburban pioneers on the outskirts of England's largest cities, including London, Birmingham, and Manchester. They sought to retreat from urban chaos and pollution and from the intrusion of industry and commerce into family life, thus resolutely splitting the spatial settings of work and home for the first time in history (Fishman 1987). This revamping of traditional notions had much to do with a redefinition of the traditional roles of men and women in family and society. In the preindustrial city, where the home was also a workshop, women participated actively in all aspects of the production process, from making tools to keeping the books. The removal of home from work also meant the removal of women (at least bourgeois women) from the city and the separation of life into two discrete spheres: public or business (to be conducted by men in the city) and private or domestic (to be conducted by women outside the city). An excellent example of how this division was supposed to work can be found in the works of reformer Catherine Beecher, who believed domesticity to be the true and honorable profession of women: "Woman, as well as man, was made to *work*; her Maker has adapted her body to its appropriate labor. The tending of children and doing house-work exercise those very muscles which are most important to womanhood." She also wrote that "it is believed that the remedy . . . is not in leading women into the professions and business of men . . . but [in] train[ing] woman properly for her own proper business" (Beecher quoted in Nicolaides and Wiese 2006, 47).[14]

This new lifestyle of separated, discrete domesticity was initially possible only for a few: the urban working masses had no choice but to live in the dark alleys between the factories and, to the horror of Victorian-era elites on both sides of the North Atlantic, to conduct whatever work they could in their cramped tenements. And poor women—that is, the overwhelming majority of women— *had* to work. But the new bourgeois model of living in purely private, domestic environments set the standard for what was seen as proper and desirable for the decades to come. In Andrew Jackson Downing's view, this model was what would distinguish a civilized people from a coarse and brutal one. By the end of the nineteenth century, a family home apart from work and the city became the widely held upper-middle-class ideal in the Anglo-Saxon world (Fishman 1987, von Hoffman 1988). To ensure a family's privacy, separation was now desirable not only from the crowded city but also from one's neighbors, separation that could be secured by a lush private yard. As Kenneth Jackson points out:

> By 1870 separateness had become essential to the identity of the suburban house. The yard was expected to be large and private and designed for both active and passive recreation, in direct antithesis to the dense lifestyle from which many families had recently moved. The new ideal was no longer to be part of a close community, but to have a self-contained unit, a private wonderland walled off from the rest of the world. (Jackson 1985, 58)

The new ideal affected the morphology of built forms over time in more ways than one: for example, it influenced street layout and residential interiors. Traditional cities are built of interconnected streets that link various neighborhoods and give passers-by access to communities of people they do not know. But the spine around which suburban subdivisions became increasingly organized was the dead-end street: the cul-de-sac. Although the cul-de-sac dates back to ancient times, it has been in common use only since the suburban era. The English designers Raymond Unwin and Barry Parker and their American colleagues Clarence Stein and Henry Wright were its chief proponents in the early 1900s, advertising it as means of assuring family privacy: by discouraging outside traffic, the cul-de-sac works "for those who desire quiet in their dwellings" (Unwin quoted in Southworth and Ben-Joseph 2004, 31). The layout of dwellings evolved significantly as well. Rooms acquired increasingly specialized functions (e.g., rooms for adults and rooms for children). Spaces that served public and private purposes became more separate (e.g., dining and living rooms on the first floor, bedrooms on the second; Archer 2005). The growing popularity of the open first-floor layout during the first half of the twentieth century was a move in the same direction, toward drawing borders around the home and the family. In older interior layouts, the kitchen and the dining room were separated by a wall. This allowed the dining room to be used as a bedroom and be rented out. The elimination of the physical separation between the kitchen and dining room minimized this possibility, reflecting the notion that "good" middle-class families did not need to invite renters (that is, outsiders) into their homes for income-producing purposes (Kelly 1993). Income generation came to be seen as utterly incompatible with good home-making: the two were to form two physically separate, mutually exclusive domains (Perrin 1977).

This ideal did not capture the imagination of the well-off in continental Europe to the same extent. The French found ways to accommodate the privacy, domesticity, and exclusivity bourgeois families desired in the apartment buildings along Haussmann's boulevards (Fishman 1987). And even the English, ostensibly the inventors of the nuclear family model, did not embrace low-density suburbia to the extent that Americans did. By the early 1900s, the desire for family cottages with generous yards in serene settings was clashing with a growing awareness of the need to protect the English countryside. When Ebenezer Howard wrote *Garden Cities of To-Morrow* ([1898] 1965)—a book that was to become a virtual blueprint for mid-century British urban policy—preservation of the countryside was already a top political concern. Howard passionately articulated this concern. His proposal sought to alleviate urban overcrowding by shifting populations from central cities to smaller "garden cities." But these garden cities had clearly defined boundaries and were surrounded by land that was designated as greenfields or farm fields for perpetuity. Post–World War II British governments institutionalized Howard's idea by surrounding major English cities with vast greenbelts to protect them from residential sprawl. Coupled with the "nationalization" of development rights that occurred during the same time, this policy ultimately produced a landscape of relatively compact cities dominated by row houses and attached single-family homes on very small lots (small from an American point of view, that is). Howard's ideas were also influential in the United States during the first few decades of twentieth century, as evidenced in the regional plan of New York City. However, English-style policies that focused on preserving the countryside never materialized in the United States. A couple of decades after Howard, the mainstream European idea of urban reform was championed by modernists such as Le Corbusier. His vision of *The City of To-Morrow and Its Planning* ([1929] 1987) focused on concentrating people in collectivist megatowers with mind-boggling densities.

The American alterative was presented most persuasively by Frank Lloyd Wright. America's most iconic architect may not be well known as an urban planner, but his urban planning proposals in the early 1930s prophesied America's development patterns in the decades to come (Fishman 1982). Responding to the European modernists, Wright argued that dense cities are examples of such "unnatural verticality" that they represent "cancerous growth." Landscapes of low population densities, examples of "natural horizontality," were for him the only type of human settlements worthy of the American aspiration for a free, individual-centered society of "space-loving human beings." Wright believed in Jeffersonian ideals and often cited Thoreau's motto: "That Government is best Government that is least Government" (10). A passionate advocate of America's frontier tradition of individual homesteads sprinkled across the land, he wrote that America's "vast territory, riches untouched, were inherited by all the breeds of the earth desiring freedom and courageous enough to come and take domain on the terms of the pioneer" and that "ground space" is the "essential basis of the new city of a new life" (Wright 1932, 5–10, 21–24, 43). His solution to urban problems was Broadacre City: a proposed city in which every household would own an individual home located on least one acre of land. Such homes, along with farms and factories, were to be connected loosely via a system of great highways (17). Broadacre City was for Wright the city of "free life" (18), the "only democratic city," "the only possible city looking toward the future" (33). In Fishman's analysis,

> Wright wanted the whole United States to become a nation of individuals. His planned city called "Broadacres" [sic] took decentralization beyond the small community (Howard's ideal) to the individual family home. . . . Wright believed that individuality must be founded on individual ownership. Decentralization would make it possible for everyone to live his chosen lifestyle on his own land. (Fishman 1982, 9)

Wright's belief was that the new city should be centered on one thing only, precisely the thing that his contemporaries put on the top of their zoning pyramid: "We come, now, to the most important unit in the [Broadacre] city, really the center and the only centralization allowable. *The individual home*" (Wright 1932, 80, my italics).

Guarding Exclusive Domesticity through Private Rules

But the vision of an America of family homes in leafy settings was not easy to defend. Well before Wright (and before zoning for that matter), the proud dweller in the individual home faced a perpetual problem: unwanted change, or what Fogelson (2005) calls "bourgeois nightmares." Since not everyone could afford a spacious home yet many craved its park-like surroundings and since many an entrepreneur figured out that money could be made by making or selling things in such surroundings, serene single-family neighborhoods were under permanent threat of "invasion"—by undesirable establishments and by lower-class residents.[15] In textbox 5.2, one of Wright's contemporaries, who, like many others, saw the situation as a key rationale for adopting municipal zoning, describes the problem.

TEXTBOX 5.2   The Perpetual "Invasion" of Residential Districts by Undesirable Land Uses, as Planners Saw It the Early Parts of the Twentieth Century.

The Home Site

It used to be quite customary to refer to a man's home as his castle. This implied that his home was a place to which he could retire when he wished to be secure from intrusion and where he would be free to carry on his life according to his own desires. In the early days of any country there was justification for this idea. When a person picked up a desirable piece of land, bought it and a built a house thereon he could feel fairly certain that he had established a residence that would continue to please him.

As population has increased ... conditions have changed. ... It was pointed out in the preceding chapter that by far the greater part of urban land is used as sites for homes. Without a city plan most of this area has been developed in a hit and miss manner. ... As a result, the seclusion of many a country estate or suburban home established with a rural setting has been destroyed.

This destruction has taken place as a result of various kinds of "invasions."

There may be a need for a grocery store, a dry-goods store or a laundry. ... Such a local store is apt to be ugly and generally comes right out to the street line, although residences alongside may have deep front yards. As a result, homes next door or across the street will no longer be desirable ... the blighted area increases. How much better it would be if the location of a neighborhood business district could be determined well in advance of its needs. ... This would prevent business structures from shutting off light and air from adjoining residences and spoiling their appearance.

A still more serious type of invasion by new uses would be the establishment of an industrial part such as a factory or warehouse, a brick yard or a coal-yard, or perhaps a junk-yard. In such a case the injury to residential property is still greater. Noise and ugliness are still more in evidence. ...

The invasion may take the form of other types of residence at a greater density or bringing in people in a lower social level. Lots on acre or more in size may be invaded by 60-foot lots, or the latter may in turn be invaded by lots of 40 feet, or only 25 feet, in width. A community of single-family homes may find itself changed to one made up of rows of box-like two-family houses with narrow dark yards between them. An apartment may be built to tower above single-family homes and take advantage of the light, air and park-like surroundings provided by its neighbors.

This all points to the need of somehow ensuring stability of use in a residential neighborhood. If only we could be sure that our home would always be in a district of homes of a quality similar to our own!

Source: Lewis 1939, 38–42.

In more vivid terms, an earlier observer, William Dean Howells, depicted the "invasions" and the degradation of property values and morale that followed in the suburbs of Boston, where the much-cherished suburban quarters of one ethnic group were infringed upon by another ethnic group. "It is amusing," pondered the author, that the Irish "would be fearful of the encroachment of the French, as we, in our turn dread the advance of the Irish":

> The householders view with fear and jealousy the erection of any dwelling of less than a stated cost, as portending a possible advent of Irish; and when the calamitous race appears, a mortal pang strikes to the bottom of every pocket. Values tremble around the neighborhood. . . . I saw more than one token of the encroachment of the Celtic army. . . . The fortunes of such a house [located in a neighborhood "invaded" by the Irish] are, of course, not to be retrieved. Where the Celt sets his foot, there the Yankee . . . rarely, if ever returns. The place remains to the intruder and his heirs forever. (Howells 1871, 70–71)

Since distance from the city alone could not guarantee the permanence of serene residential surroundings, homeowners and developers resorted to another method of protection: restrictive private covenants, or deed restrictions. Likely dating to 1826, when a "Committee of Proprietors" congregated to preserve the character of Louisburg Square, an upscale residential subdivision in Boston (McKenzie 1994, 34), housing covenants produced by homeowners' associations came into wide use during the second half of the nineteenth century—precisely when cities began to grow rapidly and new transportation technologies made it possible for the upper classes to partially withdraw from urban life. Frederick Law Olmsted's firm worked on several such covenants, including the 1871 covenant for the landmark Riverside community, a Chicago suburb whose design was completed the previous year (Nelson 2005, 32). Some of the covenants dealt with aesthetics, signs, land use, and other seemingly innocuous issues that were believed to lower home values if left unaddressed. For instance, they prohibited the sale or conversion of residential property for other uses, banned fences and billboards, required certain setbacks, regulated height, dictated that no more than one house be built per lot, mandated lawn mowing, and relegated the hanging of laundry to backyards (Young 1996; Garvin 2002, 356–357). Some of these regulations are now standard fare in zoning ordinances around the country. Other items in the covenants went well beyond the mundane to seek the outright exclusion of undesirable groups from the neighborhood, either implicitly (e.g., by requiring a minimum cost of construction) or explicitly, by listing what kind of people could and could not settle in a community. Such people, in the assessment of Olmsted's firm, tended to depreciate property values because of their "ignorance, incompetence, bad taste, or knavery" (quoted in Fogelson 2005, 29). For example, here is an excerpt from the private covenant of a subdivision in Los Angeles in the early twentieth century:

> It is hereby covenanted and agreed by and between the parties hereto and it is a part of the consideration of this indenture . . . that the said property shall not be sold, leased, or rented to any persons other than of the Caucasian race, nor shall any person or persons other than of Caucasian race be permitted to occupy said lot or lots. (Los Angeles Investment Co. v. Gary quoted in Rich and Wailes 1920, 118)

African Americans were the most common target of exclusion (Brooks and Rose 2013). But Asian Americans and several white groups were also routinely listed as undesirable owners or tenants (although members of these groups could live in the communities, if they were employed as servants). Covenants often targeted specific groups by name: one forbade "any negro or native of Ireland"; another prohibited sale or rent to "a negro or person of African or Mongolian descent"; a third barred "any person of Hungarian, Mexican, Greek, Armenian, Austrian, Italian, Russian, Polish, Slavish, or Roumanian birth" (quoted in Fogelson 2005, 95, 102–103).

These private regulations, along with nuisance laws, became building blocks for municipal proto-zoning regulations efforts in the United States (Frug 1996; Fischler and Kolnick 2006). Between 1870 and 1890, a string of northern California towns (e.g., San Francisco, Modesto) used existing nuisance laws to create municipal rules that excluded certain types of businesses—most commonly laundries—from select districts (Pollard 1931; Toll 1969; Garvin 2002, 359–360).[16] These ordinances led to a series of legal disputes known as the "laundry cases." There were some good reasons related to health and safety to impose restrictions on commercial laundries: they increased the risk of fire because of their need to boil water and heat irons when most buildings were framed with wood. But the restrictions also served other more sinister purposes: most of the laundries were owned by Chinese immigrants, and city legislators were concerned that the laundries were "becoming clubs of the Chinese" (Pollard 1931, 18). The restrictions were never applied to white owners but were readily used as rationale for expelling Asians from certain neighborhoods. As the New York Heights of Buildings Commission reported regarding Los Angeles: "When the city had been districted about 110 Chinese and Japanese laundries found themselves in the residential district [where laundries were prohibited]. The city immediately undertook to remove them to the industrial districts" (1913, 45). Notably, the line between public and private regulations was rather blurred in this case because the laws excluding the Chinese laundries were passed after the private homeowners and business owners who lived and worked in the "Anglo" districts submitted peti-tions to the city authorities (many early twentieth-century ordinances relied on a similar petitioning method: a town would pass district regulations but neighbor-hood groups had to petition the authorities for their area to be designated under any of the districts; this was the Berkeley, California case, for instance.[17]

In the early 1900s, the racially and ethnically charged private restrictions of the late nineteenth century were temporarily overshadowed by the rise of municipal zoning ordinances with the same explicit intent. Southern cities such as Atlanta, Georgia; Baltimore, Maryland; Louisville, Kentucky; and Richmond, Virginia explicitly divided their municipalities based on race (for a detailed account, see Silver 1997). But in 1917, while considering the Louisville ordinance, the Supreme Court declared such city laws unconstitutional in *Buchanan v. Warley*: "A city ordinance which forbids colored persons to occupy houses in blocks where the greater number of houses are occupied by white persons, in practical effect, pre-vents the sale of lots in such blocks to colored persons, and is unconstitutional." As overt racial segregation through zoning was no longer legally permissible, private covenants became even more popular in the early twentieth century than they had been in the late nineteenth century. The courts treated them sympa-thetically for four decades, citing the Constitution and private property rights. The tide began to turn only in 1948, when the Supreme Court declared in *Shelley v. Kraemer* that private regulations that discriminate are legally unenforceable: "Private agreements to exclude persons of designated race or color from the use or occupancy of real estate for residential purposes do not violate the Fourteenth Amendment; but it is violative of the equal protection clause of the Fourteenth Amendment for state courts to enforce them." In reality, however, discriminatory deed restrictions did not become unlawful until the Fair Housing Act of 1968. Even so, scholars point to instances where such restrictions continue to exist in a subtle form (Brooks and Rose 2013). And strangely enough, nonracial private covenants that regulate aspects of social behavior as well as the built environ-ment[18] continue to prosper in the United States; in fact, they have only increased in number with the recent explosive growth of homeowners' associations.[19]

Throughout the nineteenth century and into the twentieth, neither the public nor the private rules that existed on the books, however, could sustain an envi-ronment that was deemed suitable for private homes. The rules failed to satisfy the condition desired by the upper and, increasingly, the middle classes, "that our home would always be in a district of homes of a quality similar to our own!," as Lewis put it. In the eyes of early twentieth-century zoning proponents, the chief practical problem with the public rules, the most advanced and stringent of which were nuisance and building laws, was that they treated the city too uni-formly. They failed to categorize the built environment so that different land uses could be relegated to different parts of town in an orderly fashion.[20] Public rules could not be sufficiently stringent regarding noxious uses (say, public garages or slaughterhouses) because such stringency would likely have the effect of outlawing businesses throughout a municipality, whereas those businesses would surely be needed somewhere in the municipality. So argued Edward Bassett in his well-known zoning advocacy piece of 1922:

> Uniform building laws do not bring about the orderly condition desired. They do not recognize that the heights of buildings which may be permitted in the intensively used parts of the city should not prevail in the suburbs. They do not recognize that stores which may be built on car-lined streets should not be built promiscuously among homes. . . . In other words they apply uniformly over the entire city. The usefulness of zoning regulations consists in their being different in different districts. (Bassett 1922b, 318)

But private covenants suffered from the opposite flaw: they were not backed by a careful vision of a municipality as a whole. Instead, they targeted small areas in an ad hoc and piecemeal fashion and were often poorly drafted by nonprofessionals and thus could easily be challenged in court. Many also had an expiration date:

> The history of private covenants has been far from satisfactory. . . . Efforts are frequently made but even a small minority can usually upset even the best laid plan. Even in private residential developments the beneficial effect of private restrictions is apt to be short-lived. Usually these restrictions are for a period of up to twenty years or twenty-five years. In that time three-fourths of the lots are built upon with a uniform class of residences. As the time expires, owners begin to keep their lots, especially vacant corner lots, out of improvement so that on the lapse of the restrictions they may erect apartment houses and thus exploit the private home surroundings. . . . Often the restrictions are badly drawn and show lack of foresight. Then litigations are sure to ensue. . . . Contractual restrictions have been of great service in all cities and they will continue to be. They cannot, however, be looked upon as affording sufficient or long-term protection from an all-city point of view. (Bassett 1922b, 317)

A legal mechanism was needed to combine what was considered best in both public and private regulations while avoiding the weaknesses of each. Enter citywide zoning.

THE FORMATIVE YEARS OF AMERICAN ZONING

Between about 1910 and 1930, the United States changed from a place where the public control of private land and real-estate property consisted only of rudimentary nuisance and building laws to a place where practices related to private land, property, and construction were subject to tight public supervision in hundreds of municipalities around the country.[1] How did this change occur? How was public regulation through zoning justified in a country where the idea that "everyone was free to do what he wanted" with private land was part of the common wisdom for decades (Abeles 1989: 122)?

The classic and explicit arguments for zoning were the need to ensure public safety and protect the health and the general welfare of the population (e.g., New York City Board of Estimate and Apportionment 1913, 10). These justifications were perhaps best formulated by Bassett and articulated superbly in his later scholarly and advocacy work (1922b). They framed zoning as an exercise of the government police powers and went a long way toward ensuring that it passed the test of constitutionality. These arguments were echoed in the thousands of zoning ordinances written around the country in the past 100 years. Over time, the list was slightly expanded; for example, in 1930 the American City Planning Institute listed "health, safety, morals, convenience, prosperity and the general welfare" as the reason for zoning laws (American City Planning Institute, Committee on Zoning Standards and Principles 1930, 1). Of the primary explicit goals, the first two are perhaps easier to define. They reflected legitimate concerns related to living and working conditions in the industrialized cities of the United States at the time. One could write a book *only* on the health and safety arguments for zoning.[2] Yet the other justifications—welfare, convenience, prosperity, morals—are vague and malleable and thus, I submit, more intriguing. In this chapter, I attempt to explain why zoning—an institution that many at the dawn of the twentieth century doubted could ever take root in laissez-faire-minded America—became widely popular. I argue that zoning was successfully presented as means of enhancing Americans' welfare because:

1) As much as the zoning rules restrained the actions of private parties, they were also crafted to ensure that public authorities would have tightly defined and limited freedom of judgment (in this sense, public actions were restrained too).
2) As much as the rules placed limits on private property, they were also presented as public protections of the value of private property.
3) The rules were justified as a public guarantee of the sanctity of America's most idealized housing form: the detached private home.

Undoubtedly, racial and class prejudices played a key part in the emerging zoning story, since it was minorities and the poor who were perceived as the greatest danger to property values in general and to single-family residential areas in particular. But zoning ultimately gained legitimacy because its advocates presented it as a mechanism that was deeply embedded in the noble American traditions of political, economic, and spatial individualism. In this way, zoning appealed to the better angels of its advocates and the broader middle-class public that eventually accepted it. Because zoning conformed to these established American traditions, it developed in ways that were substantially different from the methods invented in Europe.

I start with the pioneering German experiment with citywide zoning, then move to a discussion of how the American zoning model established its own profile over time.

The German Invention

The idea that land uses should be separated and that cities should be "districted" with different rules for each district was not fully articulated until the end of the nineteenth century. No municipality before that time had divided itself into clearly delineated districts with separate regulations for each based on land use. Furthermore, although awareness was building that there is some inherent division between the spaces where social reproduction occurs (i.e., the home) and the spaces where economic production occurs (i.e., the workplace)—an awareness that was likely stronger in the nineteenth-century Anglo-Saxon world than elsewhere (Fishman 1987)—the border between homes and workplaces was not yet firmly established conceptually or legally. Who invented the idea of legally sanctioning the spatial division of human activities in cities? The foremost experts on the history of zoning in the early twentieth-century United States, such as Frank Backus Williams, author of *The Law of City Planning and Zoning* (1922) and one of the most prominent lawyers of the early twentieth century (see Buttenheim 1955), argued that the first person to express in writing the idea of full urban division based on what types of activities and what types of buildings can be located where was Reinhard Baumeister, a professor at the University of Karlsruhe (Williams 1913, 94; 1914a, 1; 1922, 210). In 1876, Baumeister published *Stadterweiterungen in Technischer, Baupolizeilicher und Wirthschaftlicher Beziehung* (Urban Expansion with Respect to Technology, Building Law and Economy), one of the most comprehensive analyses of urban problems and solutions at the time. One of Baumeister's most consequential observations was that economic activities in the industrial city were demonstrating a greater tendency to group together than in any earlier historic period. Baumeister's proposal was to reinforce this "natural" process by a municipal legal mechanism—districting or zoning. In his view, it made sense to categorize buildings and the activities within them in three classes and locate them in three types of zones:

> When we build a vision of the future . . . we want to distinguish three sections. The first consists of large-scale industry and wholesaling . . . but also the homes of workers and even factory owners; the second includes all trades which require direct contact with the public, and similarly the homes which must be united with the trade premises; the third includes homes whose owners have no trade and have different occupations (landlords, officials, merchants, factory owners, workers). (translated from Baumeister 1876, 80)[3]

The idea of three classes of buildings was not new. As I pointed out in chapter 4, London's Metropolitan Buildings Act from 1844, for example, also used three classes, albeit slightly different ones: first class ("dwelling-house," which today we would call residential), second class (which we would call commercial/industrial), and third class (which we would call public). But this act did not deliberately seek to place the different classes of buildings in different parts of the city. In that, Baumeister was likely a pioneer.

Baumeister's idea was first comprehensively implemented in Germany in Frankfurt-on-the-Main[4] under the leadership of reformist mayor Franz Adickes (Williams 1913, 1922; Lewis 1916; Logan 1976; Mullen 1976; Ladd 1990). Frankfurt's zoning act was adopted in 1891. From then on, the idea of classifying urban forms and functions and regulating them differently in different parts of the city came to be seen as a cutting-edge example of scientific municipal administration. It spread quickly across Germany: Hamburg adopted its zoning act in 1896, Berlin in 1897, Cologne in 1900, Mannheim in 1901, Hanover in 1902, Munich in 1903, Düsseldorf in 1907, and so forth (Logan 1976; Ladd 1990). From Germany, the idea travelled first to Switzerland and Scandinavia and then to England and the rest of Europe (Williams [1916] 1929, 81). The early German zoning ordinances used various mechanisms for dividing urban space: some relied heavily on requirements about density and bulk; others, like Frankfurt's, used functional categories as well as bulk and density categories, thus creating several overlapping districts. The American zoning codes that were written a few decades later initially resembled this model.

In Frankfurt's ordinance, the city was divided into two broad zones, inner and outer. The inner zone, the central city or downtown, was already densely built out with structures of various types and shapes. Although the height and bulk of buildings were strictly regulated, the functions of buildings were not. The activities inside the buildings could continue; only a few types of nuisance businesses were explicitly prohibited. The outer part of Frankfurt was divided into inner, outer, and country subzones. Outer Frankfurt had three types of districts based on land use: residential (which included two subtypes, general residential and country homes), factory, and mixed. In residential areas, despite the name, retail establishments, workshops, and industries that complied with state-level industrial performance standards were allowed. The mixed zones were just as their name suggests. The factory areas were more restrictive than the others. They housed the manufacturing establishments that did not comply with state industrial performance standards. Most types of residences were discouraged in factory zones because of concerns about workers' health. Only the dwellings of service personnel (factory watchmen, caretakers) were permitted by right (Williams 1914a; Logan 1976; Talen 2012a). Area and bulk rules were tied to each land-use type in an unprecedentedly detailed manner. As an admiring American planner noted: "In the central district one-fourth of interior and one-sixth of corner lots must be left open; in the factory zone, three-tenths; in the dwelling and mixed districts of the inner zones, four-tenths of interior and three-tenths of inner lots; in the same district of the outer or suburban zones, one-half of interior and four-tenths of inner lots, and in the country districts, seven-tenths of all lot areas" (Lewis 1916, 268; Figure 6.1 represents the zoning map of Frankfurt from 1891).

The "example of Germany" (a book with this subtitle praising German town planning was published by British expert T. Horsfall in 1904) became very popular among early urban reformers in England and other European countries in the early twentieth century. The country as a whole was seen as at the forefront of progressive and scientific city management (Mullen 1976).

Deeply impressed by what they saw in Germany, many American architects, engineers, and planners hoped that German-type public regulations would be passed on American soil. New York's Committee on Congestion of Population became a lead transmitter of ideas. In 1908–9, having returned from London where he met both German and English experts, the Committee's Secretary Benjamin Marsh organized an exhibition and published a book titled *An Introduction to City Planning* (Marsh 1909). This book introduced German planning laws to the United States, producing an effect similar to the effect that Horsfall's book on "the example of Germany" had created in England five years earlier. Although dealing with many aspects of urban policy, Marsh deemed the "zone system" as the "most important part of City Planning" (28). German influences on American planning intensified from this point on. The 1913 report of New York City's Heights of Buildings Commission included detailed notes on German cities. The first national conferences on city planning held in the United States featured a series of speeches praising German municipal planning and zoning by figures as authoritative as Marsh himself along with Frederick Law Olmsted, Lawrence Veiller, Daniel Burnham, Benjamin Marsh and Ernst Freund (Toll 1969, Scott 1971). Still, these admirers of the German model were well aware of the cultural and political obstacles of transferring zoning to the United States. As Veiller put it:

> We have cast somewhat longing eyes at the shores of Germany and wondered whether there was something so essentially different in the atmosphere of Germany and America that it would be impossible for us to engraft upon American civilization the well-established principle of zoning that has been in operation for a generation or more in that country. (Veiller 1914, 92)

Debates on the potential ideological undesirability of zoning persisted well into the 1920s. Even after *Euclid v. Ambler*—the case that established the constitutionality of the zoning principle in the United States—some observers still believed that because zoning restricted what owners could do on their private property, it was alien to American cultural and political traditions. Indeed, zoning proponents on occasion had to rebut accusations that the tool that they were proposing was an inherently anti-American and possibly even a pro-Russian, communist instrument. Alfred Bettman—the attorney whose briefs heavily influenced the outcome of *Euclid v. Ambler*—wrote a defensive letter to the *Cincinnati Enquirer* in 1929 stating that he and his close associates had never read the laws of communist Russia and thus could not have been inspired by them (Knack, Meck, and Stollman 1996, 6).

Wohnviertel.
Gemischtes Viertel.
Innenstadt.
Landhausviertel.
Fabrikviertel.
Strassen an welchen 3 Obergeschosse zulässig sind
Maßstab 1:15000
Harheim
Bonames
VILBEL
Seckbach

FIGURE 6.1   Frankfurt's zoning map of 1891.

Source: Heights of Buildings Commission (1913).

The reasons for doubt were obvious. The political context in Germany was significantly different from that in America. Not only did German cities have a centuries-long tradition of town planning and building regulation, whose "desirability is never questioned" by the wider citizenry (or so thought American planners; e.g., Lewis 1916, 13), but their powers to control their development had been greatly expanded under the Stein reforms of 1808.[5] Cities in Prussia and, later on, the German Empire had the authority to annex land and tax private property heavily. Many municipal authorities owned a large share of land within the limits of their city, and they often appropriated small private lots and packaged them into larger sites so they could build housing for workers (Howe 1911; Toll 1969; Scott 1971; Rogers 1998). These actions were not necessarily done out of pure altruism or noble concern for the well-being of workers: German governments at all levels feared workers' riots and were thus motivated to ensure minimal living standards. Monarchs most likely encouraged the urban annexations to prevent the formation of politically autonomous working-class locales (Light 1999). Small property owners had virtually no means of fighting government actions. From an American point of view, the willingness of the German populace to put up with this regime could be explained by the fact that in Germany, there was a much higher respect for municipal government since its officers were deemed the greatest city-building experts in the world. In the eyes of Germany's admirers, some of whom went so far as to claim that German authoritarianism was a "tremendous asset," as the chairman of the Syracuse Plan Commission put it (Brockway 1915: 167), this view contrasted sharply with public attitudes toward American urban politicians of the Tammany Hall era. The latter were correctly perceived not only as nonprofessionals but also as deeply corrupt. Charles Mulford Robinson, the first professor of civic design at the University of Illinois, described the attitude toward German civic officials:

> The [German] burgomaster [sic] and his magistrates are the best experts procurable, and the council of the latter does not pretend to be citizen-representative, but is made up of honored, highly-paid, professional and permanent employees, trained to the work of city administration (Robinson [1904] 1970, 22).

Six decades later, Toll summarized the perceived contrast as follows:

> For one [the American city administrator] the city was an object of rapine, for the other [the German city administrator], veneration. Corruption contrasted with duty. The American city was often governed by nothing more than a monumental crook, the German by nothing less

than the most distinguished burgher. One came to office expecting to take, the other to give. (Toll 1969, 134)

That the American municipal politicians and bureaucrats could ever be entrusted with vast regulatory powers over one of the most cherished rights of the American citizen—to freely use and enjoy private property—must have seemed in these conditions a far-fetched proposition (Mullen 1976). This ideological barrier was eventually overcome by transforming the German invention to meet American goals. Note, however, that as powerful as zoning may have seemed in the United States at the time (and still today), it was one of the *weaker* tools used by German municipalities—weaker as compared to their powers to own land, tax heavily and directly subsidize, construct and distribute housing (Rogers 1998). When in 1909 Marsh assessed that zoning was the "most important part of City Planning," he did not specify important in what context. If he was talking about Germany, where zoning was a single component of a much larger urban policy package, he was wrong. He was right, however, if he was referring to the American context, where all the other, more robust tools for shaping housing and the built environment remained far out of the reach of municipal authorities.[6] Hence in the American context, zoning truly became the most important tool of city planning at the time.

After World War I, Germany's image was tarnished and it no longer served as a model (Mullen 1976). In 1931, when zoning had already spread across America, the authors of the landmark *Regional Plan of New York and Its Environs* sought to dissociate their plan from European models generally and German models particularly. By that time, they had every reason to claim that while it had roots in Germany, "American zoning is a method of regulating building development adapted to American conditions" (Committee on the Regional Plan of New York and Its Environs 1931, 151).

In my interpretation, the essential elements that distinguished U.S. zoning from its European predecessors and contemporaries and made it acceptable to American experts and the broader public were as follows: 1) Although U.S. zoning laws gave municipal governments great powers, they deliberately sought to limit those powers by giving those who wielded them little room for discretion; hence, the laws conformed to the American tradition of political individualism. 2) Although U.S. zoning laws restricted private property rights, they also explicitly served to protect them; hence, the laws could be portrayed as befitting the American tradition of economic individualism. 3) U.S. zoning laws worked to create the kinds of private spaces that promoted the American tradition of spatial individualism.

U.S. Zoning and Government Discretion

It appears that one of the most cherished virtues zoning had in the eyes of its early supporters was uniformity—the fact that whatever written standards were put together, they were applied consistently, without variation, within their respective districts. This principle may appear mundane to casual observers, yet it played an important role in making the new regulatory mechanism acceptable in the U.S. political context. To begin with, the principle of uniformity within a district was presented as a means of achieving greater social equality. Zoning was advertised as a tool that would protect all, including those "who cannot protect themselves" (Whitten 1921, 27). Wealthy owners, this argument went, could very well find ways to avoid the harms of traffic and pollution inflicted by proximity to factories and other objectionable nonresidential uses, yet the "poor man with a family is as much entitled to live in a home neighborhood restricted from . . . undesirable buildings as is the wealthy man" (Cheney 1920, 275–276). As long as the rules were applied in the same fashion in a district where at least some social mixture occurred, the law offered the wealthy and the poor the same protections. Furthermore, the rules applied equally, at least in theory, to anyone, rich or poor, who wished to develop his or her land in a certain way in any given district. The *Zoning Primer* prepared under the leadership of Herbert Hoover emphasized that "Zoning regulations differ in different districts according to the determined uses of the land. . . . But these different regulations are *the same for all districts of the same type*. They treat all men alike" (U.S. Department of Commerce, Advisory Committee on City Planning 1926, 1). So too did the Standard Zoning Enabling Act: "All such regulations shall be uniform for each class or kind of building throughout each district" (U.S. Department of Commerce, Advisory Committee on Zoning 1926, 6). Uniformity was also essential to the justification of zoning because zoning rules could easily be struck down as violating the equal protection clause of the Fourteenth Amendment if they were applied inconsistently. "The success of any regulatory law," building officials emphasized, "is dependent upon the uniformity with which the administration of such law can be carried out" (Moomaw 1931, 85). Bassett cited uniformity as the primary reason the zoning laws were upheld by U.S. courts:

> The fact that the zoning ordinance of New York City provided that the regulations should be uniform within each district was the most powerful incentive to the court in upholding the zoning principle (Bassett 1931, 104).

But uniformity of application had another, equally important appeal. Uniformity served as a guarantee that the decision-making powers of (potentially corrupt) individual members of municipal administrations would be constrained by the detailed and uniform written rules. The key problem that zoning advocates faced at the beginning of the twentieth century, according to Frank Backus Williams, was Americans' low trust in politicians and government bureaucrats, a problem only partially offset by the high opinion Americans had of judges as the law's guardians: "In all foreign countries . . . the legislators are trusted more and the courts less than with us" (Williams [1916] 1929, 51). Cullingworth (1993, 16–17) reassessed the situation some eighty years later, reaching the same conclusion: in the United States, any land-use regime had to be explicitly rooted in the principle of "government of laws, not men,"—the tenet popularized by the 1780 Constitution of the Commonwealth of Massachusetts. This was the precise phrase Lawrence Veiller used when he argued that zoning rules should vary as little as possible in districts that were as large as possible and that zoning relief should be granted only under a very limited set of circumstances, if at all: "Instead of having a board that will grant special privileges in particular cases, let us stick to the good American principle of government by law and not government by men" (Veiller quoted in Knack, Meck, and Stollman 1996, 5). Veiller was responding not only to the widespread criticism that zoning was an example of laws that constrained private action but also to the criticism that even if zoning laws were good laws created through a virtuous process, once they fell into the hands of municipal bureaucrats, they could become their toy to play with as they wish. Gen. P. Lincoln Mitchell was one to put this sentiment in writing: zoning was not only "worse than prohibition" but also an "advanced form of communism" (quoted in Monnett 1927). This is not just because it constrained private liberties but because those liberties could be disposed with at the pleasure of bureaucratic boards of zoning appeals—a process that created a "government of men rather than of law, which is the American principle."

TEXTBOX 6.1   "Zoning Is Scored As Communistic: Puts City in Straitjacket, Hurts Growth, Says Gen. Mitchell"

By James G. Monnett Jr.

"Zoning laws are an advanced form of communism, confiscating property rights without due process of law, and have prevented proper consideration of city planning by the dust they have thrown in people's eyes."

Gen. P. L. Mitchell of Cincinnati gave this opinion in a talk yesterday before the Real Estate Board in the Hollenden hotel. He said his assertion was based upon study of the workings of zoning in his own city and in many others.

"Some features of zoning laws have been declared constitutional, but the thing as a whole never has been passed upon," he continued. "Zoning laws, like prohibition, are recent experiments and, in my opinion, both will disappear, soon to be replaced by a return to exercise of proper police power without confiscating property or preventing personal liberty."

"Worse Than Prohibition"

"Zoning probably is worse than prohibition because it establishes a precedent for complete state control and confiscation of land. Many of the zoning laws now in force serve no purpose beyond preventing orderly growth of cities.

"Great powers lodged in zoning boards of appeals make equal justice impossible. These boards are permitted to confiscate property rights at their pleasure, and thus is established a government of men rather than of law, which is the American principle.

"It is matched in part by the shocking spectacle of country squires who have handy raiding squads with both squire and squads profiting from fines they impose. Zoning and prohibition are the twin monstrosities born of the travail and abnormality of the World War."

Source: Monnett 1927.

Delafons and Cullingworth, among others, both emphasize how different views of public officials underlie the key contrasts between the English (and more broadly, the European) and U.S. cultures of governance, especially in early-twentieth-century regulation of land use:

> Americans expect corruption in government. . . . Since the values conferred or denied by land-use controls are great, their administration affords exceptional opportunities for graft and by the same token exposes them to exceptionally strong pressures. The result, in America, has been a determination to eliminate the scope for discretion in land-use controls by formalizing them in a set of standard regulations and by laying down in advance the conditions under which, if at all, change may be allowed. (Delafons 1969, 7–8)

> Americans traditionally distrust officials and favor adversary procedures and judicial interventionism. In Britain, on the other hand, people are comfortable with relying on official discretion to strike compromises

and make individualized judgments which are never reviewed by the courts. (Asimow 1983 cited by Cullingworth 1993, 198)

There is much support for such arguments in the records of the annual meetings of the National Conference on City Planning from the formative years of zoning. One finds many examples of concern among experts not just about the potential lack of constitutionality of zoning but also about the potentially unchecked powers it would hand to untrustworthy city bureaucrats. Public controls in the hands of bureaucrats were surely viewed as necessary (perhaps a necessary evil). But the key to making them acceptable was to bind the bureaucrats by written rules that were as clear and inviolable as possible. As reasonable people, of course, the experts agreed that no zoning ordinance can be so perfect that it would never need amendment. But this should happen only rarely and only under a predetermined set of conditions. The real danger lay in the possibility of freely given, potentially arbitrary zoning exceptions and modifications—that is, in the possibility of bureaucratic free will and discretion: "There is one unfortunate feature which may be is not of zoning administration but which clearly is involved in the success of zoning, and that is the ease with which a zoning ordinance can be changed," lamented one attendee at the 1931 conference (Langsdorf 1931, 102). Government corruption was very much on people's minds, likely for good reasons: "In St. Louis, citizens with an axe to grind who have influence with the board of aldermen can readily secure the passage of undermining amendments. Within the past few years there have been 114 such amendments in St. Louis and 76 resulted in planting intruding structures which were prohibited under the original zoning law" (ibid.). Mr. Langsdorf's anxiety about amendments, which he and others clearly saw as a problem, was perhaps partially offset by the assurances of the likes of Mr. Stern (1931) of Milwaukee, who proudly declared that in his city—which was home to over half a million people—no more than fifty cases for zoning exceptions were considered per year and few of them granted. Some of the discussions at the national city-planning conferences turned into quasi-support groups in which officials tried to help each other withstand the pressure to deviate from the zoning regulations. The model municipal administrators were those who achieved maximum uniformity of land use and minimal deviation from the written rules:

> The suburban city of Newton, Mass., has a most remarkable record of excellent zoning administration and strengthening of the zoning structure: since the adopting of a zoning ordinance in 1922 and the establishment of single-family zones in 1925 . . . nearly 80 per cent of the city area is now zoned for single-family residence—in this long period with only one appeal from a decision of the Board of Aldermen involving the

> change of a zone. In Grand Rapids there have been an exceedingly small number of changes in the original ordinance and excellent zoning control. . . . Madison, Wis., reported the strictest administration encountered, where no variances in use districts have been granted and 75 per cent of the variances in height and area regulations have been such as to promote a more restricted use. (Hubbard and Hubbard 1929, 175)

Limiting the discretion of local officials must have made perfect sense in the United States of the early twentieth century. Zoning was but a subpart of the much broader Progressive Era efforts to wrest power from corrupt political machines that dominated city halls and transfer it to the hands of ostensibly objective, nonpartisan, scientifically trained municipal managers who could run a city as if it were a business (and this is how Americans thought, rightly or wrongly, that German cities were administered; Toll 1969; Schwarz 1976). The first city planning commissions and zoning boards in the United States were explicitly set up with the expectation that they would be purely technocratic and nonpolitical (Levy 2006; Wolf 2008, 17–31). New York's mayor John Mitchel well expressed the ideals of his time. In a speech in which he praised "scientific" city planning and zoning (Mitchel 1916) as major policy innovations, he summed up overall progress in his city as follows:

> Partisan politics has been eliminated. With the city government out of politics and politics out of the city government, we have been free to devote our entire attention to the stupendous business of governing this great city. (ibid., 4)

Hence, American zoning was established to minimize politically (and personally) motivated decisions about land use; it was an attempt to free cities from corrupt dealings and to create "clean government, staffed by experts in technical analysis" (Haar 1989, 343). American political culture could thus accommodate only a few types of zoning relief, and reformers articulated the scope of exceptions narrowly and expressly. As I discussed in chapter 2, the first type is the variance, an administrative act under the jurisdiction of the zoning board of appeals. (These pertain to bulk and shape but not use and are granted only in rare cases of obvious individual hardship.) The other types are amendments (revisions of the text of a law) and rezonings (revisions of zoning maps); these are accomplished through legislative acts by elected officials, who are accountable to the voting public. Alfred Bettman expressed his belief in the necessity of expressly limiting the types and scope of all types of zoning relief in 1930:

> Still, in administering a zoning ordinance, there should be adherence to sound zoning principles and to the zoning ordinance. I believe that the zoning board should rather adjust the general standards of the

ordinance to exceptional and extraordinary situations rather than to get the habit of departing from the standards of the ordinance. I do not believe that boards of appeals should get into the habit of granting variations in use. This is a legislative function and should be exercised by city council. (Bettman 1930, 113–114).

Sixty years later, while acknowledging the problems the traditional system creates (e.g., large uniform districts dominated by homogeneous, cookie-cutter developments), legal experts still recognized its advantages in the U.S. context, specifically citing its capacity to limit the discretionary powers of bureaucrats; for example:

> Despite its rigidities, Euclidean zoning has many virtues. Its structure and substantive regulations allow for development predictability, certainty, and administrative accountability and objectivity. Euclidean zoning is accountable because its rules are explicit and inflexible. The clarity and consistency of the rules allow for the objective review of each individual project as-of-right. *The reviewer has virtually no discretion in administering a Euclidean ordinance. The development either complies or does not comply.* (Kwartler 1989, 191, my italics)

Of course, U.S. zoning was never immune from discretion, no matter how much the early zoning experts might have tried to prevent it. Large numbers of variances and rezonings are common in most U.S. locales, and the U.S. system has grown only more discretionary over time (Kayden 2004) through the wide application of tools such as planned unit developments, design review processes, special-purpose districts, and development agreements. The alternative to the conventional approach that has become most fashionable in recent years is form-based zoning. Like its Euclidean predecessor based on land use, form-based zoning regulates the built environment in a strict and predictable fashion, more so than, say, performance zoning, which requires a detailed case-by-case analysis of whether certain standards are met. Form-based codes are often praised because, like traditional zoning, they allow little room for government discretion:

> A form-based code supports "good" urban projects by creating a regulating plan that sets forth prescriptive building form requirements. Applications that comply with the community vision outlined in the form-based code can be approved administratively and in less time than the current process. If the proposed development project complies with the requirements within the form-based code, *there should be little, if any, discretion.* (City of Colorado Springs 2008, 6, my italics)

As strict as they are, however, form-based codes foster a greater variety in the built environment than the conventional approach. This is because their regulating plans typically apply to individual city blocks (or a small number of blocks) in contrast to the districts of many city blocks in the traditional approach. (In this respect, form-based zoning is close to today's German *Bebauungspläne.*) This shift of scale may well do away with the problem of excessive homogeneity that has plagued traditional zoning (Kayden 2004). Readers may recall from chapter 2 that America's districts based on land use have been growing in size for some hundred years (Gerckens n.d.; Talen 2012b); it is only recently that this trend has begun to reverse through the use of form-based zoning.[7] But in Germany the shift in zoning scale came in the 1920s. As Williams (1922) explains, that is when cities such as Düsseldorf and Karlsruhe began to abolish the Frankfurt-like system of a small number of large districts and adopt a more fine-grained system in which the basic unit of regulation was the street class or the individual city block. Dresden's districts were becoming much smaller than originally (and hence, the land areas they covered were subjected to more varied regulations) to the point that they were described as "kaleidoscopic," and Leipzig had no fewer than ninety-seven of them (Williams 1913, 97–98).

Today there is another significant difference between U.S. and German zoning practices that is rooted in the history of the political culture of the two countries. German *Bebauungspläne* today are very specific and detailed, but they are flexible in terms of land use. German planners use the "daily needs test" to determine which nonresidential uses can be allowed in an area designated as "exclusively residential" or "general residential." Small-scale retail establishments and offices that meet the essential everyday needs of a local neighborhood (bakeries, cafes, doctors' offices, etc.) are permissible, but retail establishments and services that will likely attract customers from a wider region and will thus cause heavy traffic and other disturbances are not (Hirt 2007a). The distinction is drawn largely at the discretion of German planners. No similar discretion is embedded in contemporary American zoning. In fact, it is not difficult to imagine that if American planners began to allow small services to intermingle with residences at their discretion, they might well be accused of practicing "spot zoning"—the "unjustifiable singling out of a piece of property for preferential treatment" (Cullingworth 1993, 49–50). Yet if one were to apply the American term to German (and other European) cities where mixed use is common, one could say that these cities are all covered in "spot" zones.

The English most fully adopted the discretionary approach with the Town and Country Planning Act of 1947. They appear to have recognized the flaws of the large homogeneous zoning district early on. English observers of the American system were criticizing it in the 1930s and praising the "more detailed and intricate approach" that European cities were developing (Mattocks 1935, 243). More recently, the English have moved slightly toward increasing the level of predictability associated with planning permissions (Cullingworth 1993; Kayden 2004). For instance, whereas the mid-twentieth-century approach was to consider the recommendations of a generalized plan as mere "material considerations" in making decisions on individual development applications, today the presumption is that compliance with the generalized plans in the local development frameworks will lead to permission. Although the U.S. system may be moving toward greater discretion and the English system toward greater certainty (Kayden 2004), distance remains between the two systems, likely because of the different levels of trust in government that Cullingworth (1993) and others have identified.

U.S. Zoning and Private Property

Zoning's capacity to preserve and even increase private property values was a constant refrain used in early advocacy of the practice. In a country such as Germany, where the government had always had greater control over private property, this rationale for the introduction of land-use control played a more tangential role. In fact, one of the express purposes of German zoning was to reduce the value of private land (e.g., by placing limits on the intensity with which it could be developed) in an attempt to make it more affordable for uses such as workers' housing (Williams 1913; Mullen 1976; Light 1999). In England, the Town Planning Acts of 1909 and 1932 stated that private property owners were to be compensated for financial losses imposed by government's "planning schemes"—the closest equivalent to a U.S. zoning ordinance—but the opposite was true as well: The government was empowered to recoup the majority of the "betterment" (the increased property value) created by these planning schemes (Purdue 2006). In other words, if the value of private property increased as a result of the planning schemes, owners could be asked to pay the government back. This was meant to bring direct and immediate resources to the government, in addition to those that would come in the long run through higher tax revenue following from increased property values. English private property owners, in other words, were not expected to make a profit from the public regulations; on the contrary, the profit was meant to "return" to the government:

> Whereby the coming into operation of any provision contained in a
> scheme, or by the execution by a responsible authority of any work
> under a scheme, any property is increased in value, the responsible

authority . . . may, subject to the provisions of this Act, recover from the person whose property is so increased in value an amount not exceeding seventy-five per cent of the amount of that increase. (United Kingdom 1932, 32)[8]

In the United States, private profit as a result of zoning ordinances that preserved and enhanced "investment values" was not only fully expected, it was a major zoning goal. In the 1913 report of the Heights of Buildings Commission in New York City, it was listed as one of three components of the "general welfare" (the other two were "comfort and convenience" and "prevention of traffic congestion"; New York City Board of Estimate and Apportionment 1913, 10). As Bassett (1922b) among many others explained, the absence of zoning resulted in financial "waste," including declining home values, falling rents, and low return on investments. The widely held theory was that strict municipal rules, including strict land-use separation via zoning, would propel private property values upward (e.g., Grinnalds 1920; Bassett 1922b). As Harvard professor of government William Murno argued, only in zoned cities, could developers and owners feel confident that their neighborhoods would never be encroached upon by undesirable uses. By zoning, governments would grant them a "touch of monopoly value," which would guarantee to them much higher and more secure returns on investments (Munro 1931, 203; see also Fischel 2001a, 2001b).

Systematic data on the relationship between zoning regulation and private property values was probably never collected. However, anecdotal evidence of declining property values in uncontrolled environments was often used even well before zoning. In *Suburban Sketches*, Howells (1871, 71) spoke semi-humorously of the "mortal pang strik[ing] to the bottom of every pocket" when unwanted uses and people, such as the "calamitous race" of the Irish, entered the "nice" neighborhoods, and the perceived link between law and property values was used as a rationale for the nineteenth-century nuisance ordinances in California (for example, in the San Francisco laundry cases; Pollard 1931). But in the early twentieth century, the story of the link between law and property told in American newspapers, professional journals, textbooks, discussions at city planning conferences, and municipal brochures became a much stronger one, likely because land-use conflicts had substantially intensified. This intensification was the result of the rapid development of cities and because improvements in transportation made the suburbs increasingly more susceptible to "invasions" from undesirable uses and populations (Fischel 2001a).

Concerns at the turn of the twentieth century that lack of regulation would cause financial harm to private property owners have been well documented by Toll (1969) and Fischler (1998a, b, c), among others, in the case of New York's high-end districts, where development pressures were especially intense. The best-known example is Fifth Avenue, where the value of the mansions and upscale retail shops and hotels was under threat of depreciation because of the "invading" garment industry, whose employees were mostly poor immigrants. The petitions of the Fifth Avenue Association provide a good illustration of how fears about declining property values were the impetus for the adoption of zoning. In 1907, the association wrote that nothing had ever been so "blasting" to the "best class of business and property interests" as the "fast flood of workers which sweeps down the pavement at noon-time every day and literally overwhelms and engulfs shops, shopkeepers, and the shopping public." (quoted in Fischler 1998a, 683). Bassett told a similar story of the relationship of property interests and zoning in a speech advocating zoning for Chicago. Before 1916, New York's authorities were not sure how to zone, he said, but they succeeded once they "went to the people, the property owners to find out, and it [the government] was advised by every section of the city and every kind of property owner, so when the plan was formed, it was purely the 'property owners' plan" (quoted in Rabin 1989, 105).[9] Bassett's conflation of "the people" and "property owners" made it clear that he saw zoning as a public policy intended to benefit private property owners. New York's Heights of Buildings Commission bemoaned the impermanence of private deed restrictions in the suburban areas of New York City, which, unlike the city itself, were dominated by detached housing already and concluded that without public regulation, no builder or owner of private homes could be guaranteed steady property values (New York City Board of Estimate and Apportionment 1913, 28). Like Bassett, the board viewed zoning as a public law that would protect the interests of private property owners. In a 1916 speech that reviewed the city's progress in zoning, New York's mayor Mitchel mentioned only one advantage brought about by zoning: property values.

> It has come to be recognized that to maintain real estate values and prevent enormous economic waste, a reasonable limitation by districts must be put upon the height of buildings to which buildings may be carried and the uses to which real estate may be devoted. It has been found, in short, that to protect values and prevent the destruction of whole districts, owners must be protected against the unrestricted use of neighboring parcels. (Mitchel 1916, 28)

In professional debates, the media and in articles and pamphlets across the nation, stories of depreciating property values where zoning laws had not been put in place were complemented by stories of appreciating values following the adoption of zoning. Business leaders from St. Louis, for example, felt that: "The greatest menace to property owners in [unzoned areas of] St. Louis today is the lack of security in present and future values. Lenders of real estate are unwilling to lend on residences unless assured that values will not be impaired by changes in the character of the neighborhood in which they were located." (Davis 1932, 97) But, according to urban planning textbooks from the 1930s, once zoning laws were passed in St. Louis, the city became "one of the best examples of the direct financial benefit to [private] property of appropriate zoning regulations which may be found in the United States"; property values in recently zoned areas reportedly quadrupled from $18,000 to $75,000 after zoning laws were adopted (Hubbard and Hubbard 1929, 188–189). Such textbooks devoted pages to detailed accounts of the beneficial effect of zoning on private property values across the nation:

> In White Plains, N.Y., it was stated that zoning is held directly responsible for an increase of $30,000,000 in assessed property values. In Oklahoma City, zoning is held to have increased property values throughout the city. In Bismarck, N.D., it is found that people are willing to pay more for a residence property now that residence districts are protected by zoning. . . . In Evansville, directly after the passage of zoning, a national insurance company authorized the issuance of 10 per cent additional loans on residential property. In the National Capital Region an insurance company was reported not interested in making loans on residential property in Virginia because it was not yet zoned, but was glad to make loans in Montgomery and Prince George's counties [which had] recently [been] zoned" (ibid., 188–189).

The federal government similarly used increasing private property values as a major justification for its advocacy of zoning: *A City Planning Primer* (U.S. Department of Commerce, Advisory Committee on Zoning 1928) asserted emphatically that planning regulation "pays."[10] And local authorities recognized that an increase in private property values improved public finances through increased tax revenues. As zoning advocates in Pittsburgh put it in 1916: "If Pittsburgh is to continue to raise practically all its revenues by taxing real estate values, steps must be taken to prevent the needless destruction of those values." Thus, there should be "no more public garages, factories or apartments in splendid residential neighborhoods" (Pittsburgh Committee on Taxation Study quoted in Fischel 2001a, 12).

But aside from the issue of increasing public revenue through taxation, there appears to have been very limited discussion in U.S. planning circles of the early twentieth century about reaping more direct public benefit from increasing private property values, as was the case in England under the town planning acts.[11]

The focus of zoning advocacy was on the benefits private property owners could extract from public regulatory action rather than on what the public sector could gain if property values would go up. Frank Backus Williams ([1916] 1929, 84) argued that although zoning was imposed on private property, it served the interests of that property and was essential to its value. City zoning, asserted John Ihlder, manager of the Civic Development Department of the U.S. Chamber of Commerce, was nothing less than "sound business" (1922).

Private property interests may have served as a stronger impetus for the adoption of zoning than concerns about public health and safety. Consider the different treatment of residential and industrial land uses in U.S. and German zoning ordinances. Here we find a commonly overlooked contrast. In Germany, the industrial zoning districts were the most restrictive ones. Dwellings were rarely allowed there. But in the United States, it was the residential districts in early zoning ordinances that became the most restrictive ones. What could be the reason for this difference? After all, in both Europe and the United States it was equally true that locating noxious industries among dwellings was detrimental to public health and safety. Indeed, this was a key rationale for creating the separate factory zones in Germany and a classic argument used in nuisance laws from the pre-zoning era.[12]

Like Frankfurt's 1891 ordinance, New York's 1916 zoning law included residential, business, and unrestricted zones based on land use (New York Board of Estimate and Apportionment 1917). But here is where the similarities end. New York embraced the hierarchical method of organizing land uses (described in chapter 2). It reversed Frankfurt's concept of restrictive industrial zoning and called its own industrial zones the *unrestricted* ones. This was an accurate label. New York's residential uses were perceived as occupying the top of an imaginary pyramid, whereas its industrial ones were at the bottom. New residences could locate everywhere in the city, including amid polluting industries. If health and safety were the primary reasons for separating dwellings and industries, shouldn't New York have banned housing next to factories just as it banned factories next to housing? Why was the building of homes (most likely the homes of poor people) permitted in heavy industrial areas, and how could allowing that practice be justified from the point of view of public health and safety?[13]

One possible answer is that health and safety were not the key motivations. New York was content to protect its nicer residential areas from industries. That the poor could continue to live amid factories in the "unrestricted zones" was not considered an issue of primary importance. But Berkeley, California, which also passed its first zoning ordinance in 1916, came up with another novel idea (City of Berkeley 1916). Berkeley adopted America's pioneering "flat" zoning code (Scott 1971, 161–162). As I mentioned in chapter 2, flat codes create districts that are mutually exclusive: no housing is allowed in industrial zones and no industries are allowed in housing zones. I will examine Berkeley's ordinance in greater detail in the next section, but the key point here is as follows: the published speeches of the key advocates of zoning in Berkeley were not particularly concerned about the health and safety effects of mixing housing with industries. They argued for the creation of restrictive, purely industrial zones because they thought that people living near manufacturing establishments would demand reductions in noise and emissions and would thereby constrain the operation of the industrial businesses. In other words, it was the factory owners who needed protection from the residents and not the other way around:

> Factories are often harassed by people who built close to them and then enter upon a course of annoyance and complaint until they are in some way pacified—when the trouble is apt to be renewed by some other similarly situated residents. In order that factory buildings may be induced to locate in Berkeley, they must be assured that they will be protected against unfair treatment so long as they conform to the municipal regulations. (Bither 1915, 168)

It was not until several decades later that the Berkeley-type restrictive, autonomous industrial district became a standard feature of U.S. zoning ordinances. The flat zoning principle did not become more popular than the hierarchical one until the mid-twentieth century (Gerckens 1994). In the 1930s, the concept of banning housing in industrial zones was still contested. Its advocates continued to argue its merits using the same rationale Berkeley's pioneers had some fifteen years earlier: it was a way to protect industrial property:

> The next important cases on zoning will probably deal with the protection of the less desirable uses from the claim of nuisance by residents or business. Thus, a manufacturer buys and builds in an industrial zone. . . . Residents move into the district who object to the noise and the confusion of the factory and seek to abate it as a nuisance. The factory must be protected in the peaceable enjoyment of the manufacturing privilege granted it by the zoning ordinance. (Pollard 1931, 31)

In addition to protecting the property values of businesses and industries, zoning also clearly aimed to protect the property investments of homeowners. The weight of this issue varied in municipalities, depending on the rate of home-ownership. In some cities like Philadelphia, homeownership was very high; in the 1920s, over 80 percent of the city's population lived in single-family dwellings they owned. In most other cities, the rates were quite a bit lower. In Dayton, Detroit, and Los Angeles, homeownership rates were about 40 percent in the early 1930s (U.S. Bureau of the Census 1932). In New York at the same time, the large majority of the population were renters living in multifamily buildings (Committee on the Regional Plan of New York and Its Environs 1931, Plunz 1990). Although zoning may have served to improve the general living conditions of the renter class (say, by prohibiting polluting industries from locating in the immediate vicinity of housing tenements), it certainly was not meant to bring them immediate financial benefits. But since zoning tended to increase home values and make banks more comfortable about giving mortgages, it was meant to help shrink the "tenant class," which the Committee on the Regional Plan of New York and Its Environs identified openly as a "source of weakness" (1931, 330). Thus, zoning was viewed as means of moving U.S. society toward mass homeownership. If that occurred, then it could be legitimately argued that the much-advertised private property gains that followed the adoption of zoning would benefit a large share of the population. This theme, that zoning would help improve the financial state of the majority of the U.S. population, was championed not only by zoning advocates and city officials but also by federal agencies. As the 1932 President's Conference on Home Building and Home Ownership put it:

> Since land and buildings used for dwellings constitute greater volume and value than land and buildings used for any other purpose in our cities, it would seem good business to conserve the enormous investment of the American people, through the application of zoning, by preventing the economic waste which accompanies unregulated use of land and buildings for dwellings. (Gries and Ford 1932, 29)

This kind of rationale allowed zoning proponents to insert (in most cases, probably sincerely) a heavily populist element into their narratives. Zoning was presented as a "poor man's bill" (Crawford 1920, 8), an institution that carried on the long-standing American tradition of securing the freedom and prosperity of its masses by granting them land and property ownership (Cullingworth 1993). Through zoning, Bassett (1922b, 322) argued, increases in property values could be distributed to the American masses "instead of being absorbed by the few." Today, given zoning's long history of excluding people from desirable districts for numerous reasons, we may take such claims with more than a grain of salt. One does not have to be a Marxist to agree that zoning favored certain groups of people (homeowners and business owners) over others (i.e., low-income renters) (Fischler 1998a; Clingermayer 2004). But against the background of turn-of-the-century Europe, where the majority of the population was both poor and property-less, where land and property were heavily concentrated in the hands of aristocrats,[14] the idea of zoning as a democratic tool was taken seriously in the United States. It presumably protected many a "common man" from losing his or her greatest investment, the home, and it was seen as an important way to enhance America's tradition of empowering—through private property ownership—a much greater share of its population than was the case in Europe. This was another way that zoning fit well into the ideology of turn-of-the-century social progressivism in the United States (Toll 1969; Wolf 2008).

Whether the views of zoning's proponents were truly democratic or not, they succeeded in making the European principle of restricting private property through zoning acceptable on American soil by emphasizing the benefits of public restrictions for private property owners. Some three decades later, after zoning was an entrenched tradition in the United States, a New Jersey court summarized these benefits succinctly: "The real object, however, of promoting the general welfare by zoning ordinances is to protect the private use and enjoyment of property and to promote the welfare of the individual property owner" (*Borough of Cresskill et al. v. Borough of Dumont*, 1953).

U.S. Zoning and the Single-Family Home

The idea of having three major zoning categories—residential, commercial, and industrial—became entrenched in the thinking of municipal planners only after a long process of discursive concept-building (see also Fischler 1998c). In this section, I will expand my account of how two conceptual (and subsequently legal and spatial) borders were constructed in the American zoning tradition: the border between home and not home and the border between a specific type of home, the detached family home, and all other types of homes.

There were many obvious and legitimate reasons to separate production activities from dwellings in the late nineteenth and early twentieth centuries. Many production activities were not only unpleasant and harmful in the long term but posed direct and immediate dangers to human life, health, and property. These activities were not limited to the polluting industries. Businesses such as laundries or restaurants, which we do not think of as dangerous today, posed serious hazards at the time because of their extensive use of wood-burning and gas stoves. These hazards may have been especially high in America where a large share of the urban fabric consisted of wood-frame buildings.[15] The final report of New York's Commission on Building Districts and Restrictions included a detailed study of several city blocks of New York that showed where fires occurred. The conclusion was that the apartment buildings "in which a large number of fires occurred had many stores on the ground floor," but "where such stores were absent the number of fires was much less" (New York City Board of Estimate and Apportionment 1916, 130).

The German zoning model also sought to reduce dangers to dwellings. However, it never eliminated all businesses (including manufacturing businesses) from housing areas. Although Frankfurt's factory zones excluded almost all housing, the city's residential districts were not solely residential, since they only prohibited industrial activities that did not comply with the performance standards established in the national industrial code.[16] In this way, the location of unsafe businesses was controlled. Furthermore, it was difficult for owners to locate large-scale factories (even ones that were not dangerous) amid dwellings because they had to meet stringent bulk standards; often these factories were simply too big to fit.[17]

The American approach began to deviate from German tradition early on. Initially, cities such as Los Angeles were content to eliminate only some noxious activities from residential areas, starting with commercial laundries. In 1909, Los Angeles extended its nuisance laws to almost completely divide its territory into three types of districts: "residence districts," "residence exceptions" (where industries were subject to conditions and could be allowed if business owners petitioned the city, neighbors agreed and the city approved), and "industrial districts" (where industries were unrestricted). Like Frankfurt some twenty years earlier, Los Angeles did not restrict its residence districts to dwellings. On the contrary, residence districts in Los Angeles excluded only the industries that could clearly be described as noxious (New York City Board of Estimate and Apportionment 1913; Logan 1976; Hirt 2007a).

But later on, it became the standard practice in American cities to ban all industries from housing zones, as New York did in 1916.[18] Another difference between the German and the American approaches was the treatment of commerce. In 1913, Los Angeles did not exclude commerce from its residential areas. But during the same year, following an act of the Wisconsin legislature, Milwaukee established a "business section" and banned certain commercial establishments (e.g., those that sold automobiles, those that produced paint) from its residence districts unless written consent was obtained from the commercial property's residential neighbors (New York City Board of Estimate and Apportionment 1913, 40–41).[19] In New York, the commercial restrictions became tighter over time. Initially, in 1916, the city allowed a limited group of small businesses (e.g., dressmakers' shops and doctors' offices) in residential districts. But eventually neighborhoods, especially in the other boroughs, were down-zoned to purely residential use and some of the uses originally permitted in residential districts were over time removed from the list of permitted uses. This contrasted sharply with the laws in Frankfurt and other German cities, where all businesses were allowed that would not have serious negative impacts (as stipulated in the national industrial performance norms) on areas dominated by residences.

German municipal authorities in fact perceived business to be so compatible with a residential lifestyle that they did not bother define a separate business zone because residential zones were open to many categories of businesses—small industries, crafts, sales, and services—as long as they were not noxious.

Some of America's greatest zoning experts were, apparently, stunned by the liberal German attitude toward the mixture of home and work. The fact that under the German system industries were not excluded from residential districts and that there was no commercial districting struck Frank Backus Williams, for instance, who was otherwise a great admirer of German planning, as inexplicable.[20] He commented on this repeatedly in his writings:

> **Absence of Business Districts.** It will be noticed that the Frankfort ordinance does not establish districts for business, from which manufacturing is excluded, as the zoning ordinances in this country do; nor does it forbid business, in residential districts. . . . In Berlin there is not a single block where business has driven out residences. . . . Nor could business and industry in Germany be completely excluded from any district by law (Williams 1922, 215).

> This differentiation between industrial and residential districts in Frankfort, although far advanced, is not complete. The mixed districts, for instance, contain both residences and factories. . . . [T]he results of the mixed district . . . have not been altogether good. . . . A better solution would be to create separate residential and industrial streets. . . . Another instance of incomplete differentiation between residential and industrial districts occurs in German cities in the case of chief traffic streets. Here may be seen shops and minor industries and residences also; offices too are found here. . . . In [German] cities, residences in the upper stories of buildings occupied on their lower floors by shops and offices are found not only on chief traffic streets, but wherever shops and offices are to be found. In none of the continental cities is there an actual business district (Williams 1914b, 28).

> The real trouble with the business district in Germany and all continental cities is that there is none. Business is universally done in the lower stories of buildings, with residences above. This is true even in Berlin, and on Berlin's principal street, Friedrich Strasse (Williams 1914a, 5).

Williams's observations point to an important but much-overlooked point: although the concept of citywide zoning was a German invention, it was the Americans who developed the idea of zoning cities in ways that clearly separated home and work. As Williams (1922) noted, Americans were somewhat like the English: English town-planning schemes also talked about business zones. Yet the English planning schemes appear to have given the concept of separating home and business less weight than American zoning ordinances. For example, in 1913, when the city of Birmingham became the first English city to adopt a set of planning schemes (Birmingham City Council n.d.; Delafons 2005, 35), it discussed areas suitable for shopping centers, but it did not exclude most businesses from the areas designated for housing. The basic division was between housing and factory areas (City of Birmingham 1913).[21] The areas labeled for dwelling houses banned new industrial establishments, but authorities were required to justify in writing why they withheld consent for the erection and operation of shops.[22] Further, English cities such as Birmingham initially passed planning schemes only for undeveloped areas. Thus, unlike New York's ordinance, they did not legally impose separation of land uses on areas that were already built out. Some of the prominent planning experts of the early twentieth century recognized the emerging exceptionalism of the U.S. approach to land-use separation. John Nolen, for example, posited in a 1914 speech in London that the separation of home from work was among the "principal" contributions of American planning to the world's planning tradition (quoted in Talen 2005, 154).[23] On the tenth anniversary of New York's zoning code, in a speech titled "Stores in Residence Zones," Edward Bassett expressed a similar opinion when he praised the separation of homes and businesses as evidence of American progress:

> Before the zoning resolution was adopted ten years ago[,] the occasional grocer or butcher would jump his shop into some street corner in the heart of a residential district, thinking he could short-circuit the business of the neighborhood. Wagon deliveries, noise, litter and increased fire risk were introduced into a quiet home district. . . . The zoning plan seeks to keep stores on business streets and residences on residence streets. . . . Stores with families above should be relegated to the dark ages of the past. The play space of small children ought not to be near fruits and vegetables for sale. . . . Sanitary streets should be all business and no families. One of the best tendencies of zoning is to make business streets business only and residence streets residences only. (Bassett 1927, 2)[24]

What explanations did leading American zoning advocates offer for setting such a rigid border between home and work? In addition to their concerns about health and fire safety, zoning's early proponents pointed to a number of practical factors that, in their view, necessitated the separation of land uses. These included traffic patterns, sanitation, street cleaning, and water and other infrastructure requirements related to the different land uses. Zoning advocates argued that these differential needs made it more efficient to place businesses, factories, and homes in different parts of the city. During the twentieth National Conference on City Planning, for instance, detailed calculations were presented on the different transport and other infrastructure needs of the different land uses as part of an ostensibly scientific argument for legally and spatially dividing them (Goodrich 1928). These arguments were expanded by later advocates of the "scientific" planning method such as Clarence Perry, the author of the "neighborhood unit formula," who in *Housing for the Machine Age* argued for careful calculating of the needs of the different land-use classes and placing them in strictly predetermined areas (Perry 1939, 49–82). It was also believed that the separation of home and work would reduce traffic accidents by reducing congestion. The final report of the New York City Board of Estimate and Apportionment included the opinions of many experts that improvement in traffic safety would follow from the introduction of zoning (1916, 11–12, 20–22, 98, 101). Finally, it was believed that zoning would reduce work-related accidents because certain labor safety standards could be enforced in factory settings through existing factory laws. But if the work was conducted in residential setting (e.g., in the tenements, which often housed sweatshops for the garment and other industries), these laws could not be enforced (ibid. 104).

While these arguments for land-use separation seem legitimate, others seem to fall into the category of pseudoscience, at least from today's point of view. The presence of stores along residential districts, for instance, was lambasted as harmful since it made streets unfit for children's play and thus contributed to juvenile delinquency and psychological disorders, eventually converting youth to criminals. "Nervous diseases," leading zoning proponents like Alfred Bettman suspected, might be caused by exposure to "noises and turmoil and hurly-burly" (Bettman 1914, 113). In explaining the need for a zoning law, the New York City Board of Estimate and Apportionment put it this way:

> In the crowded tenement districts having stores on the ground floor, the roads are congested with vehicular and push carts and the sidewalks with business encroachments and pedestrians. There is absolutely no place for the child to exercise natural play instincts. Play is as necessary to the child as food and clothing. It is this thwarting of the boy's craving for play that leads to a large proportion of the juvenile delinquency that comes before the Children's Court. (New York City Board of Estimate and Apportionment 1916, 22)

In *Euclid v. Ambler*, the Supreme Court summarized the findings of many such studies and used them as a justification for separating, homes, businesses, and industries:

These reports, which bear every evidence of painstaking consideration, concur in the view that the segregation of residential, business and industrial buildings will make it easier to provide fire apparatus suitable for the character and intensity of the development in each section; that it will increase the safety and security of home life, greatly tend to prevent street accidents, especially to children, by reducing the traffic and resulting confusion in residential sections, decrease noise and other conditions which produce or intensify nervous disorders, preserve a more favorable environment in which to rear children, etc. (*Euclid v. Ambler Realty Company*, 1926)

Yet into the late 1920s and early 1930s, even after *Euclid v. Ambler* and after the land-use-separation system became local law in many American cities, people intuitively questioned whether some of the explanations flew in the face of common sense. Segregating dwellings and industries was indeed hard to object to. But separating homes and shops was not as easy to accept. A full-blown debate erupted during the twenty-first National Conference on City Planning. Alfred Bettman— the man who suspected that traffic noise brings nervous disorders and whose arguments helped seal the triumph of zoning in *Euclid v. Ambler*—argued, hesitantly:

I am rather skeptical as to whether a grocery store next door is to my house is going to affect seriously the health of my children. There have been mighty healthy children raised over grocery stores. (Bettman 1929, 98)

And even Edward Bassett, who enthusiastically welcomed the separation of homes and businesses in some of his other writings, acknowledged that he had to fight his initial hesitation for some time:

It was a little hard to see why retail business coming into a residence district really affected health and safety, but after the testimony of Dr. Kober in a case under the city of Washington zoning ordinance, the judge decided much to his own surprise that a grocery store was such an invasion of a residence district as to be excluded by zoning. Dr. Kober gave an instance of the transmission of disease not by anything poisonous which the flies would take from the grocery store, but by the germs carried by flies flying to the foodstuffs in the grocery store. The other side had nothing to meet this evidence. Little by little the cases favoring zoning have been increasing. (Bassett 1929, 97)

Separating homes from businesses by law was difficult enough, but separating homes *by type*, separating homes from other homes, required an even greater leap of the imagination. Should housing be at all categorized and then divided? Or should the people—housing's occupants—be categorized and then divided? As with the separation of home from work, American zoning developed a distinct approach. The early European attempts at zoning started with only rudimentary housing taxonomies. Frankfurt's 1891 ordinance created two types of residential districts: the first for the "country dwellings" and the second for dwellings generally. The authors of the ordinance were clearly motivated by considerations of class. The country-dwellings quarter was meant for the affluent: it was located in the more scenic, peripheral parts of the city, farther from heavy industries. In this district, seven-tenths of the individual lots had to be left open, thus encouraging detached housing. The second, less desirable residential zone was intended for the homes of workers. But the ordinance relied on its bulk rules to distinguish between the districts for country homes and those for small homes without setting a firm legal border between them. A similar approach was adopted at the turn of the twentieth century in Berlin, Hamburg, Stuttgart, Munich, and other German cities (Logan 1976), where a distinction was made between detached and block housing, but the two could be mixed in the same area without violating the law (Logan 1976, Liebmann 1996). In Essen, the 1907 ordinance defined a zone for single-family houses, but the authorities reserved discretion to permit two-family houses and multiple (attached) houses in that zone. According to Frank Backus Williams, "practically everybody [in Essen] applies for permission to build double houses or groups" (Williams 1913, 97).[25] Joseph Stübben, the grand master of German planning thought, concluded that pure single-family zones were "extremely unusual" in his country (quoted in Logan 1976, 383).

The early English approach to zoning for housing types appears to have been somewhere between those of Germany and the United States. The first "planning scheme" in Britain, in Birmingham, established three districts of housing types in undeveloped parts of the city. Although it used a definition of "dwelling houses" that became a hallmark of U.S. zoning, "houses designed for occupation by not more than one family" (City of Birmingham 1913, 11), it did not distinguish detached houses from row housing in the dwelling districts. Some dwelling districts allowed, say, up to twelve "dwelling houses" per acre, others up to fifteen, and a third type up to eighteen. The houses could be either detached or attached as long as they complied with rules such as the following: "no more than eight dwellings shall in any place be built under one continuous roof or without a break in building from the ground upwards" (ibid., 14). All the way to the mid-1940s, when zoning in the form of planning schemes ceased to be routine English practice after the adoption of the 1947 Town and Country Planning Act, English towns still tended to use a "general residence" category rather than multiple categories that distinguished between detached single-family housing and apartment blocks. Larger cities used basic residential and density categories (e.g., less than twenty-four houses per acre and more than twenty-four houses per acre; City of Manchester 1945) without routinely carving out exclusive space for detached single-family homes.

In the United States, many believed that single-family, two-family, and multi-family housing somehow represent principally different types of human environment. An early example is model national building code that was prepared in New York in 1907, which proposed that for the purposes of safety, housing be divided into several types. The "private dwelling" was one that could be occupied by no more than "two separate and distinct families or households, and in which no more than fifteen rooms shall be used for the accommodation of boarders, and no part of which structure is used as a store or for any business purpose" (National Board of Fire Underwriters 1907, 17).[26] The other types were the apartment house, the tenement house, the lodging house, and the apartment hotel. Like London's 1844 building act, the American model code of 1907 only proposed a system of building classification and did not envision that different classes of residential buildings should be located in different parts of town (that is not what building codes do anyway). It was up to others to convert the system of residential classification into a system of residential separation. The idea was discussed by Benjamin Marsh, secretary of New York's Committee on Congestion of Population, in his book *An Introduction to City Planning* where he envisioned multifamily housing "only in the neighborhood of factories and business centers" and separated from one-family homes (1909, 130).[27] It was also proposed at the first National Conference on City Planning, where Henry Morgenthau, chair of the same committee, stated that "we can make city plans establishing factory zones and residence zones . . . and then restrict certain zones to . . . one- or two-family houses" (Morgenthau 1909, 60). A few years later, New York City's Heights of Buildings Commission included the "maintenance of the essentially residential character of the neighborhood" in its definition of "general welfare" (1913, 10) and saw a clear dichotomy between single-family homes and all other types of housing, arguing that stable property values, health, and comfort justified this position:

> Again take the case of the man who builds a home in a district which at the time seems peculiarly suited for single family dwellings. In a few years the value of his property may be largely destroyed by the erection of apartment houses, shutting off light and air and completely changing the character of the neighborhood. When single family dwellings, apartment houses, stores and factories are thrown together indiscriminately, the health and comfort of home life are destroyed and property and rental values are reduced. (New York City Board of Estimate and Apportionment 1913, 72)

Yet Bassett did not include the idea of an exclusive single-family district in New York's 1916 zoning resolution. Although New York's residence districts excluded most businesses, they included all types of dwellings: detached houses, apartments, and even hotels (hotels do not fall under the commercial designation until later). New York's resolution did not define a district for detached homes based on land use because of concerns that such a policy might be viewed unfavorably by the courts. The solution was the E area district, which prescribed the lowest lot coverage in the city (this was a bulk approach, like the approach Frankfurt used). Bassett explained that the E area districts were created using language that he hoped would pass the test of constitutionality in what were intended as districts for spacious single-family homes:

> In New York it is not practical to put up any residential building on 30 per cent of the lot except a one-family private residence. . . . One may ask why they are called E districts instead of private residential districts. The reason is that the method of creating districts graduating from 100 per cent to 30 per cent is a plain employment of the police power with a recognition of health and safety considerations, and the courts will protect a plan which is based on such a foundation. (Bassett 1922b, 323)

By the time New York had passed its resolution, in 1916, at least two other approaches to the classification of residences (and therefore of residents) had developed. Both divided the population to a greater extent than New York City did. The most extreme approach was taken by laws in southern cities that mandated racial segregation. In 1910, Baltimore was the first city to adopt a racially divisive law (Silver 1997). In 1914, Louisville adopted an ordinance that prohibited blacks and whites from living in houses on blocks where most houses were inhabited by people of the other race (Toll 1969).[28] But three years later the Supreme Court struck down the idea of overt racial segregation via municipal law in *Buchanan v. Warley* (1917).

An alternative approach emerged in Berkeley, California. This method ultimately became the blueprint for housing taxonomies used in zoning ordinances around the country. Berkeley passed its first zoning ordinance in 1916, the same year as New York. This ordinance created eight principal land-use classes.[29] In Class I districts, "no building or structure shall be erected, constructed or maintained which shall be used for or designed or intended to be used for any purpose other than that of a single family dwelling" (City of Berkeley 1916, 1). Using similar language, the ordinance set aside Class II districts for single- and two-family homes, thus establishing a legal distinction between single- and two-family homes. Class III was for row houses and single- and two-family homes; Class IV was for boarding houses, fraternities, and dormitories plus the housing types in the previous three use classes; Class V was for apartments, hotels, and restaurants and the housing types from the previous classes; Class VI was for religious and cultural buildings; Class VII was for warehouses and some light industries; and Class VIII was for the remaining industries (ibid., 1–2).

Berkeley's ordinance was a trendsetter in at least two important ways. First, it was likely the first U.S. zoning ordinance to define a principal zone exclusively for single-family homes (Fischler 1998b). Surely, there were some earlier experiments. Utica and Syracuse in the state of New York had enacted "residence districts" in 1913,[30] but these districts included both single- and two-family homes (Scott 1971, 152).[31] In 1916, Minneapolis went a step further. It passed ordinances for a series of small "residence districts," which were defined in a way to exclude apartments and potentially, duplexes (City of Minneapolis 1917, Cheney 1917). But Berkeley established an exclusively single-family category as a principal, Class I district, thus setting a new standard. Second, Berkeley's zoning law was novel because it used the hierarchical zoning principle that had formed the conceptual core of New York's zoning resolution *only* in Berkeley's housing areas. Elsewhere, it adopted the "flat" zoning principle. Its land-use districts were defined in a mutually exclusive way; they permitted a single land-use class such as only residential, only business, or only industrial (Scott 1971, 161). Berkeley's ordinance was adopted after intense advocacy by J. Bither, director of the Manufacturers Association, who argued that "factories are often harassed by people who build close to them" and that "apartment houses are the bane of the owner of the single family dwelling" (Bither 1915, 168, 174); and by Charles Cheney, a leading architect and zoning activist,[32] who felt that an apartment house will "condemn the whole tract . . . of fine residences" (Cheney 1915, 165). Duncan McDuffie, president of the Civic Art Commission, also played a key role. Once Berkeley passed its ordinance, McDuffie wrote the first petition to request that a neighborhood (Elmwood Park) be labeled as a Class I zone.[33]

The Berkeley method was eventually upheld in the courts; the U.S. Supreme Court endorsed the concept of the exclusive single-family zone in 1926 in *Euclid v. Ambler*. Writing for the majority, Justice George Sutherland (in)famously stated that an apartment house in the vicinity of "fine detached homes" is a "parasite" and a "nuisance:

> With particular reference to apartment houses, it is pointed out that the development of detached house sections is greatly retarded by the coming of apartment houses, which has sometimes resulted in destroying the entire section for private house purposes; that in such sections very often the apartment house is a mere parasite, constructed in order to

take advantage of the open spaces and attractive surroundings created by the residential character of the district. Moreover, the coming of one apartment house is followed by others, interfering by their height and bulk with the free circulation of air and monopolizing the rays of the sun which otherwise would fall upon the smaller homes, and bringing, as their necessary accompaniments, the disturbing noises incident to increased traffic and business, and the occupation, by means of moving and parked automobiles, of larger portions of the streets, thus detracting from their safety and depriving children of the privilege of quiet and open spaces for play, enjoyed by those in more favored localities—until, finally, the residential character of the neighborhood and its desirability as a place of detached residences are utterly destroyed. Under these circumstances, apartment houses, which in a different environment would be not only entirely unobjectionable but highly desirable, come very near to being nuisances. (*Euclid v. Ambler Realty Company*, 1926)

The New York City Board of Estimate and Apportionment had reached a similar conclusion some ten years later, in 1917, when it stated that in sections occupied by "private houses," the "apartment house is a mere parasite" (New York City Board of Estimate and Apportionment 1916, 31). But the Supreme Court ruling made this view a matter of law, thus settling a quarter-century-long debate on whether residential typology and residential division were appropriate methods of urban development control. This ruling elevated the detached single-family home as the most desirable form of human habitation and placed apartments in a category that was alien to the "true" residential districts, indeed as alien as stores or slaughterhouses. Bassett appears to have been concerned about separating apartments from single-family homes on legal grounds, but other American intellectuals objected to it on moral grounds. The Ambler Realty lawyers in *Euclid v. Ambler*, whatever their ulterior motivations were, argued forcefully against exclusive single-family zoning because it would oppress "all the people" who "are not able to maintain a single-family home"—an argument the Supreme Court obviously did not find compelling. But the district court judge in the Euclid case, David Westenhaver, put his moral objections as follows: "The result to be accomplished [by having exclusive single-family zoning in Euclid] is to classify the population and segregate them according to their income or situation in life." Zoning, in his opinion, would only increase "such class tendencies" (quoted in Toll 1969, 224).[34]

In hindsight, we may say that such concerns were well founded: zoning was from its very onset and to a large extent concerned as much with who should be located where as with what should be located where (e.g., Babcock 1966). Indeed, once the dichotomy of detached family homes versus apartments was upheld in the courts, cities—including those whose leaders wished to make racial segregation the law—could use residential zoning for racist purposes without fear of legal reprisal. Baltimore, the pioneer in racial zoning, discarded its ordinance in the years after *Buchanan v. Warley*. But, as its assistant civil engineer, J. Grinnalds, noted in a newspaper article, there was a "tendency of [a certain kind] of people to live in a certain kind of house." A "scientific" survey of housing using the legal housing categories, he continued, would reveal that: "Some sections of the city will show a preponderance of one family homes. Some will indicate that there is a considerable grouping into two family houses. Other neighborhoods will appear to be tenement or apartment districts almost as if by segregation." Zoning could use these categories to keep the districts generally as they were (and thus eliminate the danger of future crossover between the residential types and, potentially, between the types of people) (Grinnalds 1921, 2).

The voices that feared the exclusionary potential of zoning and were drowned out in the early years of zoning reappeared with renewed vigor in the 1960s. But in the 1920s and 1930s, those who argued for the benefits of exclusionary zoning who won the debate. Land-use taxonomy and division, including the separation of single-family from multifamily housing, became the established wisdom—so established as to be assumed natural and unquestionable. Zoning maps throughout the country displayed districts that used the same terminology: residential, business, and industrial—all divided into similar subcategories. These subcategories were illustrated in countless brochures, textbooks, pamphlets, and papers (figures 6.2, 6.3, 6.4 and 6.5).

The assumption was that it was possible to define, in a universal way, for all cities, the correct location and distribution of urban land uses (Bartholomew 1928, 1932, 11–14; Hubbard and Hubbard 1929, 184–185; Lewis 1939; see also Fischler 1998c). The position of federal bodies shifted notably from the mid-1920s (when residential separation through zoning was still debatable) to the 1930s (when it became the standard practice). Although the Standard Zoning Enabling Act mentioned, and only in a footnote, that one-family residence districts *might be* possible (U.S. Department of Commerce, Advisory Committee on Zoning 1926, 5), the President's Conference on Home Building and Home Ownership boldly recommended "that zoning separate residence districts by homogeneous types of dwellings" and that "in residential districts they [zoning codes] should provide for one-family dwelling districts, two-family dwelling districts, multiple dwelling districts" in order to "encourage the development of neighborhoods with such uniformity of type of dwelling as will secure the best social and economic conditions" (Gries and Ford 1932, 31–32, 44).[35]

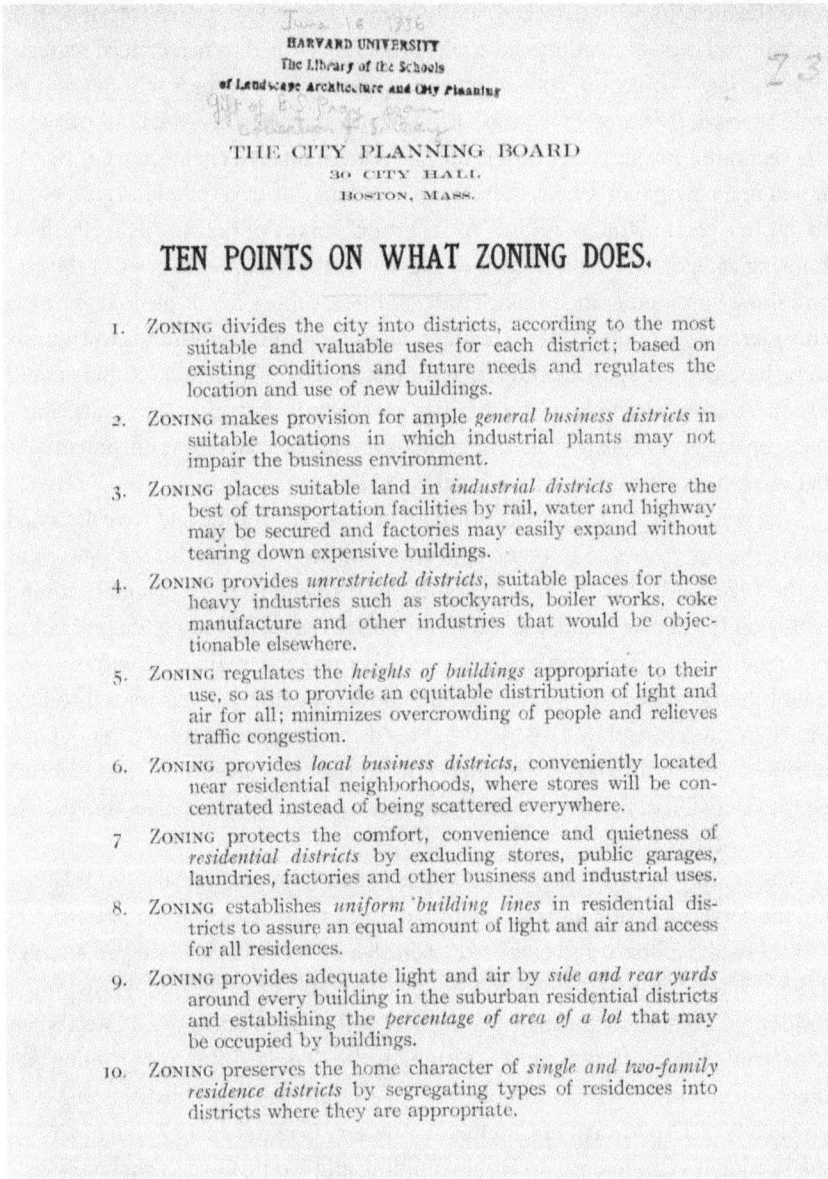

THE CITY PLANNING BOARD
30 CITY HALL
BOSTON, MASS.

TEN POINTS ON WHAT ZONING DOES.

1. ZONING divides the city into districts, according to the most suitable and valuable uses for each district; based on existing conditions and future needs and regulates the location and use of new buildings.

2. ZONING makes provision for ample *general business districts* in suitable locations in which industrial plants may not impair the business environment.

3. ZONING places suitable land in *industrial districts* where the best of transportation facilities by rail, water and highway may be secured and factories may easily expand without tearing down expensive buildings.

4. ZONING provides *unrestricted districts*, suitable places for those heavy industries such as stockyards, boiler works, coke manufacture and other industries that would be objectionable elsewhere.

5. ZONING regulates the *heights of buildings* appropriate to their use, so as to provide an equitable distribution of light and air for all; minimizes overcrowding of people and relieves traffic congestion.

6. ZONING provides *local business districts*, conveniently located near residential neighborhoods, where stores will be concentrated instead of being scattered everywhere.

7. ZONING protects the comfort, convenience and quietness of *residential districts* by excluding stores, public garages, laundries, factories and other business and industrial uses.

8. ZONING establishes *uniform building lines* in residential districts to assure an equal amount of light and air and access for all residences.

9. ZONING provides adequate light and air by *side and rear yards* around every building in the suburban residential districts and establishing the *percentage of area of a lot* that may be occupied by buildings.

10. ZONING preserves the home character of *single and two-family residence districts* by segregating types of residences into districts where they are appropriate.

FIGURE 6.2 By the 1930s, the land-use categories were well established. Courtesy of the Frances Loeb Library, Harvard University.

That a desire to exclude certain people on the basis of class or race was a driving force behind residential typology must by this point be evident to all readers. Early zoning advocates of some 80–100 years ago were simply too open to leave us in doubt. The Fifth Avenue Association, which wanted to

Zoning Will Prevent This

Courtesy of Evansville Courier and Journal

A Cartoon used in the Zoning Publicity Campaign
at Evansville, Indiana

FIGURE 6.3 The standard land-use taxonomy, this time illustrated humorously. Hubbard and Hubbard (1929).

expel the garment industry from New York's posh streets, referred to the ethnic immigrants the industry employed as "flies" (quoted in Wolf 1989, 257). The New York City Board of Estimate and Apportionment was a bit more tactful, explaining that the differences between the office workers and retailers on Fifth Avenue and garment workers existed primarily because the latter were

FIGURE 6.4 More humor and politics, this time from the *Atlanta Journal* (March 30, 1922). The idea of land-use segregation acquired a heavy populist tone: in this case, the message is that without zoning, the heavily muscled factory will easily defeat the defenseless single-family home.

FIGURE 6.5   The conflict between private residences and apartments as illustrated by the City of Philadelphia Zoning Commission (1921). The caption: "Fifteenth Street and Allegheny Avenue—apartment house built to street line, projecting 25 feet beyond other buildings, cutting off light and air and depreciating property values."

not "familiar with the English language" and "do not readily fit themselves into the conditions which are so different from those under which they have lived in their native countries" (1916, 115–116). B. J. Bither, one of the key actors in the Berkeley story, reflected on California's leading role in developing zoning in the United States in the explicitly racist terms: "We [Californians] are ahead of most states [in adopting zoning]. . . thanks to the persistent proclivity of the 'heathen Chinese' to clean our garments in our midst" (Bither 1915, 175). It may be difficult to grasp the extent to which some Americans of the early twentieth century sincerely (if erroneously) believed that ethnic and class differences were *natural* phenomena, a matter of fact, not of theory and not of prejudice. In 1903, in *Principles of City Land Values*, real-estate expert Robert Hurd explained the growth patterns of the industrial city by referring to the "natural" desire "to live among one's friends or those whom one desires to have for friends," concluding that "there will be as many residence neighborhoods in a city as there are social strata" (quoted in Fischler 1998a, 697). Three decades later, Harold Lewis echoed this opinion in a well-regarded planning textbook: "Nearly all people like to feel they are a part of a certain neighborhood. They like to keep such neighborhoods free from intrusion by those in other ranks of life. In other words, they wish to stay where they feel at home and where they have some assurance that their children will find suitable associations" (Lewis

1939, 46). The famous landscape architect S. R. De Boer who was a leading proponent of zoning to Denver, praised municipal zoning as the thoughtful extension of "natural zoning," which he defined as "the subconscious grouping together of business houses or of residences of a similar nature." He further observed that "in residential sections [zoning] is carried out in the desire of people in one type of house and hating to have another type enter their neighborhood. The type in this case is based mainly on wealth." He also noted that "this natural grouping of similar interests . . . runs though the life of the whole city" (De Boer 1937, 12–14). For Robert Whitten, who worked with Edward Bassett on New York's zoning, it was not only natural for people of different classes to wish to live separately but also beneficial to society as a whole. Thus, it was something that governments should promote: "Bankers and leading business men should live in one part of town, storekeepers, clerks and technicians in another, and working people in yet others where they enjoy the association of neighbors more or less of their own kind" (1922, 205). Whitten's held similar convictions regarding race. He became main author of Atlanta's post-Buchanan zoning ordinance, in which the standard residential categories were designated "colored": R1-white, R2-colored, and R3-undetermined. Racial division, Whitten believed, would help social stability (Toll 1969, 262–263).

Nonresidential land-use taxonomies were also grounded, at least partially, in the desire for exclusion on the basis of class or race. Opening a shop in a stately residential area would surely bring lower-class outsiders, if not the shoppers themselves (assuming the store was as high end as the residences around it), then the salespeople and various dubious others. The same concern applied to the opening of a production facility that would likely employ lower-class workers. This was plainly stated in cases that were heard in the courts before *Euclid v. Ambler*. In *Civello v. New Orleans*, for instance, the Supreme Court of Louisiana justified the legal separation of homes and businesses primarily on the ground that it would protect neighborhood residents from outsiders:

> A place of business in a residence neighborhood furnishes an excuse for any criminal to go into the neighborhood, where, otherwise, a stranger would be under the ban of suspicion. Besides, open shops invite loiterers and idlers to congregate. (*Civello v. New Orleans*, 1923)

The same logic of class exclusion was applied to the idea of separating businesses from industries, as in the hallmark example of New York's Fifth Avenue merchants who felt that their businesses would wither if garment industry workers were allowed to perpetually engulf "the shops, shopkeeper, and the [respectable] shopping public" (quoted in Fischler 1998a, 683). It also was also used in arguments for the business subcategories that proliferated in zoning ordinances in later decades. As Charles Cheney, one of the key advocates of zoning in Berkeley, put it:

> Garages, oil stations, tin shops, plumbing shops, dying and cleaning works and undertakers are not good bedfellows for high class retail stores nor do they attract the same kind of customers; also they are almost always of the lesser rent-paying class ... [and will] seriously deter needed high class retailers from coming in. Hence two kinds of retail business zones need to be established. (Cheney 1929, 33)

The perpetual concern about falling property values following the "invasion" of a stable (i.e., functionally and demographically homogeneous) area by "others" was one consequence of these deep race- and class-based fears. Indeed, high-class property values *did* fall, as the previous section discussed, likely for a combination of factors that had to do with the declining desirability of the area in which the property was located. Factors that decreased the value of property could include the traffic and pollution that accompanied uncontrolled mixture of land uses, much as they included a strong distaste for people perceived as of low class or of different race. But here is a puzzle for the student of comparative legal regimes: why did the single-family district establish itself as a more popular tool for excluding certain categories, classes, and groups in America than in Europe? It is hardly a viable hypothesis that European elites at height of European imperialism were somehow less prone to deep class prejudices (see, for example, Panayi 1994; Fetzer 2000; Nightingale 2012). Why didn't they seek to defend their turf, including their property values, by legally excluding all businesses and flats? Did Europeans have other means of exclusion? Did they have fewer others to fear (since fewer foreign immigrants were coming to Europe)? Or, accustomed to the tree-lined boulevards of Berlin, Paris and London, did they *not* associate class supremacy with exclusively single-family neighborhoods? After all, although single-family dwellings tend to cost more than multifamily ones because of their size and the land they occupy, the relationship is not absolute. The occupants of flats *could* be rich and the occupants of single-family homes *could* be poor. There are countless examples of cities in the world with highly desirable and thus highly priced neighborhoods of apartment buildings and cheap peripheral areas of self-built family huts. Why did exclusionary policies surrounding the detached home develop more systematically in the United States than in Europe?

Here, I think, we should emphasize the exceptional role that the individual home played in the imagination of early twentieth-century American elites, including the leading urban reformers and zoning advocates. They believed that, "It needs no argument to demonstrate that a business or industrial street does not furnish the most favorable environment for a home" (New York City Board

of Estimate and Apportionment 1916, 20). The family home that was protected
from interaction with those engaged in other activities was more than a housing type associated with wealth. It was a *normative* position—the spatial form
that was uniquely able to deliver stable family life. It was, also, much as Andrew
Jackson Downing and Frank Lloyd Wright believed, the only spatial form that
could deliver the homeownership-based democracy that America sought to be,
a democracy centered on the family's spatial autonomy. Good citizens, good
families—both the poor who couldn't afford an individual home and the rich
who lived in apartments—could do better by acquiring the ideal housing form.
As a matter of fact, wishing to live in a single-family home was a sign of individual normalcy: "The normal man, with wife and children, wants a house to
himself" (Williams 1920, 4); the opposite wish may just as well have been a sign
of delinquency. That someone could live in dense and mixed urban surroundings by *choice* rather than by economic necessity was, apparently, a foreign idea
to people such as renowned planner Clarence Perry. A single-family homeowner,
Perry described himself as "naturally biased in favor of that form of living." He
had difficulty conceiving that others would prefer to live in an apartment building. He thought that for all sorts of people, "building the home may be the cherished ideal" (Perry 1939, 108). Even in New York City, where the majority of the
population lived in apartments—some of which were very upscale—the single-
family home was seen as the form that citizens should aspire to. With regret, the
Committee on the Regional Plan of New York and Its Environs acknowledged
that many people, some well-to-do, liked their apartments: "We have to face the
fact that in New York public opinion will always largely be influenced by a population living in multi-family apartments." But these people, the text went on,
needed "*more education* on housing" (my italics). Recognizing that it might be
impossible to place the entire population into luxurious single-family homes, the
report emphasized the "importance of the small [single-family] home," as small
as it needed to be for its dwellers' economic situation, yet a single-family home
nonetheless (Committee on the Regional Plan of New York and Its Environs 1931,
330–331, 337–338). The report cited Edward Bassett's warning of a "Harlemized"
future for greater New York (a term that he used to mean the spread of universal
"solid apartment house construction"; 159) and regarded Philadelphia to be the
model American city because it was a "city of homes." Philadelphia's Americanness,
its distinction from foreign cities, was well articulated by the managing director
of its housing association, whom the report quoted:

> Housing in Philadelphia for almost 300 years has disregarded the Tower
> of Babel prototype of living and has spread over the land. . . . Over
> 80 per cent of our families live in single dwellings. . . . [the] conviction

has been bred into Philadelphians that they are entitled to a home and not simply a cross-section of an ant-hill! (Committee on the Regional Plan of New York and Its Environs 1931, 223)

The single-family home was deemed superior for many reasons. It was the housing form thought to be "best adapted for home ownership"; in fact, single-family housing and homeownership were viewed as nearly synonymous (ibid., 255). And homeownership in itself led to better lives and a better citizenry, as Bassett put it in the very title of one of his articles: "Home Owners Make Good Citizens" (Bassett 1922a). A decade later, the accumulated wisdom on the matter was eloquently summarized by Herbert Hoover:

> To possess one's own home is the hope and ambition of almost every individual in our country, whether he lives in hotel, apartment, or tenement. . . [There is] the high ideal and aspiration that each family may pass their days in the home which they own; that they may nurture it as theirs; that it may be their castle in all that exquisite sentiment which it surrounds with the sweetness of family life. This aspiration penetrates the heart of our national well-being. It makes for happier married life, it makes for better children, it makes for confidence and security, it makes for courage to meet the battle of life, it makes for better citizenship. There can be no fear for a democracy or self-government or for liberty or freedom from homeowners no matter how humble they may be. (Hoover 1931)

The single-family home was also said to provide not just more light and air, less traffic, less noise, and better health conditions, but also more favorable conditions for the development of children and thus a superior family life. The apartment building was seen as inherently less capable of delivering these social and moral goods. It was an unfit place to raise a good family: not only did it bring noise, street danger, litter, dust, contagion and fire risk (Bassett 1923, 130–131), but it was also "children-devouring" and "family-destroying" (Crawford 1920, 7). And it devoured children not just physically, by fire or traffic accidents, but also by moral corruption. The single-home family, in sharp contrast, carried the values of American "civilization" and thus had to be defended in the same way the republic should be defended. As the New York City Board of Estimate and Apportionment explained it (1916, 20–22, 31):

> The moral influences surrounding the homes are of greatest importance. The sordid atmosphere of the ordinary business street is not a favorable environment in which to rear children. Immediate and

continuous proximity to the moving picture show, the dance hall, pool room, cigar store, saloon, candy store, and other institutions for the creation and satisfaction of appetites and habits is not good for the development of the child. Influences and temptations resulting from the proximity of such business to the homes may affect seriously the morals of the youth of the community. Under such conditions it is difficult to cultivate the ideals of life that are essential to the preservation of our civilization.

The protection of the home environment is vital to the welfare of the state. . . . It is important from the standpoint of citizenship as well as from health, safety and comfort that sections be set aside where a man can own a home and have a little open space about it. It makes a man take a keener interest in his neighborhood and city. It has undoubted advantages in the rearing of future citizens.

Apparently, these values of "civilization" so vital to the "welfare of the state" could not be transmitted equally well in environments dominated by apartment buildings. In fact, according to Lawrence Veiller, in an area of family homes, apartment buildings were a "source of detriment to the development of any city"; they interfered with the "proper social conditions and the development of the proper civic spirit" (Veiller 1914, 104). According to the health expert George C. Whipple, so ruinous was the addition of multifamily structures to a single-family neighborhood that once "infected with an apartment house [the area] tends to accumulate other apartments and the neighborhood tends to change from a stable, homeowning class to a shifting, renting class, a class lacking in neighborliness and civic life and leading an impoverished civic life" (Whipple quoted in Schwartz 1976, 29). Sociologist Nels Anderson wrote, "If an area of single homes can keep out apartments, it is better able to retain face-to-face community relationships. The apartment breaks down neighborhood spirit and is not congenial to family life" (Anderson 1925, 159). So undesirable was the apartment that it could not be considered a residence at all: "The attractive cottages with a vacant lot between, gave the "*semi-residence* interloper" (i.e., the apartment building) a chance to steal his lights and air and view and to ruin the other properties" (cited by Talen 2012, 97).

In the emerging American planning and zoning tradition of the early twentieth century, then, the apartment building came to play the role of the intruder, the interloper, the thief, the parasite, the infection that came upon a neighborhood of single-family homes. New York's Secretary of the Zoning Committee Herbert S. Swan summarized this attitude succinctly: "The apartment building took, took, took. It never gave!" (Swan 1920, 46). The single-family home had the *right to the city*: it was always seen as being there first. It was the gracious host, the delicate victim, and the original citizen that was always haunted, followed, invaded, and taken advantage of by other housing types. It is both easy and correct to read class and racial exclusion in the legal shield around the single-family home that American zoning had created by the 1930s. However, it is also the case that many of zoning's propagandists who supported class segregation, such as Edward Bassett, also wished to spread the perceived benefits of the single-family home to the American masses. Residential zoning, he proudly noted, is having the desired effect as neighborhoods were rapidly building up with the homes of the "best sort of the citizens who are not wealthy" (Bassett 1922). Zoning gave more and more Americans the gift that they desired (or should desire), privacy in private homes, and it taught them the kind of values that would allow American "civilization" to go on. In creating the single-family district, American urban reformers of the 1900s in fact pursued conflicting goals—segregation *and* equalitarianism. Many of them like Bassett and Whitten could somehow embrace these two values simultaneously. Thus, they created a tool that helped make American cities what European cities were not: neatly ordered spaces in which the single-family home was the primary element of the composition—an element to be protected from other housing types to the greatest extent possible. The single-family home, which in Europe at the time was generally either the shabby village hut, the English row house, or the wealthy country estate, became the hallmark of the large American middle class. Over time, the single-family home of the United States took on some functions, such as family entertainment, that in European cities remained in the public street and square for much longer. And it exported other functions, especially work and services, in ways that carved out a distinctly private American spatial realm. The primacy of the home set apart American built forms (especially those in today's massive urban peripheries) from those of most other industrialized countries. To paraphrase Lewis Mumford (1938), the detached home in a district all to itself represented Americans' collective effort to lead a private life, a life of "quiet seclusion," "where yards are wide" and "people few," in a "land use project addressed to family needs" (*Belle Terre v. Boraas* 1974). And it is doubtful that this life that so defined and continues to define the American metropolis could have been maintained through the last century had zoning not kept the alternatives at bay.

THE PROMISES AND PARADOXES OF RESIDENTIAL ZONING

Every one knows that the crux of the zoning problem lies in the residential district.

—Ernst Freund, 1929

The U.S. model of public land-use regulation deserves its own category. Among its distinct features are the fact that land-use regulation is practiced primarily at the municipal level (whereas in the other countries I surveyed, it is embedded in national legislation and is practiced by higher-tier governments which work with the locales); the fact that the regulation is the key mechanism for municipal intervention in the built environment (whereas in West European countries, for example, governments play a much larger role in the production of the built environment through higher levels of public property ownership and more aggressive public planning and investment, including the direct construction and distribution of housing for sizable shares of the population); the fact that regulation is detailed and prescriptive (at least compared to regulation in countries such as England, Canada, and Australia, where government discretion plays a greater role); the fact that the system operates under tight constitutional limits on public infringement on private property rights; and the fact that the system is heavily dependent on court rulings. In this last chapter, I will focus on the part of the U.S. land-use regulatory model that continues to intrigue me most: the model's reliance on narrowly defined, often mutually exclusive land-use categories that are perhaps the model's basic organizing element. I will also focus on the privileged position that one particular type of human habitat, the detached home, continues to occupy in the U.S. model.

From the beginning, my intent has been to show that the standard rules of U.S. zoning are not mere technical tools but are culturally loaded constructs that were invented at a particular place and time. They were not a straightforward response to the operation of the market, since the market itself is embedded in society and culture, as we know from Polanyi (1944) and many others. In the U.S. case, zoning advocates legitimized a seemingly technical land-use tool that certainly did respond to market conditions but ran contrary to Americans' aversion to authority by appealing to other dominant ideals of the time; specifically, those regarding the proper scope for government (limited), the proper role of government (to help private interests), and the definition of a good city (one that maximizes individual and family space). My conclusion is similar to that of Matthew Light:

> National land-use regimes do not arise in response to universal laws of the market that exert the same influence at any location on the planet. Rather, land-use regimes differ from country to country. They are embedded in a complex, historically developing framework of ideology, law and culture. If land-use controls regulate the physical shape of the communities we live in, then it is history itself that regulates what kind of community we view as wholesome, normal and desirable—our ideas of what "the city" and "the good city" mean. (Light 1999, 577)

Implicitly throughout the book and especially in the previous two chapters, I have tried to do what discursive institutionalists do (e.g., Schmidt 2008): examine how specific rules and institutions—those of land use—came to be made at specific times in history as a partial consequence of ideas and discourses. These rules and institutions may by now have become a matter of habit (Wickersham 2001). But as Foucault (1972, 1980) teaches us, rules and institutions that we often take for granted are far from "natural"; they were simply *made up* at some point in time.

By highlighting the historic and ideological specificity of America's land-use categories, I hope to break the "perceptual spell" they hold over us (Fischler 1998c, 392). I hope that readers will ask themselves whether these constructs are still useful to us. Categories are never trivial: to categorize is always to theorize. We should know this from the likes of Linnaeus, Darwin, and Mendeleev. As biologist and science historian Stephen Jay Gould (1989, 98) put it:

> Taxonomy (the science of classification) is often undervalued as a glorified system of filing—with each species in its prescribed place in the album . . .; but taxonomy is a fundamental and dynamic science, dedicated to exploring the causes of relationships and similarities among organisms. Classifications are theories about the basic natural order, not dull catalogues compiled only to avoid chaos.

The land-use categories America embraced at the beginning of the twenti-eth century were based on a theory that posited that if activities on land were classified in a certain way,[1] if homes were separated from offices, services, and industries, certain benefits would follow. This is what we may call zoning's original "promises" (Haar and Kayden 1989). These benefits ranged from the practical to the abstract and included fewer fires, traffic accidents, and work-related accidents, more efficient cities, and better public health. The theory also held that a natural social order exists that would be maintained by institu-tionalizing a particular residential taxonomy—single-family versus multifam-ily housing in various sizes and densities—to the benefit of society as a whole. Finally, the theory held that the detached single-family home is a supreme type of habitat that gives Americans what they want—privacy, peace, space, seclusion, and so forth—and that it strengthens the American individual and family, and helps produce civic-minded citizens who would in turn make bet-ter communities and a better nation. So widespread was this theory of the single-family home that Ernst Freund (1929, 92) could conclude—in my view, correctly—that "every one knows that the crux of the zoning problem lies in the residential district."

But what if parts of the theory are wrong, or what if the theory was originally right but parts of it no longer apply? Institutional theorists often use the term "path dependence" to describe a situation in which the initial setup of an institu-tion constrains its ability to respond to changing external conditions (see Hall and Taylor 1996). My reading of the current state of American zoning is very much along these lines. Yes, we see a lot of changes: states have become more involved in local land-use matters (mostly to counter environmental degradation and pro-mote affordable housing), the discretionary powers of municipalities have grown significantly, and various more flexible zoning tools are now in play. But if we place the American land-use control system and especially American residential zoning in comparative perspective, it is clear that we still have an unusually high level of legally mandated separation of residential from other land uses and an unusually radical way of legally guarding the single-family home. The issue is not simply that large parts of U.S. urban areas are taken by residential uses—some 50 percent according to Nelson (2004), a number that has stayed roughly stable over nearly a century if we accept Harold Bartholomew's calculations (1928, 1932) for the 1920s and one that is bound to be much larger in suburbs and exurbs. Now, I would be surprised if any large and living metropolis exists in the world where residential uses account for a minority of land uses. But in cities elsewhere in the world, the areas where people live are not *necessarily* reserved for that one type of human activity alone by legal mandate.

I am not suggesting that something is inherently wrong with having the space and privacy that usually come from living in a single-family home (I live in one myself). My concern is whether making it a widespread legal norm is bringing about the benefits originally promised. To begin with, some of the problems that zoning sought to resolve through land-use separation either do not exist today or have been solved through other means, to the point that a zoning solution is no longer necessary. No doubt polluting and hazardous production activities should be kept far from where most people live, work, and play. But the list of such activities is shorter now than it was 100 years ago. Thanks to better building construction and state-of-the-art fire-safety mechanisms, ordinary businesses such as laundries and restaurants no longer pose a danger to human life and health, yet they continue to be zoned out of most residential areas and relegated to strictly demarcated commercial nodes. Today, theories such as the one that grocery stores attract flies that transmit disease to children would probably bring a smile to most people's faces; like Alfred Bettman did in 1929, I know a lot of "mighty healthy children raised over grocery stores," although most of them (myself included) were not raised in America. The work-related safety concerns that early zoning sought to address have dissipated. It may have been admirable to try to remove exploitive business (e.g., the garment industry) from tenements and relocate them into factories so that the conditions in which people work could be better regulated. But any remaining American sweatshops should clearly be eliminated through means other than zoning.

There is no reasonable justification for the ongoing legally mandated separation of home and work—especially the type of work that most of us conduct today, when so much can be done via telecommuting. Today there are some 30 million home-based businesses in the United States (a new one is started every twelve seconds; Nuyten 2012; Small Business Administration 2012). In the Internet age their number is bound to grow, posing a fundamental challenge to the basic premise of land-use separation: that life can be divided into discrete spheres, home and work. The overwhelming majority of home-based business activities pose no threat to health and safety and provide an opportunity for zero-commute lifestyles (Dolan 2012).[2] Such businesses often operate in housing areas as "home occupations," but in many cases this zoning category is highly restrictive and does not allow much opportunity for growth (Garnett 2000).

Zoning's early proponents believed that separating land uses would make society safer by lowering crime and minimizing traffic accidents. The belief about crime was based on the theory that if densities were reduced and the mixture of land uses were constrained, the temptation and opportunity to commit crime would decrease. This was a particularly far-fetched proposition. Today we know enough about crime to realize that it is a social problem too complex to be resolved through changes in the physical environment, especially through reshuffling land uses on a map. Jane Jacobs (1961) countered this thesis of early zoning advocates by arguing that separating land uses creates areas that are empty of people during certain parts of the day, thus affording criminals more opportunities (this is her famous "eyes on the street" proposition: that the natural surveillance that occurs when people watch each other at all hours of the day constrains criminal actions). Jacobs's thesis may also be critiqued for placing too much emphasis on the physical environment as a determinant of social behavior. One way or the other, however, studies in criminology and in environment and behavior have shown that a simple relationship between crime and space (including between crime and land-use structure) is difficult to demonstrate (for a summary, see Cozens and Hillier 2012).

The early assertions that zoning would improve traffic safety also remain unproven. While the relationship between transportation and land use is more straightforward than that between crime and land use, it is not clear whether it works as zoning's early advocates claimed. Their prediction of greatly reduced traffic and therefore fewer traffic accidents may have been accurate for particular sections of a metropolis (e.g., where only dwellings were prescribed by law), but how were people supposed to get from the residential areas of the metropolis to all the other areas, including where they worked and shopped? To the credit of zoning's early U.S. advocates, the land-use segregation they proposed was fine grained (see Talen 2012b). They often talked of separate business and residential streets framing the same city block (rather than whole sections of the city dedicated to either residential or commercial use). They assumed that most essential land uses, even though they may be separated, would still be accessible on foot. But once the principle of land-use separation was applied to much larger areas, as they were later in the twentieth century, the connective tissue of the American metropolis—the highways that link residential suburbs to commercial strips and business nodes—became unbearably congested.[3] According to 2009 data, over 75 percent of Americans drive alone to work (McKenzie and Rapino 2011). The average American spends about 50 minutes a day traveling from home to work and back again, longer than in most European countries (The Economist 2011). According to 2001–2002 data, the average distance traveled in the United States each day is 40 miles. The number of vehicle miles traveled per capita per year approaches 15,000, over five times the distance between the East Coast and the West Coast. In Germany, the average distance traveled per day per person is 23 miles and the average miles of car travel per person per year is less than 7,000 (Buehler, Picher, and Kunert 2009, 9). The traffic safety comparison is not in America's favor, either. Likely in part because Americans drive so much more, between 2002 and 2005 the United States has 14.7 traffic fatalities per 100,000 people; Germany has only 6.5 (Buehler, Picher, and Kunert 2009, 7).[4] A long list of economic, cultural and policy differences may explain these contrasts. But the large distance between homes and workplaces and services traditional American zoning has imposed is surely one. This seems to be the hidden price of privacy: if you wish to live in a purely residential area as far as possible from "noises and turmoil and hurly-burly" (Alfred Bettman's terms), then to get to business areas, you have to sit in traffic. There are heavy costs to this behavior in addition to the mere annoyance of spending extended time with yourself in the car. These include the economic costs of congestion stemming from reduced labor productivity, delays in deliveries, business and personal travel expenses, and so forth (e.g., see Economic Development Research Group 2005). There are also environmental costs. The majority of greenhouse gas emissions in the United States originate from the transportation and building sectors; they are directly impacted by land-use patterns (e.g., Dale 1997; Kalnay and Cai 2003). In 2005, per capita car emissions of CO_2 in the United States were about 8,600 pounds; in Germany, only 2,900 pounds (Buehler, Picher, and Kunert 2009, 7). Environmental costs are also related to building type. Bigger single-family houses on bigger lots—which have been the U.S. trend for some time—lead, quite obviously, to greater consumption of natural resources: larger urbanized areas, greater runoff of storm water due to larger impermeable surface areas, higher energy use, and consumption of more building materials. According to the National Association of Home Builders—which can scarcely be faulted for its environmentalist bias—a 5,000-square-foot house consumes about three times as much material as a 2,000-square-foot house (Wilson and Boehland 2005, 278).

In addition, the land-use patterns traditional zoning helped create may be working against one of its most important original promises: the improvement of public health. Eliminating polluting and hazardous industries from residential areas and enforcing minimum standards for access to light and air must surely have improved human health, but highly segregated and sprawling patterns may today be having the opposite effect. This is for at least two reasons: the relationship between ambient air pollution and health (see Ren and Tong 2008) and the relationship between land-use patterns and obesity and the resultant chronic diseases. Spread-out built landscapes, where homes are far from other destinations and where the primary routes to these destinations are arterial roads, are associated with higher rates of automobile use, which then are associated with higher body mass index.[5]

Finally, what may well have been the grandest promise of zoning—increasing homeownership and thus producing a greater civic-mindedness and a better citizenry—today seems hopelessly naïve and simplistic. As chapter 1 showed, with or without zoning, homeownership rates are higher in a long list of countries than they are in the United States (and only in the ownership of detached homes is the United States near the top). But even if the United States were the world's leader—in homeownership generally or in single-family ownership specifically—does a high rate of homeownership lead to a more civic-minded citizenry? The positive social externalities of homeownership continue to be debated (especially in the aftermath of housing crises[6]; see for example, Stern 2009), but even if some benefit exists, nobody I have ever heard of or read still believes that owning a single-family home teaches people the essential values of "civilization," as early U.S. zoning advocates expected. To believe that would be to believe that New Yorkers are predisposed to be worse citizens that most other Americans or that the Swiss are predisposed to be worse citizens than the Swedish. And I don't see the Swiss worrying.

Arguably, zoning—the kind of zoning that makes explicitly private space the formative compositional element of America's settlements—does deliver the gift of privacy to American families. But put all the other arguments mentioned in the previous paragraphs together, and one begins to wonder whether the original promises of zoning were either highly suspect from the beginning or have since been turned on their heads. Paradoxically (from the viewpoint of zoning's founders), we may now have more pollution and worse public health with our current zoning than we would have if we had modified our land-use laws more substantially over the last hundred years.

There are persistent paradoxes embedded in the U.S. zoning system. My focus in this book has been on what I thought was the most obvious paradox, that of freedom (or at least, perceived freedom) versus authority. Indeed, how could one account for the remarkable extent to which otherwise authority-resistant Americans are willing to subject themselves to strikingly detailed municipal rules such as those on land use and building (and the rules adopted by homeowners' associations) in order to preserve the status quo of their residential surroundings? How was the idea sold to begin with? My argument was that the original aversion to authority was overcome by the arguments advanced by the early zoning advocates, who made clear that zoning regulation would not threaten the American idea of limited government, would benefit private property, and would help defend the much-cherished single-family home.[7] But there are other paradoxes, to some of which I only alluded in the introduction (perhaps they would make good topics for follow-up books). One of them (let's call it the change-and-stability paradox) is the dedication to preserving the status quo in land use and buildings in the country where growth, mobility, and breathtaking change have been an integral part of the national life story. Ernst Freund commented on it early on, suspecting that Americans needed strict zoning more than Europeans perhaps to resist such breathtaking change:

> I wish to dwell on the instability of American neighborhoods, the lack of attachment to a local habitat. . . . I note a contrast between American and European conditions. . . . In the [eighteen seventies my father bought a new house in a new residence district [in Dresden]. When I go back to Dresden now, that house is exactly as it was and the neighborhood is exactly as it was, and a relative of mine lives in that house now. The whole thing is unchanged. . . . On the other hand, the house in New York, where I was born, I suppose would be entirely out of the question for living purposes. I probably wouldn't recognize it at all. . . . I just wonder whether zoning will produce that stability which does not seem to be comfortable to American mobility. (Freund 1926, 80–81)

Another one (let's call it the home-versus-property paradox) stems from Fischel's (2001b) theory that zoning's popularity in the United States can be explained by homeowners' concern with their property values. To protect these values, homeowners need a way to control their surroundings. Yet we are talking about America here—the land where people constantly leave one home for another to follow better jobs, schools or services,[8] the land where people are more likely to see their homes as financial assets, as wealth generators, and as retirement plans than anywhere else in the world (Wasik 2009). Isn't it ironic that American residential space is so sacredly residential (so protected from intrusion through land-use law, that is) only because it is so commercial (because it is an object of trade rather than an object of our sentiments)?

I could go on. The moral of the story is that zoning does not seem to perform according to the explicit theories it was based on. And I hope that most Americans no longer subscribe to the implicit theory that underpinned zoning—that public institutions should be in the business of enforcing a "natural" social order. What, then, does the future hold? Institutional theorists often talk about policy windows: openings that create the possibility of change in a path-dependent policy system. Are we there yet?

Notes

INTRODUCTION

1. Excerpt from a conference speech quoted by Fischel (2001b, 258). In the post–World War II decades, Babcock was widely considered the dean of American land-use lawyers. His most famous work is *The Zoning Game*. On his legacy, see Bosselman (2008).

2. When I use the term "American cities," I often include cities, towns, suburbs, exurbs, etc. This is not to say that the distinction between cities and other types of settlements in America is immaterial. It is undisputable that suburbs and exurbs have much lower population and housing densities than cities and that they are much more heavily dominated by private spaces. Also, American suburbs and exurbs usually have more restrictive zoning laws. Still, I believe the distinction between U.S. cities and U.S. suburbs is highly consequential only if we maintain a self-referential discussion: if we compare certain things in the United States to other things in the United States (e.g., U.S. cities to U.S. suburbs or zoning in U.S. cities to zoning in U.S. suburbs). But if we choose to switch our reference point and compare U.S. settlements to settlements elsewhere (e.g., in Europe), the intra-U.S. differences become less prominent. For example, some 35 percent of the city of Seattle is zoned for single-family homes, and the number for Seattle's suburbs is bound to be larger. But does that matter if we know that in Stuttgart, Germany, the percentage of the territory covered by such zoning is in the single digits (Hirt 2007a)?

3. The only large city in America that does not have municipal zoning is Houston, Texas. However, it has private regulations that are enforced by the municipal government. Scholars have argued that the effect of Houston's private regulations is similar to that of public zoning regulations in other cities (Berry 2001; Lewyin 2005). See also notes in chapter 2.

4. I use the term "American model" of land-use regulation here without endowing it with normative content. Alternative terms such as "the American way" or "the American system" work just as well. I do not seek to either praise or criticize American land-use practices. I only scrutinize them and compare them to practices elsewhere and let the reader judge. I do point out, however, in the concluding chapter, that the U.S. model entails some paradoxes: i.e., it promises to do some things, yet does others.

5. Of course, I cannot claim that the American land-use control model is truly unique unless I investigate the models used in all other countries of the world. I can't wait for *someone else* to do this, although I doubt that it is possible. Most book-length monographs on the subject have focused on the United States and one other country, most commonly England (Delafons 1969; Haar 1984; Cullingworth 1993). I expand the comparison and include a few other countries for which we commonly expect certain economic, institutional, and lifestyle similarities: the countries in the industrialized world. I am especially interested in Germany, but the reader will find notes on other industrialized countries, such as France, Sweden, Russia, Australia, Japan, and Canada. Most of the pertinent text is in Chapter 3. The bulk of the international discussion is based on secondary sources. However, I interviewed land-use experts in each selected country and analyzed legal materials available on the Internet (e.g., national and municipal land-use laws).

6. The closest cousin of the U.S. land-use control model can most likely be found in Canada; still, there are noteworthy differences between the two neighbors, as Chapter 3 points out.

7. This is especially the case in northwestern Europe. The city of Helsinki, for instance, owns two-thirds of the land in its jurisdiction; the city of Amsterdam owns 85 percent (Dornette and van Veen n.d.; Clark, Notay, and Evans 2010). Such high numbers are unknown in American cities.

8. In the post–World War II period, many European governments (of the United Kingdom, France, the Netherlands, Sweden, etc.) built and controlled the distribution process of millions of middle-class housing units. In the United States, government construction of new housing targets only the poorest members of society and the overwhelming amount of new housing is constructed by the private sector. But in the Netherlands, for example, 35 percent of housing is publicly owned. The Dutch capital Amsterdam has fourteen public housing associations, which own 55 percent of the city's housing stock and control 80 percent of the production of new units (Schuiling and van der Veer 2004).

9. Here I refer to the fact that most European governments are not hindered by "taking" clauses in their constitutions. In other words, they are less legally bound to pay compensation to private owners for restricting private development opportunities. The U.S. Constitution includes several amendments that guard against government taking of private property. More on this in Chapter 2.

10. Although other nations have national-identity formulae, none of the ones I am familiar with center on individualism to the extent one finds in the United States. The French, for instance, embrace "liberte, egalite, fraternite" as a key part of their national ethos and as part of their world's "civilizing mission" ("mission civilisatrice") (see Roos 2011). The Russians have a soft spot for a loose set of vague spiritual-communitarian ideals that, in the Good-Bye-Lenin era, claim lineage to Tolstoy and Dostoevsky. And before the recent European crisis, it was quite feasible to talk about a "European Dream"—ostensibly, one of connectivity, sustainability, and human rights that flattered itself as being counterposed to the American Dream, with its focus on competition and individual wealth and advancement (Rifkin 2004).

11. A perfect example is the outrage among conservatives about President Obama's remark in 2012 that "if you've got a business, you didn't build that." The president said that he was referring to public infrastructure, but his words were widely interpreted as an insult to the American tradition of individual achievement (e.g., Krauthammer 2012).

12. See, for instance, G. Hoftstede (2001), who showed that Americans embrace the highest degree of individualism of people in the industrialized nations he studied. One expression of this trait is Americans' appreciation of competition between individuals in the free market. The 2005–2006 World Values Survey—the largest international study of cultural preferences—asked respondents to express their views on whether competition is good because "it stimulates people to work hard and develop new ideas" or harmful because "it brings out the worst in people." The question used a scale of 1 (full agreement with "competition is good") to 10 (full agreement with "competition is harmful"). Whereas 21.3 percent of U.S. respondents gave the answer "1" (strongest support for competition), the numbers for West European countries were significantly lower: e.g., 10.2 percent in Germany, 10.9 percent in France, and 15.5 percent in the UK. Or compare American and German attitudes toward private business ownership. A question in the World Values Survey asked whether private ownership of business should be increased at the expense of government ownership of business on a scale of 1 to 10 (1 = more private ownership and 10 = more government ownership). Some 20 percent of Americans fully agreed that private business ownership should be expanded, but only 7 percent of Germans felt this way (World Values Survey n.d.). This in the context of the already slightly

higher share of GDP held by the private sector in the United States than in Germany (90 and 85 percent respectively; Bitzenis and Rodrik 2008). Lastly, consider the fact that even though income inequality in America is greater than in most other western nations (e.g., if we compare the U.S. Gini coefficient to the average coefficient for the twenty-seven countries in the Organization for Economic Cooperation and Development; OECD 2011), Americans today are less supportive of the idea that the government should do something to soften inequality compared to citizens of other nations (see Sachweh and Olafsdottir 2010). The 2005–2006 World Values Survey asked respondents to indicate which of two statements more closely expressed their views: "Incomes should be made more equal" and "We need larger income differences as incentives for individual effort." The question used a scale of 1 (more equal incomes) to 10 (less equal incomes). Only 6.1 percent of US respondents gave the answer "1" (strongest support for greater income equality), compared to 12.2 percent of respondents in Germany, 12.9 percent in the UK, and 16.4 percent in France (World Values Survey n.d.). Another question asked on a scale from 1 to 10 whether taxing the rich and subsidizing the poor is an essential feature of democracy (1 = full disagreement with the statement that taxing the rich and subsidizing the poor is essential to democracy) and 10 (full agreement with the same idea). Whereas 16.4 percent of U.S. respondents thought taxing the rich to subsidize the poor is *not* an essential feature of democracy, the numbers for Germany, the UK, and France were only 4.4, 7.1, and 7.9, respectively (World Values Survey n.d.).

13. The U.S. Constitution does not treat the accumulation of property as a right, but references to property are included in some state constitutions. For example, the 1776 Virginia Declaration of Rights stated "that all men are by nature equally free and independent, and have certain inherent rights, of which, when they enter into a state of society, they cannot, by any compact, deprive or divest their posterity; namely, the enjoyment of life and liberty, with the means of acquiring and possessing property, and pursuing and obtaining happiness and safety." (See http://www.constitution.org/bcp/virg_dor.htm)

14. The idea is well articulated by Benjamin Franklin too. Note how in his "Advice to a Young Tradesman" he suggests that money-making is virtuous, that *not* to make money is to harm future generations: "Remember, that money is the prolific, generating nature. Money can beget money, and its offspring can beget more, and so on. Five shillings turned is six, turned again is seven and three pence, and so on, till it becomes a hundred pounds. The more there is of it, the more it produces every turning, so that the profits rise quicker and quicker, he that kills a breeding sow, destroys all her offspring to the thousandth generation. He that murders a crown destroys all that it might have produced, even scores of pounds"

15. In the admiring eyes of one European-turned-American, Italian-born Los Angeles architect Edgardo Contini, "The suburban dream house is the idealization of every immigrant's Dream—the vassal's dream of his own castle. Europeans who come here are delighted by our suburbs. Not to live in an apartment!" (quoted in Forman 2011).

16. Sociologist Claude Fischer (2010) points to another answer. Americans, in his view, are willing to obey strict regulations because they think they *select the authority* that passes them (in this case, the locale where they live or their homeowners' association). This way they feel the regulations are not imposed but chosen.

17. In Nelson's (1977) formulation, zoning is an exercise of collectively held property rights.

18. Fischel credits a few American economists from the 1970s (e.g., Sonstelie and Portney 1978) with the initial formulation of the homevoter hypothesis. But I would argue that its seeds were sown much earlier, precisely when zoning began to capture the American imagination. Take, for example, Frank Backus Williams, a contemporary of Ernst Freund and also a distinguished law professor and "father" of zoning. In Williams's views, homeownership and the desire to control the home's environs are directly related: "In a residential district where men own their homes, the exclusion of business ... increases health and comfort, and will without doubt increase the satisfaction of those concerned,

as it might not do in a city in which only a small percentage of homes were owned by their occupants" (Williams 1922, 208). Four decades later, John Delafons (1969), a scholar who analyzed U.S. land-use law from a British perspective, echoed the homeownership hypothesis. He used it to explain why British town planners tended to designate "general residential" areas without distinguishing between attached and detached housing, whereas their U.S. colleagues tended to employ complicated housing subcategories, thus placing housing types in different parts of the city and protecting the exclusivity of the single-family areas. When looking at a city layout, "the British planner," Delafons noted, "would probably say 'Let the whole place be "general residence"', but the more exclusive [American] zones do reflect the very marked preferences held by the American homeowner" (47).

19. These perceptions are deeply ingrained, despite the fact that empirical evidence that commercial establishments and high-density rental housing projects have a depreciating effect of on predominantly single-family neighborhoods has been mixed (e.g., Stull 1975; Polakowski, Ritchay, and Weinrobe 2005; Mathews 2006).

20. There are about 39,000 general-purpose governments in the United States, including counties, municipalities, and townships (Hogue 2013). The average number of residents in a municipality is just over 6,000 (Cox 2008).

21. In the United States, about 75 percent of local revenue comes from local property taxes (Tax Policy Center 2013). Thus, to maintain their finances, municipalities need the "good" taxpayers. These include not only single-family homeowners but also large commercial and industrial businesses. Zoning can be used for the purpose of winning this intermunicipal competition ("fiscal zoning"). In Europe, municipal governments are typically more dependent on higher-tier governments for revenue. In Great Britain, for example, local council taxes comprise only about 25 percent of local revenue; the rest comes from various central government sources (Barker 2006).

22. This is the basis of Tiebout's 1956 model and what has been labeled as "freedom of choice in the public sector" (Brueckner 2000, 169).

23. This is a tall order when one keeps in mind how difficult it is to measure government decentralization and fragmentation comparatively (Martinez-Vazquez and Timofeev 2009).

24. France, a country whose population is five times smaller than that of the United States, has over 35,000 communes (similar to the number in the United States). Metropolitan Paris dwarfs metropolitan Pittsburgh with its 1,500 local governments (Encyclopedia of the Nations n.d.;; Cox 2008).

25. Even in American markets, residential values in mixed-use environments do not always decline, as is evidenced by the very high prices in fashionable New Urbanist developments.

26. Canada, Australia, and New Zealand probably come closest to the United States in this respect.

27. I realize that making a case for an "American culture" is controversial. American society is complex and fragmented. How can there be such a thing as a "national temperament," as quintessentially American values? These are of course valid questions. But as Claude Fischer—author of one of the best recent cultural biographies of America—recently noted, despite all our talk of diversity, all our celebrations of cultural pluralism, there still are "important [cultural] distinctions that do coincide with [our] national borders" (2010: 12).

CHAPTER 1

1. The rate of homeownership in the United States significantly surpasses that of only two EU countries, Germany and Austria, which at 53 and 58 percent respectively are outliers on the European continent. Perhaps unexpectedly, the homeownership

"champions" are post-communist nations such as Romania, Lithuania, Croatia, Hungary, and Slovakia, all of which are much poorer than the United States but have homeownership rates near or exceeding 90 percent. To add insult to injury, although homeownership is integral to the American Dream, even the Russians and the Chinese—those formerly "misguided" collectivists—achieve the dream in higher numbers. Their homeownership rates are about 80 percent (Kosareva, Puzanov, and Tumanov 2010; European Mortgage Federation 2013; Nacionalnoe Agentstvo Razvitiya Jiliyshtnyih Fondov n.d.; Deng, Shen, and Wang 2009).

2. Note that Americans do not own their homes more "absolutely" than the citizens of other nations, either. On the contrary, Americans are more heavily indebted to banks. Greater percentages of citizens of several European nations own the places they dwell in *without* a mortgage (again, the postcommunist nations, headed by Romania, have really excelled on this front, as Table 2.1 illustrates). The Eurozone's average percentage of homeowners without mortgages is more than double that of the United States (44 percent as compared to 20 percent).

3. The U.S. number becomes higher if manufactured homes, which are typically single-family units, are included.

4. From Europe's largest cities, only London is an exception, with about half of its housing in apartments. This data, however, is reported for Greater London, rather than the city itself.

5. The statistics for large Canadian cities are generally between the U.S. and European ones. In Montreal, for example, about 85 percent of occupied private dwellings are in multifamily structures; in Vancouver, about 75 percent (Statistics Canada 2006).

6. In the United States, however, a potentially important trend has developed. As a result of the Great Recession and demographic change (e.g., a higher percentage of Hispanic citizens, who typically have larger extended families), single-family homes may be becoming multigenerational dwellings (Alcantara 2012).

7. Data is for detached homes and mobile homes.

8. In terms of size of new dwellings, America shares world leadership with Australia: in both countries, the average size of recently constructed dwellings is about 2,200 square feet (Demographia n.d.)

9. One of my favorite portrayals of an American lawn comes from *The Great Gatsby*, which describes a lawn as a living being nearly capable of animation: "The lawn started at the beach and ran toward the front door for a quarter of a mile, jumping over sun-dials and brick walks and burning gardens—finally when it reached the house drifting up the side in bright vines as though from the momentum of its run" (Fitzgerald [1925] 1993, 6). The fascinating story of the American lawn is told in Schroeder (1993).

10. This is according to "Lot Size of New Single-Family Homes Sold Excluding Condominiums," www.census.gov/const/C25Ann/malotsizesold.pdf, accessed February 15, 2012. I have not been able to find corresponding statistics for other countries, but the urban density figures cited earlier speak for themselves.

11. According to McCahill and Garrick (2012), one way of quantifying the relationship between automobile use and urban density is as follows: for every additional 10 percent of residents who commute by automobile, parking areas in cities grow by about 2,500 square meters per 1,000 people and density drops by about 1,700 people per square kilometer.

12. I often start a class with this question, and my undergraduate students always give the same answer: land.

13. If the abundance of land itself was the key explanatory variable in land-use laws and land development patterns, countries such as Kazakhstan and Russia, which have relatively small populations for their large territories, should have developed in a more land-extensive manner and their cities should have low population densities. Cities in

these countries should have also adopted laws facilitating low-density urban development. But I have seen no evidence that this is the case.

14. Turner further argued that the key difference in character that emerged between Europeans and Americans of European ancestry was based on the fact that the former lived in lands defined by fortified boundaries surrounding dense populations, whereas the latter faced boundless land.

15. See also Forrest n.d.

16. Bruegmann (2007, 2008) has also sought to counter the conventional wisdom that Anglo-Saxon elites have been uniquely enchanted with living in sprawling out-of-town environments. His argument is that at least in the western world, "urban sprawl" dates back all the way to the Romans. He also asserts that sprawl is pervasive today in many other affluent countries besides the United States.

17. My favorite quote on homeownership comes from William Levitt—the builder of Levittown, the most paradigmatic community of generic suburban American single-family homes: "No man who owns his house and lot can be a Communist; he has too much to do" (quoted in Kelly 1993, 164).

18. A year earlier he declared that homeownership "lies at the heart of the American Dream" (quoted in Archer 2005, 260). The housing crisis appears to have slightly altered the position of the current U.S. president, Barack Obama (see Goldstein 2011). I should also point out here that America's top politicians are not the only ones who have prioritized homeownership. Australian politicians have talked about (and worked to implement) the "Great Australian Dream" of homeownership for several decades now (e.g., see Donoghue, Tranter, and White 2002), and the idea has been recently hailed by two Russian presidents, Putin and Medvedev, who called it a "Russian Dream" (Gillis 2010).

19. As most people know, gas prices are much higher in Europe. As of March 2012, one gallon of gas cost about $4 in the United States, compared to $8.20 in the UK, $8.00 in France, and $8.80 in the Netherlands. In the latter, taxation of gas comprises nearly 69 percent of the price of fuel, whereas in the United States federal excise tax is about 18 percent (when state taxes are added, the U.S. percentage goes to about 48). Another difference in transport policy is that the U.S. highway funds are revolving: gas tax revenues are earmarked for highway improvement alone. In European countries, revenues from gas taxes typically go into a general fund and may be used for purposes other than highway improvement; highway investment must compete with other government priorities (Nivola 1999).

20. Some European countries have partial deductions or credits to help homeowners. But the U.S. pro-homeownership tax break appears to exceed what exists internationally.

21. It is very difficult to assess the extent to which the policies really *cause* sprawl (U.S. General Accounting Office 1999). Studies such as Knaap et al. (2001) have tried to make a case for the causal relationship.

22. For comprehensive analyses of the housing crisis and its impact on America's urbanization patterns, see the following excellent books: William Rohe and Harry Watson's *Chasing the American Dream: New Perspectives on Affordable Homeownership* (2007); John Wasik's *The Cul-de-Sac Syndrome: Turning around the Unsustainable American Dream* (2009); and William Lucy's *Foreclosing the Dream: How America's Housing Crisis Is Reshaping Our Cities and Suburbs* (2010). Not surprisingly, the topic has become popular in the mainstream media too and I will not cover it in greater depth here.

23. Another recent survey concluded that only 8 percent of Americans wish to live in dense urban environments (Braddy 2012).

CHAPTER 2

1. In the United States, zoning is supplemented by another major means of municipal regulation—subdivision controls. Unlike zoning, subdivision controls prescribe no functional specialization for particular areas. Instead, they constitute detailed rules pertaining to the

subdivision of land and the design and layout of roads and utilities (Levy 2006: 120). Despite the obvious differences, zoning and subdivision controls are examples of the same preemptive and detailed approach to regulating urban space. In many communities, they are included in a single ordinance.

2. Districts are then formed based on each of the three criteria—land use, shape, and bulk—so that if a private party were to build something, she or he would have to comply with the rules related to all three.

3. This is calculated as total covered area on all floors of all buildings on a certain plot divided by the area of the plot.

4. Some cities have begun to require minimum density (and/or maximum lot size) along with maximum density (and/or minimum lot size) in residential districts in an effort to encourage urban living and curb urban sprawl. Portland, Oregon, is a good example. But this approach is rare.

5. At least in extreme cases; for example, when owners can demonstrate that they have experienced devastating financial harm.

6. Compensation is provided for regulatory taking in Germany under certain rare circumstances (see Richter 2003).

7. One could argue that the label is misleading because it eventually came to symbolize only a particular type of exclusionary and land-use-segregationist zoning, but the term has endured.

8. Some states, such as Florida and Maryland, have ventured into statewide land-use planning. The federal government has not (Kayden 1999).

9. John Dillon (1831–1914) was an American jurist who wrote a treatise on the relationship between states and municipalities (see Schulz 1989, 66–75).

10. In practice, Dillon's doctrine is not as clear cut (see Briffault 1990a, 1990b).

11. A companion federal Standard City Planning Enabling Act was published in 1928.

12. For such a law to pass the constitutional test, it would likely need to be grounded in a source of federal authority. However, federal environmental laws are typically grounded in the Interstate Commerce clause of the U.S. Constitution, which would be difficult to use as source of authority for zoning since its impacts are perceived as primarily local.

13. This remains so despite the fact that proposals for transferring zoning functions to metropolitan or state authorities have been discussed for quite some time, primarily with the purpose of forcing suburban locales to accept their "fair share" of low-income housing (see Downs 1973).

14. This fact has led some to argue that far from being a German import (Logan 1976), zoning was actually a domestic product (Frug 1996; Fischler and Kolnick 2006). I will return to this subject later on.

15. In 1928, Harold Bartholomew, city planning engineer of St. Louis, reported the percentage of developed land occupied by residential zones in several American cities during the mid- and late 1920s: for instance, 47 percent in Minneapolis, 43 percent in Memphis, 39 percent in Kenosha, 38 percent in South Bend, 30 percent in Toledo, 27 percent in Buffalo, and 20 percent in Washington. He also reported percentages for areas zoned for apartments in three cities (Minneapolis, South Bend, and Washington): all were less than 1 percent (Bartholomew 1928, 61–62). This number has increased over time, but only moderately so. In another article, Bartholomew (1932, 12) estimated the "average" amount of land zoned for single-family residential purposes in American cities as 36.1 percent. All other uses occupied smaller amounts of land: e.g., streets occupied 33.6 percent, industry occupied 10.8 percent, railroads occupied 5.5 percent, two-family dwellings occupied 2.1 percent, and multifamily dwellings occupied 1.1 percent.

16. For instance, in 1923, Denver had only thirteen districts; in 1957, there were nineteen; and in 1994, there were forty-two (Elliott 2008, 12).

17. Since a greater number of permitted uses accumulate at the bottom of the pyramid, this type of zoning is also referred to as cumulative.

18. As zoning districts of all types—land-use, bulk, density, overlay, floating, form-based, etc.—proliferated during the mid-twentieth century, it became increasingly more difficult to represent them on a single map. The human eye simply could not deal with the visual representation of such complexity. So in most cities, especially large ones, if you were to request the zoning map, you would get a very large set of maps, each covering a part of town. Geographic Information Systems (GIS) have of course made representation much easier (and more accurate). Today, if one wants to find how a particular lot is zoned, he or she would typically visit a city's Web site and query the online system regarding this lot. Some cities have managed to fit all their information on a single zoning map (e.g., Fort Worth and Seattle), but having multiple maps that cover the city sector by sector continues to be more common.

19. Zoning ordinances can also list the uses that are explicitly prohibited.

20. Home-based businesses, also known as home occupations, are defined as small businesses operated by a homeowner whose residence is on site (e.g., architect's office). They have strict size limits and restrictions on the number of people employed. Sometimes the homeowner can be the only person engaged in the business. Most commonly, two or three people can be employed. In Jacksonville (2011, 183), for instance, "home occupations shall have no more than three persons engaged in operating the businesses at one time." Food or drink sales and tutoring of more than two students at a time are specifically banned as home-based businesses.

21. "Nonconforming" uses may be referred to as another type of zoning relief. Under this status, a use that is not in conformance with the zoning ordinance is allowed to exist because it has been grandfathered.

22. Houston, Texas, the largest American city without municipal zoning, is often brought up as the proof that markets without zoning bring about similar outcome as markets with zoning: Houston looks "for the most part . . . [like] any other large North American city" (Coy 2007); it has many low-density monofunctional areas. But this is a misleading argument because Houston is covered by private neighborhood deed restrictions that the municipality enforces. They appear to have an effect similar to that of municipal zoning. Houston is thus a city without zoning but is not an unregulated city (Berry 2001; Lewyn 2004).

23. For example, discretion has been increasing by granting large amounts of variances or by purposefully zoning areas for low-intensity uses, thus inviting rezoning demands from developers—demands that then become subject to municipal discretionary judgment.

24. These tools are called Purchase of Development Rights (PDR) and Transfer of Development Rights (TDR).

25. For example, based on the cost of new public green space that should be provided for residents brought in by a new development.

26. For example, cluster zoning typically allows developers to locate houses on smaller lots than regular zoning, as long as the developers designate land for common open space. Under cluster zoning, the permitted density of a development is determined for an entire area, rather than on a lot-by-lot basis.

27. Mixed-use districts have many names: downtown districts, traditional neighborhood districts, live-work districts, etc. Examples are given later in this chapter.

28. PUD can be tied to pre-selected tracts of land much as traditional zoning districts or can be used as overlay or floating zones (i.e., developers may propose PUD in an area of town that is otherwise covered by traditional zoning).

29. The assumption here is that the distribution of land uses is "naturally" controlled, since certain uses can or cannot be located in certain size "containers." For instance, a large shopping center cannot be located in an area where an ordinance prescribes small-scale built forms and limited parking. Hence, controlling built form indirectly controls use.

30. New Urbanists such as Emily Talen have wondered whether the focus on "non-representative, popularized accounts" of individual pioneering (rather than "typical") U.S. municipalities is leading to a false sense of ubiquity among proponents of zoning reform (Talen and Knaap 2003, 346).

31. What if mixed-use districts exist nominally but they allow an extremely limited mixture of uses, such as a mix of retail and offices? It is likely that local officials would respond affirmatively were they to be asked if they employ mixed-use zoning. But the de facto situation may be different (Hirt 2007b). A review of the actual legal texts and maps would eliminate this problem.

32. I randomly selected twenty-five of the fifty largest cities in the United States. Undoubtedly, the largest cities are not representative of the entire U.S. municipal landscape, which is dominated by suburbs. Large cities have long been more open to integrating land uses and eliminating exclusionary zoning than suburban locales. This is because most large cities are older and they developed a higher share of their built fabric prior to the advent of traditional zoning. Furthermore, large cities typically have higher densities and are more open to diverse populations. They also have larger, more sophisticated planning departments that can be expected to be more in tune with recent planning trends. If, as this chapter section shows, even large cities still embrace traditional zoning, what shall we say about suburbs?

33. Only a few cities allowed some residential uses in industrial districts, typically in unique areas, such as those dominated by old warehouses that are commonly converted into live-work spaces.

34. For example, residential mixed-use districts, neighborhood business districts, downtown districts.

35. Perhaps predictably, New York City's code appears to be the most liberal in "nesting" services within residential zones: for example, certain services such as those related to health care are generally allowed in "regular" residential zones, and certain floor-area percentages can be designated for office use in otherwise residential buildings located in residential zones (City of New York 2011).

36. Las Vegas has about thirty "regular" base and overlay zoning districts (City of Las Vegas 2010). Many of them conform to traditional U.S. practice. There are several exclusively single-family districts (Ranch Acres, Residence Estates, Single Family Residential-Restricted, Single Family Residential, and Single Family Residential-Compact Lot) and a few more that allow some mixing of housing types. The residential part of the code is generally organized according to the hierarchical principle, while the rest of the code is not. Mixed-use projects may be proposed in several of the commercial districts. There is a Traditional Development category and a Main Street Mixed Use category. What makes Las Vegas unique is its reliance on discretionary zoning; that is, on regulation plans adopted after negotiation between planners and developers through a PUD process. Residential land takes about 40 percent of the city, and about half of it is taken by Residential Planned Developments (R-PDs). While there are dozens of R-PDs in the city, the operative word is *residential*—these are not mixed-use PUDs. The city also has many commercial and industrial PUDs. For our purposes, it is important to note that the Planned Community (PC) and Planned Development (PD) categories are meant for mixed-use projects. But without reviewing every individual PC and PD, it is impossible to say whether they are mixed-use or not and whether they are low-density or high-density. The city's zoning map, however, shows that most of the PCs and PDs have a standard suburban-like street layout, one that is closely associated with traditional monofunctional low-density residential or commercial development. Thus it is unclear whether the PUD mechanism so popular in Las Vegas has been truly reformist.

37. Sometimes such standards are embedded in the zoning code; in other cases, they are listed in detail in an environmental code or in several topic-focused ordinances (noise ordinances, emissions ordinances, etc.).

38. In Colorado Springs, a Form-Based Zone (FBZ) is listed after the traditional base and overlay zoning districts. An FBZ may be proposed for any tract of land in the city by a private developer or a public body. If an FBZ regulation plan is approved, it will replace the regulations pertaining to an existing base zoning district (see City of Colorado Springs 2011). Dallas has more detailed form-based regulations in three zoning districts: Walkable Urban Mixed Use (WMU), Walkable Urban Residential (WR), and Residential Transition (RT) (City of Dallas 1997, 2009). As the names hint, however, only the WMU allows residential and nonresidential uses. The WMU occupies a small part of the city and no projects have yet been developed in it. Although El Paso has a 91-page Smart Code in addition to its traditional code (City of El Paso 2011a, 2011b), its use is not mandatory. It does not replace parts of the standard zoning code but rather paves the way for rezoning applications from property owners seeking to convert a particular lot from a standard designation to a SmartCode Zone. Four small SmartCode Zones have been adopted, but specific plans have not yet been approved at the time of writing. In Omaha, a form-based code was developed for a particular area in Midtown but has not yet become part of the main zoning ordinance (City of Omaha 2011). San Antonio, which has a number of mixed-use districts, also has a Form Based Zoning Development District—an optional designation that may be granted upon a developer's request (City of San Antonio 2011). Tulsa has adopted a Form-Based Code that *may* be used throughout the city, but so far only a small pilot area has been rezoned (City of Tulsa 2011).

39. The single-family category is also used in the other well-known form-based ordinance in the United States: that of Miami, Florida (City of Miami 2012).

40. And we are talking about *low-density* single-family areas. Atlanta's R-1 single-family zone, for example, permits one dwelling per two acres and restricts maximum lot coverage to 25 percent. Atlanta's highest-density single-family zone (R4-B) permits standards that are better fit for affordable housing: an area of not less than 2800 square feet and a frontage of not less than 40 feet and lot coverage of 85 percent. In Dallas, the single-family districts require minimum lot sizes varying from one acre to 5,000 square feet. In Jacksonville, the variation spans from one acre to 4,000 square feet. Typically, the low-density single-family districts occupy a much greater part of a city than the high-density ones.

41. Corresponding numbers for residential land in small towns (even historic ones) and in suburban areas are almost invariably much greater than in big cities. In Brookhaven, New York, for instance, land zoned exclusively for residential purposes occupies about 85 percent of the town's area (Town of Brookhaven n.d.). In Concord, Massachusetts, the home of Henry Thoreau, the percentage is 95 (Town of Concord n.d.)

CHAPTER 3

1. The basic variables that distinguish the five European families from each other are legal tradition (specifically, whether a given country uses common or civil law) and administrative structure (i.e., the power relationship between national and subnational governments in a country). Great Britain is the only European country that uses common law (thus warranting the existence of an autonomous British family); all others use civil law. With respect to the relationship between the central and the local government, the Scandinavian countries are likely the most decentralized in Europe, followed by the Germanic ones.

2. The planning family is called "British," but for historical reasons, the Scottish and Irish planning systems are actually closer to those of the European continent (Newman and Thornley 1996). This chapter discusses the planning system in England.

3. Even before that time, some land-use separation—an outcome typically pursued by zoning—occurred in Britain through market processes, as happened elsewhere in the industrializing world. The centers of cities were being increasingly used for office and

commercial purposes; the owners of those companies were able to outbid the residential owners in the competition for scarce space in prime locations. As central areas became less and less hospitable, the English bourgeoisie became the first to suburbanize, a process that began as early as the 1700s (Fishman 1987). Thus, single-use areas were already forming both in the centers and at the periphery of the large industrial cities.

4. This is very different from the nationalization of land that was carried in communist countries such as the Soviet Union. Land remained in private ownership in England. Private owners lost "only" the right to develop it, but they were paid off with hefty sums. The country established a fund of £300 million to compensate private landowners for the loss of development rights (Delafons 1969). At the time, this was a vast sum, although it could hardly compensate for losses that were to occur over an indefinite period of time.

5. This refers to the English Planning Policy Statements (PPS), of which there are currently twenty-five on topics that range from housing to climate change.

6. The term "zoning" is commonly used in Britain in reference to Enterprise Zones (EZ) and Simplified Planning Zones (SPZ). These were recently introduced to create greater certainty for developers pursuing key economic development projects. However, the number of such zones across English municipalities is small. Thus, zoning continues to represent "a fundamental break from the UK system of planning" (Cullingworth and Nadin 2006, 140–141).

7. This is not to say that English authorities deny development proposals capriciously. Precedent is extremely important, and if a private party was given a green light to develop a piece of land under certain circumstances, it can be expected that other private parties operating under similar circumstances will also be allowed to proceed.

8. To mitigate some of these concerns and provide greater certainty for the development process, the English system has been slightly modified since the early 1990s. If a private development proposal is in general agreement with the objectives expressed in a generalized plan, it is presumed that planning permission will be granted. Previously, this was not the case.

9. The greenbelt idea stemmed from Ebenezer Howard's ([1898] 1965) proposal for urban reform as outlined in his famous *Garden Cities of Tomorrow*. Currently, about 13 percent of the total area of England is covered by greenbelts surrounding the major cities. There has been criticism of the greenbelt approach because of some evidence that development has been pushed further into rural territory, beyond the greenbelts. Still, the policy remains very popular among politicians and citizens alike. For the history of the English greenbelts, see Natural England and Campaign to Protect Rural England (2010).

10. Conservation easements are legally enforceable agreements between private landowners and government agencies or nonprofit land preservation organizations (often called land trusts). In these agreements, land remains in private hands but the right to develop is limited. Various tax incentives make conservation easements attractive to private landowners. Like other tools I mentioned earlier (e.g., transfer of development rights and purchase of development rights), conservation easements are similar to the English approach in some respects: for example, the right to develop is severed from the right to own. However, conservation easements are voluntary; the English greenbelts are not. Furthermore, in England, the right to develop is divorced from the right to own in principle and universally; it pertains to more than specific chunks of land.

11. In the English tradition, locales play the function of "deliverers" of services envisioned by the central government. The latter plays the stronger role in local land-use planning and regulation matters. Although there is no national land-use plan for the territory of England, the national PPS are a powerful shaper of local land-use decision making. Local plans may be called into question and nullified if they are seen to be in violation of

national priorities. Also, the role of the courts is limited; a private applicant who is denied planning permission typically appeals to the central government as the ultimate decision maker (Cullingworth 1993; Newman and Thornley 1996).

12. Booth (2000b) highlights the feudal origins of the idea of separating the right to own land from the right to develop it in England.

13. However, the French bourgeoisie was not inclined to suburbanize in single-family dwellings at that time. On the contrary, the grand restructuring of Paris carried out under Baron Haussmann between 1853 and 1870 served the opposite purpose: the bourgeoisie expelled the poor and reclaimed the central parts of Paris by moving into fashionable apartment buildings (Fishman 1987). The districts under construction were subject to design rules, and the charm of the boulevards derived partially from the fact that the elegant buildings flanking them were (and still are) mixed-use.

14. This zone includes the large public facilities, such as train stations, railroad lines, water reservoirs, and hospitals.

15. In the twenty-first century, Germany is widely considered to be a model planning country again.

16. Note that German municipalities typically account for larger territorial and population units than French ones. There are about 14,000 municipalities in Germany compared to the nearly 40,000 ones in France (Gosniak and Stevens 2006).

17. The standards for "non-disturbing industries" were set in another federal law, the German Industrial Norms (Deutsche Industrienorm), which regulates the permissible emissions, vibrations, noise, etc. for each BauNVO residential class.

18. This is like in England and unlike in France. In the U.S. system, some states require local planning and others do not. In Sweden and Russia, which I review later, local planning is also mandated by the state.

19. There are 290 municipalities and twenty-one counties in Sweden.

20. I will not delve here into how political realities in Russia may make its land-use planning and regulation system work quite differently from what we find in the "western democracies" (see Pagonis and Thornley 1999; Golubchikov 2004; and Hirt and Stanilov 2009).

21. Veliky Novgorod (Novgorod the Great) was a medieval state that eventually became part of Russia. Because for part of its history it was a republic (rather than a kingdom) and because of its role as the easternmost port of the Hanseatic League, Veliky Novgorod is commonly considered the seat of Russian democracy. Thus, the fact that it was the first Russian city to adopt rules for private construction in the post-Soviet period was seen as a deeply symbolic sign of the state's loosening of control over the actions of its citizenry (Trutnev and Bandorin 2010).

22. There are about 25,000 self-government units in Russia today.

23. However, some building regulations existed as early as the late medieval age (Baba 2011).

24. This is hardly surprising, since Ikeda Hiroshi, the head of Japan's Home Ministry Roads Bureau and primary author of the land-use classification idea, had just traveled through Britain, Germany, and the United States (Sorensen 2002, 115).

25. After the national land-use classification system was formulated, only six Japanese cities adopted zonal plans right away. Zoning proliferated at a much slower pace there than in the United States. By 1930, only twenty-seven Japanese cities and towns had zonal plans (Sorensen 2002, 118); in the United States, the number was well into the hundreds. Furthermore, even the pioneering cities applied zoning for only parts of their territory. In 1925, areas without zonal designation occupied about 40 percent of Tokyo and about 50 percent of Osaka (Shibata 2008, 22).

26. An earlier, the 1950 law postulated the need for a national land development plan (Oshugi 2010). The national government today defines two broad types of zones in the

country: urban promotion areas, in which the local governments are expected to promote further development (these are already urbanized areas and areas where urbanization is expected and/or encouraged) and urban control areas, where building is restricted (Goto 1999).

27. There are about 1,800 local governments in today's Japan. For an excellent account of the evolving relationship between state and substate governments in the country, see Jacobs (2011).

28. According to a 1975 count, 68 percent of the zoned territory of Japanese cities was under one of the three residential classifications (Sorensen 2002, 222). The comparable figure for the United States is about 50 percent (Nelson 2004; see Hirt 2007b and 2013a for data on individual U.S. cities). But note that in the United States, "residential" generally means areas occupied only by housing, whereas in Japan these areas are essentially mixed-use.

29. The term "zoning" is also used in Australia today.

30. There are about 600 local governments in Australia.

31. Roughly speaking, the term "preferred uses" is similar to the term "principal uses" in the standard U.S. zoning vocabulary, and "contemplated uses" is similar to the U.S. "special" or "conditional uses."

32. This is not to say that the term is nonexistent in Australia. For example, the Territory Plan (Government of Australian Capital Territory 2008) designates suburban core zones in which "single dwelling housing" is the only main use that does not require seeking development approval (i.e., in U.S. terms, single-family uses are permitted by right). This is of course similar to U.S. practice, except that the Territory Plan lists several other land uses (e.g., multi-unit housing, guest houses, health facilities) as "assessable" (i.e., as potentially permissible) in these suburban zones. For the purposes of the comparison, consider that the suburban zone in Miami—the city with the most advanced form-based code in the United States—allows single- and two-family housing but does not allow commercial uses by right.

33. There are 5,600 municipal governments in Canada (Statistics Canada 2001).

34. There are major differences in the roles provinces play vis-à-vis municipalities (Rogers 1991).

35. This act was modeled after the U.S. Homestead Act, which I discuss later on.

36. Fischler and Kolnick (2006) and Fischler (2007) have shown that the idea of an inherent distinction between residential and nonresidential uses developed in Canadian cities such as Toronto as early as 1850.

37. For example, J. Kitchen, assistant engineer to the Town Planning Commission of Canada, wrote: "The use and development of land should be zoned in two fundamental classifications, Home Districts and Work Districts, subdivided by degrees and intensity" (1926, 7). He argued that the Home Districts should be subdivided in Minimum Density (individual detached dwellings with accessories on individual lots), Medium Density (semi-detached dwellings and duplexes), and Maximum Density (apartment houses, flats, tenements, and boarding and rooming houses). Similar arguments for the necessity of separating home and work and classifying housing by type were widespread in the United States at the time (for more on this, see the later chapters).

38. Vancouver applies discretionary control in its Comprehensive Development Districts.

39. For comparative purposes, consider that in Atlanta only the highest-density single-family zones have comparable minimum lot sizes, whereas the lowest-density zone requires a two-thirds of an acre minimum lot size. Even in New York, the lowest-density single-family zones (R1-1) require a 0.21 acre minimum lot size. To come close to Vancouver's metrics of minimum lot size of 0.08 acres, one must look at New York City's

R2 districts (City of New York 2014). The fact that regulations in land-rich Canada and Australia prescribe higher densities than the ones typically found in the United States should settle once and for all the question of whether the presence of large chunks of vacant space explains why Americans prescribe low-density patterns. Clearly, not all land-rich countries have chosen American-style densities as their norm.

40. Here I am not referring to the English home zones or the Dutch *woonerven*, the various community-building and traffic-calming techniques that are used in English and Dutch urban neighborhoods. I refer here to exclusive residential zoning.

CHAPTER 4

1. As Talen (2009b) notes, other authorities such as religious orders can write and enforce codes. Also, unwritten codes may get implemented by virtue of social custom.

2. Catherine the Great credited Peter's urban decree with making urban inhabitants "more docile and polite, less superstitious" (quoted in Kostof 1991, 256).

3. The Vedic treatises are from roughly 1500–500 BCE. However, the plans cited here may have been idealized proposals and it is not clear whether they were enacted on the ground.

4. In Egypt, some rules for construction may have existed as far back as Kahun (about 1800 BCE) (LeGates [1935] 2004; Marshall 2009) and Tell-al-Almarna (1350 BCE) (Hugo-Brunt 1972; Ben-Joseph 2005).

5. For example, during the reign of Augustus, building standards linked the width of streets to their location in the city: streets could vary in width from fifteen to forty feet depending on how close they were to the city's center. Building heights were limited to sixty-six feet. Later, Nero linked building height to street width: building height could not exceed two times the street width (Southworth and Ben-Joseph 2003; Ben-Joseph 2005; Talen 2009b, 2012a).

6. The same could be said for the emergence of specialized quarters in buildings. For example, on the increased specialization of rooms in ancient Greek dwellings, see Nevett (2010).

7. As earlier mentioned, it is unclear whether these idealized schemes were enforced on the ground.

8. For instance, it was expected that new buildings would not deprive their neighbors of adequate light (Robinson [1922] 1992).

9. According to Hugo-Brunt (1972, 73), the density of ancient Rome was about 20,000 people per square mile. In the most populated Roman districts, density may have come close to 100,000 per square mile.

10. The same applies to residential quarters. For example, baths in some upscale Roman villas were used not only by the families residing in the villas but also by outsiders for pay. So were such baths residential or commercial, if we are to use modern dichotomies? Rooms in ancient houses were also more multifunctional than they are today: dining rooms were used for sleeping, courtyards for stabling animals, bedrooms for parties or storage (Bowes 2010). A similar multifunctionality of spaces in medieval Chinese dwellings is discussed in Xie (2012a, 2012b).

11. This is not to say that there were no functional groupings of buildings. The area next to the forum, for instance, had a heavy concentration of inns, bakeries, and workshops (Laurence 1996).

12. The census at the end of the third century recorded only 1,790 *domus* and 44,300 *insulae* in Rome (Benevolo 1981, 176).

13. According to Nelson (1977, 112–121), modern zoning is rooted in the eighteenth-century enclosure movement that put an end to the English commons.

14. But, as earlier noted, many of the medieval municipal ordinances were limited in scope and were poorly enforced (Ben-Joseph 2005).

15. According to Rasmussen (1937, 166): 'When an earl or a duke did turn his property to account, he wanted to determine what neighbors he got. The great landlord and the speculative builder found each other, and together they created the London square with its character of unity, surrounded as it is by dignified houses all alike."

16. Banking business, for example, was conducted in private houses in England throughout most of the seventeenth century. The first specialized bank building, the Bank of England, was completed in London in 1734 (Abramson 1993; Xie 2012b: 135).

17. This is the title of a book chapter in Peter Hall's very well-known book (1996). I am borrowing it as a section title.

18. London's death rate during the mid-nineteenth century was about 25 per 1,000 (Brown 2004).

19. In this sense, the Germans introduced not only land-use-based zoning but also performance zoning—an approach which, as I mentioned in the previous chapter, was first championed in the United States by Kendig et al. (1980) some 100 years after the German invention.

20. As Habermas put it (1966, 45): "Partisans of the enlightenment such as Condorcet could still entertain the extravagant expectation that the arts and sciences would not merely promote the control of the forces of nature, but also further understanding of self and world, the progress of morality, justice in social institutions, and even human happiness."

21. Although rulers of all ages had an inherent interest in making their subjects better off (e.g., so that they could obtain higher taxes or lead stronger armies), the idea that many aspects of human life could be and should be improved through government action did not develop until the age of reason (Scott 1998).

22. These methods to study cities crystallized in the later part of the nineteenth century in the works of Scottish biologist and sociologist Patrick Geddes. He pioneered the comprehensive urban analysis method (or the civic survey, as he called it) as a precondition for urban planning. The use of quantification and standardization as methods of studying and reforming urban life peaked in the mid-twentieth century, during the "high modern" period (Scott 1998), when several other aspects of the urban fabric became the subject of not only classification (e.g., roads) but also of "high-tech" modeling (e.g., making forecasts about population, land use, and transportation). Zoning can certainly be regarded as one of the modernist means through which cities have been categorized and controlled. Since the 1960s, however, such methods have been subjected to intense critique in tandem with the rise of postmodern philosophy. The critique of zoning by Jane Jacobs and others can well be described as postmodern (Hirt 2005).

23. This approach is similar to urban growth management techniques practiced in contemporary cities.

CHAPTER 5

1. For instance, during the sixteenth century, the Aztec capital of Tenochtitlan had some 300,000 inhabitants, making its population comparable to that of Paris, Venice, and Constantinople during the same time.

2. However, some included relatively intricate design standards. For Philadelphia, William Penn posited "let the houses be built in a line, or upon a line, as much as may be." In their plans for Washington, D.C., Pierre L'Enfant and Thomas Jefferson prescribed street standards and included rules regarding street frontage: "Houses shall range even and stand just six feet in their own ground from the street" (quoted in Talen 2009b, 151). L'Enfant's plan was exceptional for its masterful treatment of important public buildings and vistas (see Berg 2008).

3. Based on such statements, some authors point to Jefferson as the "founding father of sprawl" (Vazquez 2006), fairly or not.

4. See, for example, Fishman (2000, 6), who claims that the idea that American culture is anti-urban is a "persistent misunderstanding." Talen (2005) also provides useful insights on this topic.

5. The famous 1855 speech attributed to Chief Seattle sums this up: "The Great Chief in Washington sends word that he wishes to buy our land. . .. How can you buy or sell the sky—the warmth of the land? The idea is strange to us. If we do not own the freshness of the air or the sparkle of the water, how can you buy them from us. . .. Every part of this earth is sacred to my people." (Quoted in Swann and Krupat 1987, 525).

6. Leo Marx (1991) points that among the Enlightenment philosophers, John Locke exerted the greatest influence on America's founders.

7. In 1800, 85 percent of the U.S. labor force was engaged in agriculture. By 1880, the number had decreased to 50 percent (Levy 2006, 9).

8. The *New York Times* commented in 1892 that America is being invaded by "the physical, moral and mental wrecks" from Europe "of a kind which we are better off without" (quoted in Hall 1996, 34).

9. Late into the nineteenth century, many tenements were simultaneously sweatshops and were thus immune from factory laws. The work did not move to larger factories until the early twentieth century (Toll 1969, 112).

10. Some viewed cities so negatively that they believed a Sodom-and-Gomorrah solution might be appropriate (e.g., as F. J. Kingsbury did in 1895; quoted by Hall 1996, 35). In 1897, the *American Journal of Sociology* claimed that the popular belief that cities were centers of "corruption" and "degradation" was correct (Hall 1996, 34).

11. That is not to say that there were not many important government interventions in the U.S. economy (e.g. transportation bills and anti-trust laws) in the nineteenth century, only that national and municipal regulations that targeted urban development were more limited than in Europe.

12. A perfect example of the judges' continuous hesitation to impose limits on the actions of private parties in turn-of-the-century America is the famous and controversial case of *Lochner v. New York* from 1905. In this case, the Supreme Court overturned an 1895 New York law that limited the daily working hours of bakery-shop workers to a maximum of ten. The court argued that this would amount to "unreasonable, unnecessary and arbitrary interference with the right and liberty of the individual to contract." On the intersection of *Lochner v. New York* and early zoning law, see Williams (1989).

13. In one indicative later example of public-private overlap that pertains directly to the history of zoning, the Chamber of Commerce, a private body, established its Special Committee on the Height of Buildings the same day in 1913 that the City of New York's Board of Estimate and Apportionment, a public body, established its own Commission to study the same subject. The two organizations had overlapping memberships. As H. Smith, the chair of the chamber's committee, remarked, the public commission "embodies in its membership some of our best judges of real estate as well as members of this Chamber." The public commission in fact reported to the Chamber of Commerce, which adopted the report after it had the opportunity to view the proposed zoning maps (Chamber of Commerce of the State of New York 1916, 170).

14. It is ironic that at the time when some expected that middle- and upper-class women to retreat to the domestic sphere, many of the organizations that aimed to reform the city were led by women. And this is probably truer in the United States than in Europe because the U.S. reform movements relied more heavily on voluntary organizations than on male-dominated professional bureaucracies. Daphne Spain (2001) tells the story of "how women saved the city."

15. These consecutive "invasions" formed the conceptual bass of the ecological model developed by the Chicago School. The model presented neighborhood change partially as the outcome of the struggles of ethnic communities to occupy desirable city districts.

16. For example, a 1885 ordinance declared that "it shall be unlawful for any purpose to establish, maintain, or carry on the business of a public laundry or washhouse where articles are washed and cleansed for hire, within the City of Modesto, except within that part of the city which lies west of the railroad track and south of G Street" (quoted in Pollard 1931).

17. This border continues to be blurred in Houston, where public authorities have the power to enforce private regulations.

18. Some bizarre contemporary rules include limits on the number of rose bushes that can be planted, demanding that all dogs be carried (not walked) at all times, and prohibiting grandchildren from residing at their grandparents' houses since the community is restricted to people fifty-five years of age or older (see "Top 7 Insane Homeowners' Association Rules," *The Week*, December 15, 2009, http://theweek.com/article/index/104150/top-7-insane-homeowners-association-rules).

19. In 1975, 340,000 dwelling units were located in communities with private homeowners' associations in the United States. By 2000, there were 6 million units in 200,000 such communities, housing some 40 million Americans (Levy 2006, 98). By 2005, the number of private communities had reached 250,000 and the number of people living in them had increased to over 50 million (Weinstein 2005).

20. It should be noted, however, that some cities in North America used fire districting. Unlike nuisance laws, fire safety laws divided cities into districts that had different rules about building materials. This approach followed the example of London after the Great Fire. Fire districting can also be deemed a zoning predecessor (Kolnick 2008).

CHAPTER 6

1. In 1916, only 8 cities had adopted zoning ordinances. By 1921, the number had increased to 76. At the end of 1926, right after the *Euclid v. Ambler* decision, the total was 564. By the close of the twenties, the total was about 800 (Hubbard and Hubbard 1929, 162; Toll 1969, 193).

2. Note, however, that health and safety rationales could be easily manipulated. We saw in the previous chapter that valid health and safety concerns stemming from the operation of laundries in late nineteenth-century California cities were used for racist purposes. See also Fischler (1998a, b).

3. The Heights of Buildings Commission produced a nearly identical statement thirty-seven years later: "Moreover, advantage of location and the resulting enormous difference in land values tend strongly toward differentiation in the character and intensity of use and this and other social and economic factors tend toward a natural segregation of buildings according to type and use. The city *is* divided into building districts. We believe that these natural districts must be recognized in any complete and generally effective system of building restriction" (1913, 67).

4. However, seven years before Frankfurt, in 1884, the small town of Altona near Hamburg divided its territory into districts with different bulk rules for each (Williams 1922, 212).

5. Baron von Stein (1757–1831) was a Prussian lawyer and public administrator who convinced Prince Wilhelm to issue a decree granting greater autonomy to Prussian cities. Later, the idea spread to several other states of the German Empire (Toll 1969, 132).

6. To put this in comparative perspective: Rogers (1998, 198) estimates that municipal authorities in Berlin alone had built 11,000 new dwellings by 1914, whereas the total number of dwellings constructed by public authorities across all of the United States was in the very low hundreds. He cites U.S. housing reformer Edith Elmor Wood, who in 1913 remarked that: "Municipal housing or municipal slum clearance, or any form of government aid . . . were a taboo and anathema. They were un-American. They were something pertaining to the effete monarchies of Europe."

7. Emily Talen (2012 b) specifically discusses how zoning districts based on land use were initially, at the beginning of the twentieth century, fairly small because it was expected that people would have to walk from the areas where they lived to the areas where they shopped and worked. The districts grew much larger over time as the automobile became the chief means of transportation.

8. The earlier Housing and Town Planning Act (1909) entitled authorities to recover up to half of the value increase following from the adoption of a planning scheme.

9. In a later recognition of the role of private property interests in the adoption of zoning, the Committee on the Regional Plan of New York praised the Fifth Avenue Association: "The owners in this district have been organized for many years for the defense of certain property and business interests" (1931, 33–34).

10. On the key role of the federal government in zoning see also Whittemore (2012).

11. It could be said that U.S. governments eventually began to collect revenue from regulatory changes through the concept of value capture (e.g., through exactions and impact fees). However, this did not happen until the 1950s. The idea was advocated by very few in the early twentieth century. For example, at the Third National Conference on City Planning, Lawson Purdy argued that "when land is put to its best use the maximum land value is often one of the results. Land is the kind of property that is increased in value by improvements in the city plan. Land, therefore, ought to pay the bill and can well afford to pay it" (Purdy 1911, 124). However, the link between zoning and value capture was not formalized in early twentieth-century America in the way it was in English legislation. Thanks to Nico Calavita for pointing out Purdy's speech to me.

12. We saw in the previous chapter that this argument was advanced in the California laundry cases (racism, undoubtedly, was an underlying motive).

13. Of course, workers' dwellings had to be close to the factories since most workers still walked to work. Hence, in German ordinances, some dwellings were permitted in industrial districts. But in the United States, hierarchical zoning permitted all dwellings in the industrial districts (accurately called the "unrestricted" districts in 1916 New York).

14. In Scotland, for instance, 100 aristocrats owned half of all private land (Wightman 1999).

15. One observer estimated that "the average loss by fire in a purely residential neighborhood, that is, in one or two family houses, was about $250 a fire . . . [but] in a dwelling over a store, $600. . . . [Therefore] the [fire] hazard in the combined residence and store building . . . is greater than in a purely residential building" (Miller 1929, 101).

16. We could perhaps call this an early attempt at performance zoning.

17. We could perhaps call this an early attempt at form-based zoning.

18. Although Bassett (1914) noted in some of his writings that he favored the elimination of only large-scale industry from certain districts, New York's 1916 resolution excluded practically all industry from the residential areas.

19. In 1913, Minnesota authorized the cities of Duluth, Minneapolis, and Saint Paul to create residential districts from which all business might be excluded (Heights of Buildings Commission 1913, 39–40).

20. Note, however, that Williams proposed a fourth basic category for New York that would include apartment buildings with commercial ground floors. Today, we would call it a mixed-use district.

21. See, for example, George Cadbury (1915), a member of the City of Birmingham Town Planning Committee, who gives a comprehensive account of the development of the Birmingham planning scheme. The author acknowledges that "too frequently the intrusion of a factory into an area which is otherwise residential has done much to remove the good effect of the re-construction scheme" (Cadbury 1915, 148) and that this might lower existing property values. However, his text does not include a similar concern about the intrusion of commercial facilities in residential areas.

22. Planning schemes incorporated language such as this: "By the consent of the Corporation [i.e., the authorities], but not otherwise, such consent to be expressed by sanction as aforesaid in the orders to be made under sub-clause c (iii) of this clause, there may be erected such shops or buildings other than dwelling-houses as the Corporation may see fit" (City of Birmingham 1913). In other words, whether shops or other nonresidential buildings could be built in the residential areas was left to the discretion of municipal authorities. In London's suburbs such as Ruislip-Northwood, there were separate zones for shops and businesses, but the residential areas could include "professional dwelling houses" including those that allowed for "the carrying on of handicrafts and the selling of the products thereof" if the products sold and the materials used were not displayed in the windows (National Housing and Town Planning Council 1914, 28). In Doncaster, streets of continuous shops were "desirable," but while the housing areas could not include industry and agriculture, they could include "roads, local playgrounds and open spaces, churches, shops and civic centers" (City of Doncaster 1922, 25–26).

23. Some courts continued to strike down the zoning-induced separation of home and business into the early 1920s. For example, in 1921, the Texas Supreme Court declared "idle" the attempts of municipalities to ban "ordinary retail stores" from residential districts on health and safety grounds (Williams 1989, 281).

24. Note that Bassett thought of separating residential streets from business streets (not entire city blocks). He assumed that the residential and the business streets should be close enough so that the stores can accessed by walking (this point is also raised by Talen 2012b). Still, a European-American difference was emerging in the treatment of land-use separation. Unlike what became standard in the United States, English definitions of a "private house" did not exclude the possibility of conducting business in the house. According to the Greater London Regional Planning Committee, "Where an undivided private house is used partly for business and professional purposes, it is treated as occupied by a private family unless the portion for non-domestic purposes consists of at least three rooms and is more than one quarter of the whole" (Greater London Regional Planning Committee 1933, 27).

25. As we saw in chapter 3, current German regulations do not define an exclusive single-family category at all and rely heavily on the general residential category (Light 1999; Hirt 2007a, 2012).

26. Note that the one- and two-family homes were in the same category and a homeowner could have as many as fifteen rooms for tenants. No current zoning code that I know of uses such a liberal definition.

27. Marsh claimed that this view was underpinned by economic principles developed by R. Hurd in his 1903 book *Principles of City Land Values*.

28. Other Southern cities with explicitly racially based ordinances included Atlanta, New Orleans and Richmond.

29. Unlike New York, not all of Berkeley was immediately zoned. Berkeley's districts were defined by the municipal ordinance but citizens had to petition the city in order for their area to be designated under a zoning category (City of Berkeley 1916; see also Babcock 1966).

30. The cities followed an act of the New York State legislature from 1913 that stated that residence districts could legally be limited to one- and two-family homes, if two-thirds of the property owners in a neighborhood would submit such a petition (New York City Board of Estimate and Apportionment 1913, 38–39).

31. Also, according to the New York City Board of Estimate and Apportionment (1913, 41), an area of Baltimore, Forest Park, was designated in 1912 for houses which had to be "separate and unattached buildings."

32. For a positive recent assessment of his work, see Akimoto (2013).

33. The petition stated: "The property owners of Elmwood Park and vicinity ask that their district be classified under the District Ordinance as a District of Class I . . . in which

no buildings shall be erected or maintained other than single-family dwellings with the appurtenant outbuildings. The petitioners make this request on the ground that such classification will afford them a protection against the invasion of their district by flats, apartment houses and stores, with the deterioration of values that is sure to follow" (McDuffie 1916, 12).

34. Westenhaver also objected to Euclid's zoning on economic and property-rights grounds.

35. Note that during the same time period, the Greater London Regional Planning Committee made exactly the opposite statement: "The development of large areas with dwellings suitable for occupation by persons of one class is undesirable and can be avoided by suitable planning" (1933, 9).

CONCLUSION

1. We could choose to classify land and buildings based on all sorts of other criteria (instead of the conventional rules about land use, bulk, and shape). We could classify buildings, for example, based on the ratio of window space to solid façade. Nobody does that, apparently because we consider it unimportant. But if I were a prisoner I would consider it very important.

2. For decades before 1990, the number of people in the United States who were occupied in income-generating activities conducted at home had been decreasing. However, the decline reversed about that time and since then the number of people working at home has been increasing (U.S. Department of Commerce 1998; Dolan 2012, 78–80).

3. Levine et al. (2012, 157) have recently argued that "having destinations nearby, as when densities are high, offers benefits even when the associated congestion slows traffic. Where land use policy frequently seeks to support low-development densities in part in an attempt to maintain travel speeds and forestall traffic congestion, our findings suggest that compact development can often improve transportation outcomes."

4. Sweden seems to be the international superstar in transport safety. In 2010–11, road user fatalities in Sweden were 2.9 per 100,000 people, compared to 10.6 in the United States They were 4.9 in Germany (International Transport Forum 2012).

5. According to a much-publicized study by McCann and Ewing (2003), people living in the most sprawling counties in America weigh on average six pounds more than people in the most compact county.

6. I am going to leave aside the question of how the high homeownership rates U.S. policymakers pushed and the concomitant irresponsible behavior of mortgage lenders contributed to the recent housing crisis. There is hardly a major media outlet in America that has not already reported on this link (e.g., Kiviat 2010; Zuckerman 2010; Cox 2011) and there are several excellent academic books on the topic (e.g., Lucy 2010).

7. I have for some time tried to explain to many of my European friends how American zoning works. Once I tried to explain it to a Czech friend. After answering a series of his questions with: "No, in America, you cannot sell cookies on the ground floor of your house," "No, in America, you cannot build a house for your son on your lot in a single-family district," "No, in America you cannot rent your third floor to another family in a single-family district," my friend acquired an increasingly worried look. He finally concluded that such heavy state regulation will eventually convert America to become a "communist country"—precisely what property-rights advocates from the early 1900s thought zoning would do.

8. Reportedly, a person in the United States can expect to move 11.7 times in his or her lifetime (U.S. Census Bureau 2012a).

References

Abeles, P. 1989. "Planning and Zoning." In *Zoning and the American Dream: Promises Still to Keep*, edited by C. Haar and J. Kayden, 122–153. Chicago: Planners Press.

Abrams, R., and V. Washington. 1989. "The Misunderstood Law of Public Nuisance: A Comparison with Private Nuisance Twenty Years after Boomer." *Albany Law Review* 54: 359.

Abramson, D. *Money's Architecture: The Building of the Bank of England, 1731–1833.* Ph.D. dissertation, Harvard University.

Adams, J. 1851. *The Works of John Adams, Second President of the United States.* Boston: Harvard College Library. Vol. IV.

Adams, T. 1934. *The Design of Residential Areas: Basic Considerations, Principles and Methods.* Cambridge: Harvard University Press.

Akimoto, F. 2013. "Charles H. Cheney of California." *Planning Perspectives* 18: 253–275.

Alcantara, K. 2012. "Multigenerational Homes: Real Estate's Next Big Thing as More Families Share a Space." AOL Real Estate, November 16. http://realestate.aol.com/blog/2012/11/16/multigenerational-homes-real-estates-next-big-thing-as-more-fa/. Accessed March 5, 2013.

Ali, A. 2008. "Greenbelts to Contain Urban Growth in Ontario, Canada: Promises and Prospects." *Planning, Practice & Research* 23(4): 533–548.

Alterman, R. 1997. "The Challenge of Farmland Preservation: Lessons from a Six-Nation Comparison." *Journal of the American Planning Association* 63, no. 2: 220–243.

———. 2010. *Takings International: A Comparative Perspective on Land Use Regulations and Compensation Rights.* Washington, D.C.: American Bar Association.

Amati, M., ed. 2012. *Urban Green Belts in the Twenty-first Century.* London: Ashgate.

American City Planning Institute, Committee on Zoning Standards and Principles. 1930. Report. Chicago: American City Planning Institute.

American Public Health Association. 2010. *The Hidden Health Costs of Transportation.* Washington, DC: American Public Health Association.

Anderson, N. 1925. "Zoning and the Mobility of Urban Population." *City Planning* 1, no. 3: 155–159.

Archer, J. 2005. *Architecture and Suburbia: From English Villa to American Dream House, 1690–2000.* Minneapolis: University of Minnesota Press.

Aristotle. 1912. *A Treatise on Government. Book II.* Translated by William Ellis. London: J. M. Dent and Sons. http://www.gutenberg.org/files/6762/6762-h/6762-h.htm#2HCH0020. Accessed July 18, 2012.

Arntz, K. 2002. *Building Regulation and the Shaping of Urban Form in Germany.* Birmingham: University of Central England in Birmingham, School of Planning and Housing.

Ashton, P., and R. Freestone. 2008. "Town planning." *Sydney Journal* 1, no. 2: 11–23.

Asimow, M. 1983. "Delegated Legislation: United States and United Kingdom." *Oxford Journal of Legal Studies* 3: 253–276.

Australia Bureau of Statistics. 2007. "Wealth in Homes of Owner-Occupied Households." http://www.ausstats.abs.gov.au/ausstats/subscriber.nsf/0/3033607B0D

8EF88BCA25732F001CA261/$File/41020_Wealth%20in%20homes%20of%20
owner-occupier%20households_2007.pdf. Accessed March 12, 2012.
———. 2013. "2011 Census QuickStats: Australia." http://www.censusdata.abs.gov.
au/census_services/getproduct/census/2011/quickstat/0?opendocument&nav
pos=220. Accessed July 16, 2012.

Baba, Y. 2011. "*Machizukuri* and Urban Codes in Historical and Contemporary Kyoto."
In *Urban Coding and Planning*, edited by S. Marshall, 120–135. New York:
Routledge.

Babcock, R. 1966. *The Zoning Game: Municipal Practices and Policies.* Madison: University of Wisconsin Press.

Bairoch, P. and G. Goertz. 1986. "Factors of Urbanisation in the Nineteenth Century
Developed Countries: A Descriptive and Econometric Analysis." *Urban Studies*
23(4): 285–305.

Barker, K. 2006. *Barker Review of Land-Use Planning: Final Report—Recommendations.*
London: HMSO.

Barnett, J. 1987. *The Elusive City: Five Centuries of Design, Ambition and Miscalculation.*
New York: Harper & Row.

Bartholomew, H. 1928. "What Is Comprehensive Zoning?" In *Planning Problems of
Town, City and Region: Papers and Discussions at the Twentieth National Conference on City Planning Held at Dallas and Fort Worth, Texas on May 7–10, 1928,*
47–71. Philadelphia: W. Fell.

———. 1932. "A Program to Prevent Economic Disintegration in American Cities."
In *Planning Problems of Town, City and Region: Papers and Discussions at the
Twenty-Fourth National Conference on City Planning Held at Pittsburgh, Penn-
sylvania,* 1–16. Philadelphia: W. Fell.

Bassett, E. 1914. "The Regulation of Building Heights: Value of Zone Plan." *New York
Times,* May 10.

———. 1922a. "Home Owners Make Better Citizens." *Baltimore Municipal Journal,*
March 10.

———. 1922b. *Zoning.* New York: National Municipal League.

———. 1923. "Present Attitudes of Courts toward Zoning." In *Planning Problems of
Town, City and Region: Papers and Discussions at the Fifteenth National Confer-
ence on City Planning Held at Buffalo and Niagara Falls, New York,* 115–134.
Philadelphia: Fell.

———. 1927. "Stores in Residence Zones." *National Municipal Review* 16, no. 4: 285–286.

———. 1929. "Discussion." In *Planning Problems of Town, City and Region: Papers and
Discussions at the Twenty-Third National Conference on City Planning Held at
Buffalo and Niagara Falls, New York,* 96–101. Philadelphia: Fell.

———. 1931. "Discussion." In *Planning Problems of Town, City and Region: Papers and
Discussions at the Twenty-Third National Conference on City Planning* held in
Denver, Colorado, 109–115. Philadelphia: Fell.

Baumeister, R. 1876. *Stadterweiterungen in Technischer, Baupolizeilicher und Wirthschaftlicher Beziehung.* Berlin: Verlag von Ernst & Horn.

Baunutzungsverordnung (BauNVO)(Federal Land-Use Ordinance) (1993). Accessed
at http://www.bauarchiv.de/neu/baurecht/baunutzungsverordnung/baunvo_
main.htm on September 30, 2011 (in German).

Beatley, T. 2000. *Green Urbanism: Learning from European Cities.* Washington, D.C.:
Island Press.

Beauregard, R. 2006. *When America Became Suburban.* Minneapolis: University of
Minnesota Press.

————. 2009. "Antiurbanism in the United States, England and China." In *Fleeing the City: Studies in the Culture and Politics of Antiurbanism*, edited by M. Thompson, 35–52. New York: Palgrave Macmillan.

Bender, T. 1975. *Toward an Urban Vision: Ideas and Institutions in Nineteenth-Century America*. Lexington: University of Kentucky Press.

Benevolo, L. 1981. *The History of the City*. Translated by G. Culverwell. Cambridge: MIT Press.

Ben-Joseph, E. 2005. *The Code of the City: Standards and the Hidden Language of Place Making*. Cambridge: MIT Press.

Berg, S. 2008. *Grand Avenues: The Story of the French Visionary Who Designed Washington, D.C.* New York: Random House.

Berry, C. 2001. "Land Use Regulation and Residential Segregation: Does Zoning Matter?" *American Law and Economics Review* 3, no. 2: 251–274.

Best, G. 1971. *Mid-Victorian Britain, 1851–75*. London: Fontana Press.

Bettman, A. 1914. "Discussion." In *Planning Problems of Town, City and Region: Papers and Discussions at the Sixth National Conference on City Planning Held at Toronto, Ontario*, 111–114. Philadelphia: Fell.

————. 1929. "Discussion." In *Planning Problems of Town, City and Region: Papers and Discussions at the Twenty-Second National Conference on City Planning Held at Buffalo and Niagara Falls, New York*, 96–101. Philadelphia: Fell.

————. 1930. "Discussion." In *Planning Problems of Town, City and Region: Papers and Discussions at the Twenty-Second National Conference on City Planning Held at Denver, Colorado*, 109–115. Philadelphia: Fell.

Birmingham City Council. N.d. "Chronology of Birmingham 1883–1950." Birmingham City Council. http://www.birmingham.gov.uk/cs/Satellite?c=Page&childpagename=Lib-Central-Archives-and-Heritage%2FPageLayout&cid=1223092760254&pagename=BCC%2FCommon%2FWrapper%2FWrapper. Accessed November 12, 2012.

Bither, B. J. 1915. "A Factory Zone Necessary for Industrial Development in Berkeley." *Berkeley Civic Bulletin* 3, no. 10, 167–177.

Bitzenis, J., and D. Rodrik. 2008. "The Private Sector." In *International Encyclopedia of the Social Sciences*. http://www.encyclopedia.com/topic/Private_sector.aspx. Accessed June 25, 2012.

Booth, P. 1996. *Controlling Development: Certainty and Discretion in Europe, the USA and Hong Kong*. London: UCL Press Limited.

————. 2000a. "From Property Rights to Public Control: The Quest for Public Interest in the Control of Urban Development." *Town Planning Review* 73, no. 2: 153–169.

————. 2000b. "Nationalizing Development Rights: The Feudal Origins of the British Planning System." *Environment and Planning B: Planning and Design* 29, no. 1: 129–139.

————. 2003. *Planning by Consent: The Origins and Nature of British Development Control*. London: Routledge.

Booth, P., M. Breuillard, C. Fraser, and D. Paris, eds. 2007. *Spatial Planning Systems of Britain and France: A Comparative Analysis*. London: Routledge.

Bosselman, F. 2008. "Richard Babcock: Zoning Game Troubadour." *Planning and Environmental Law* 60, no. 5: 3–5.

Bosselman, F., and D. Callies. 1971. *The Quiet Revolution in Land Use Control*. Washington, D.C.: Council on Environmental Quality.

Boverket. 2002. *Boken on detajlplan och områdesbestämmelser*. http://www.boverket.se/Global/Webbokhandel/Dokument/2002/Boken_om_detaljplan.pdf. Accessed October 7, 2011.

Bowes, K. 2010. *Houses and Society in the Late Roman Empire*. London: Duckworth.

Boyer, M. C. 1983. *Dreaming the Rational City: The Myth of American City Planning.* Cambridge, Mass.: MIT Press.

Braddy, E. 2012. "Smart Growth and the New Newspeak." *New Geography,* April 4. http://www.newgeography.com/content/002740-smart-growth-and-the-new-newspeak. Accessed August 4, 2012.

Briffault, R. 1990a. "Our Localism: Part I—The Structure of Local Government Law." *Columbia Law Review* 90, no. 1: 1–115.

———. 1990b. "Our Localism: Part II—Localism and Legal Theory." *Columbia Law Review* 90, no. 2: 346–454.

Brockway, L. 1915. "Discussion on Some Aspects of City Planning Administration in Europe." *Proceedings of the Seventh National Conference in City Planning.* Boston: MCMXV.

Brooks, R., and C. Rose. 2013. *Saving the Neighborhood: Racially Restrictive Covenants, Law, and Social Norms.* Cambridge, MA: Harvard University Press.

Brown, R. 2004. "The City in European History: London in the Nineteenth Century." University of North Carolina at Pembroke. http://www.uncp.edu/home/rwb/london_19c.html. Accessed August 14, 2012.

Brueckner, J. 2000. "Urban Sprawl: Diagnosis and Remedies." *International Regional Science Review* 23, no. 2: 160–171.

Bruegmann, R. 2007. *Sprawl: A Compact History.* Chicago: University of Chicago Press.

———. 2008. "Sprawl and Accessibility." *Journal of Transport and Land Use* 1, no. 1: 1–7.

Buehler, R., and J. Pucher. 2009. "Sustainable Transport that Works: Lessons from Germany." *World Transport Policy and Practice* 15, no. 1: 13–46.

Buehler, R., J. Picher, and U. Kunert. 2009. *Making Transportation Sustainable: Insights from Germany.* Washington, D.C.: Brookings Institution Metropolitan Policy Program.

Burchell, R. 1972. *Planned Unit Development: New Communities American Style.* New Brunswick: MacCrellish & Quigley.

Buttenheim, H. 1955. "Frank Backus Williams." *Journal of the American Institute of Planners* 21, no. 1: 61.

Cable, F. 2009. "Design First, Codify Later: Germany Offers Lessons for US Planners." *Planning* (July): 25–27.

Cadbury, G. 1915. *Town Planning with Special Reference to the Birmingham Schemes.* London: Longmans, Green and Co.

Cai, Y. 2011. *Chinese Architecture.* Cambridge: Cambridge University Press.

Calavita, N. 1998. "Inclusionary Housing in California: The Experience of Two Decades." *Journal of the American Planning Association* 64, no. 2: 150–169.

Calthorpe, P. 1993. *The Next American Metropolis: Ecology, Community, and the American Dream.* Princeton, N.J.: Princeton Architectural Press.

Canada Housing and Mortgage Corporation. 2013. Housing and Market Information; CHS Demography. schl.gc.ca/odpub/esub/64693/64693_2013_A01.pdf?fr=1396561837173. Accessed April 7, 2014.

Ceginskas, K. 2000. "Sweden." Compendium of Spatial Planning Systems in the Baltic Region. http://vasab.leontief.net/countries/sweden.htm. Accessed October 5, 2011.

Chamber of Commerce of the State of New York. 1916. *Annual Report of the Corporation of the Chamber of Commerce of the State of New York for the Year 1915–1916.* New York: Chamber of Commerce.

Charles II. 1666. "An Act for Erecting a Judicature for Determination of Differences Touching Houses Burned or Demolished in the Late Fire Which Happened in

London." In *Status of the Realm*. Vol. 5, *1628–80*, ed. John Raithby, 801–803. http://www.british-history.ac.uk/report.aspx?compid=47389. Accessed February 5, 2014.

Cheney, C. 1915. "The Necessity for a Zone Ordinance in Berkeley." *Berkeley Civic Bulletin* 3, no. 10: 162–167.

———. 1917. "Districting Process and Procedure in California." *Proceedings of the Ninth National Conference in City Planning*. New York: MCM XVII.

———. 1920. "Removing Social Barriers through Zoning." *Survey* 44, no. 11: 275–278.

———. 1929. "Discussion." In *Planning Problems of Town, City, and Region: Papers and Discussions of the Twenty-First National Conference on City Planning Held at Buffalo and Niagara Falls, New York*, 31–34. Philadelphia: Fell.

Cherry, G. 1996. *Town Planning in Britain since 1900: The Rise and Fall of the Planning Ideal*. Oxford: Blackwell.

Choppin, T. 1996. "Breaking the Exclusionary Land Use Regulation Barrier: Policies to Promote Affordable Housing in the Suburbs." *Georgetown Law Journal* 82: 2039–2077.

CIAM (International Congress of Modern Architecture). [1934] 1973. *Athens Charter*. New York: Grossman Publishers.

City of Atlanta, Georgia. 2013. "Code of Ordinances, City of Atlanta, Georgia." http://library.municode.com/index.aspx?clientID=10376&stateID=10&statename=Georgia. Accessed August 10, 2011.

City of Baltimore, Maryland. 2012. "Zoning Code of Baltimore City." http://www.baltimorecity.gov/Portals/0/Charter%20and%20Codes/Code/Art%2000%20-%20Zoning.pdf. Accessed August 12, 2011.

City of Berkeley, California. 1916. *Districting Ordinance No. 452-N.S.* Berkeley: City of Berkeley.

City of Birmingham, UK. 1913. *Quinton, Harborne and Edgbaston Town Planning Scheme*. Birmingham: City of Birmingham.

City of Chicago, Illinois. 2011. "Title 17 Chicago Zoning Ordinance and Land Use Ordinance." http://www.amlegal.com/nxt/gateway.dll/Illinois/chicagozoning/chicagozoningordinanceandlanduseordinanc?f=templates$fn=default.htm$3.0$vid=amlegal:chicagozoning_il. Accessed on August 13, 2011.

City of Cleveland, Ohio. 2011. "Part ThreeB: Land Use Code – Zoning Code Title VII: Zoning Code." http://www.amlegal.com/nxt/gateway.dll/Ohio/cleveland_oh/cityofclevelandohiocodeofordinances?f=templates$fn=default.htm$3.0$vid=amlegal:cleveland_oh. Accessed August 15, 2011.

City of Colorado Springs, Colorado. 2008. "Why Form-Based Code? A New Code for the Heart of Downtown Colorado Springs." http://www.springsgov.com/Files/FBCBooklet-FINAL.pdf. Accessed November 9, 2012.

———. 2011. "Colorado Springs, Colorado, City Code." http://www.sterlingcodifiers.com/codebook/index.php?book_id=855. Accessed August 15, 2011.

City of Dallas, Texas. 1997. "The Dallas City Code." http://www.amlegal.com/nxt/gateway.dll/Texas/dallas/volumei/preface?f=templates$fn=default.htm$3.0$vid=amlegal:dallas_tx. Accessed August 16, 2011.

———. 2009. "Chapter 51A Article XIII: Form Districts" http://www.dallascityattorney.com/51A/article13.pdf. Accessed April 28, 2014.

City of Denver, Colorado. 2010. "Denver Zoning Code." http://www.denvergov.org/tabid/432507/Default.aspx. Accessed August 20, 2011.

City of Detroit, Michigan. 2011. "Code City of Detroit, Michigan." http://library.municode.com/index.aspx?clientId=10649. Accessed August 22, 2011.

City of Doncaster, UK. 1922. *The Doncaster Regional Planning Scheme: The Report*. Liverpool: University of Liverpool.

City of El Paso, Texas. 2011a. "Municipal Code City of El Paso, Texas." http://library. municode.com/index.aspx?clientID=16180&stateID=43&statename=Texas. Accessed August 25, 2011.

City of El Paso, Texas. 2011b. "Municipal Code. Title 21 – Smart Code." http://library.municode.com/index.aspx?clientID=16180&stateID=43&statena me=Texas. Accessed on August 31, 2011.City of Fort Worth, Texas. 2011. "[City of Fort Worth] Zoning Ordinance." http://www.fortworthgov.org/zoning/. Accessed September 17, 2011.

City of Jacksonville, Florida. 2011. "Ordinance Code City of Jacksonville, Florida." http://library.municode.com/index.aspx?clientId=12174&stateId=9&stateName= Florida. Accessed September 28, 2011.

City of Las Vegas, Nevada. 2010. "Zoning and Subdivision Laws." http://www. lasvegasnevada.gov/LawsCodes/zoning_laws.htm. Accessed September 29, 2011.

City of Long Beach, California. "Long Beach Municipal Code." http://library.municode. com/index.aspx?clientID=16115&stateID=5&statename=California. Accessed September 30, 2011.

City of Manchester, UK. 1945. *City of Manchester Plan*. Norwich and London: Jarrold & Sons.

City of Mesa, Arizona. 2011. "Zoning Ordinance: Title 11 of the Mesa City Code." http://www.mesaaz.gov/planning/PDF/ZoningOrd/Full_Document.pdf. Accessed October 5, 2011.

City of Miami, Florida. 2012. "Miami 21 Code." http://www.miami21.org/PDFs/ AsAmended-April2012.pdf. Accessed July 12, 2012.

City of Milwaukee, Wisconsin. 2008. "City Charter." http://city.milwaukee.gov/ TableofContents. Accessed October 7, 2011.

City of Minneapolis. 1917. *Proceedings of the City Council of the City of Minneapolis from January 1, 1916 to January 1, 1917*. Minneapolis: City of Minneapolis.

City of Nashville and Davidson County, Tennessee. "The Code of the Metropolitan Government of Nashville and Davidson County, Tennessee." http://library. municode.com/index.aspx?clientID=14214&stateID=42&statename=Tennessee. Accessed October 8, 2011.

City of New York, New York. 2011. "Zoning Resolution." http://www.nyc.gov/html/ dcp/pdf/zone/allarticles.pdf. Accessed October 10, 2011.

City of New York, Department of City Planning. 2014. "Zoning Districts: Residence Districts." http://www.nyc.gov/html/dcp/html/zone/zh_resdistricts.shtml. Accessed July 19, 2012.

City of Oklahoma City, Oklahoma. 2010. "Oklahoma City Municipal Code 2010." http://library.municode.com/index.aspx?clientID=17000&stateID=36&statena me=Oklahoma. Accessed October 12, 2011.

City of Omaha, Nebraska. 2011. "Municipal Code." http://library.municode.com/ index.aspx?clientID=10945&stateID=27&statename=Nebraska. Accessed October 13, 2011.

City of Perth, Australia. 2013. "Scheme Text Schedules 1 to 9." http://www.perth. wa.gov.au/static_files/cityplanningscheme2/scheme_text/scheme_text_ schedules.pdf. Accessed March 7, 2014.

City of Philadelphia. 1921. *Annual Report of the Zoning Commission of the City of Philadelphia*. Philadelphia: Author.

City of Phoenix, Arizona. 2013. "Phoenix City Code." http://www.codepublishing. com/az/phoenix/. Accessed October 16, 2011.

City of San Antonio, Texas. 2011. "Unified Development Code." http://library. municode.com/index.aspx?clientID=14228&stateID=43&statename=Texas. Accessed October 17, 2011.

City of San Diego, California. 2009. "San Diego Municipal Code." http://docs. sandiego.gov/municode/MuniCodeChapter13/Ch13Art01Division01.pdf. Accessed December 12, 2013.

City of San Jose, California. 2014. "San Jose Municipal Code." http://sanjose.amlegal. com/nxt/gateway.dll/California/sanjose_ca/sanjosemunicipalcode?f=templates$ fn=default.htm3.0vid=amlegal:sanjose_ca. Accessed February 10, 2014.

City of Stockholm, Sweden. 1999. *Stockholm City Plan 1999: Planning Strategies.* Stockholm: City of Stockholm.

City of Tulsa, Oklahoma. 2011. "Tulsa Code of Ordinances." http://library.municode. com/index.aspx?clientID=14783&stateID=36&statename=Oklahoma. Accessed October 23, 2011.

City of Vancouver, Canada. 2012. "Zoning and Development Bylaw." https://vancouver. ca/your-government/zoning-development-bylaw.aspx. Accessed July 12, 2012.

City of Wichita, Kansas. 2009. "City of Wichita Ordinance No. 48-451. Unified Zoning Code." http://www.wichita.gov/Government/Departments/Planning/ PlanningDocument/Wichita-Sedgwick%20County%20Zoning%20Code.pdf. Accessed October 26, 2011.

City Planning Administration. 2009. "Stockholm City Plan: Summary, May 2009." international.stockholm.se/PageFiles/165973/Cityplan_short.pdf. Accessed October 7, 2011.

Clark, G., Notay, A. and Evans, G. 2010. *Leveraging Public Land to Attract Urban Investment.* Washington, DC: Urban Land Institute.

Clingermayer, J. 2004. "Heresthetics and Happenstance: Intentional and Unintentional Exclusionary Impacts of the Zoning Decision-Making Process." *Urban Studies* 41, no. 2: 377–388.

COMMIN: The Baltic Spatial Conceptshare. N.d. "BSR Interreg III B Project: Promoting Spatial Development by Creating COMmon MINdscapes: Sweden." http:// commin.org/upload/Sweden/SE_Country_in_English.pdf. Accessed October 4, 2011.

Concerned Neighbors of Wellington. N.d. Blog and reader comments. http://www. wellington-neighborhood.com/wellington-neighborhood/NeighborFeedback. htm www.wellington-neighborhood.com/wellington-neighborhood/ NeighborFeedback.htm. Accessed February 28, 2012.

Committee on the Regional Plan of New York and Its Environs. 1931. *Buildings, Their Uses and the Spaces about Them.* Vol. 6 of *Regional Plan of New York and Its Environs.* New York: Committee on the Regional Plan of New York and Its Environs.

Congress for the New Urbanism. 2001. "Charter of the New Urbanism." http://www. cnu.org/charter. Accessed November 7, 2011.

Continental Congress. 1785. "An Ordinance for Ascertaining the Mode of Disposing of Lands in the Western Territory." http://www.loc.gov/teachers/classroommaterials/presentationsandactivities/presentations/timeline/newnatn/confed/docsix. html. Accessed February 6, 2014.

Conzen, M. 1996. "The Moral Tenets of American Urban Form." In *Human Geography in North America: New Perspectives and Trends in Research,* edited by K. Frantz, 275–287. Innsbruck: Selbstverlag des Instituts für Geographie der Universität Innsbruck.

Coolidge, C. 1925. "Address to the American Society of Newspaper Editors, Washington, D.C." The American Presidency Project. http://www.presidency.ucsb.edu/ws/index.php?pid=24180. Accessed October 3, 2012.

Coppa, F. 1976. "Cities and Suburbs in Europe and the United States." In *Suburbia: American Dream and Dilemma*, edited by P. Dolce, 167–192. Garden City: Anchor Books.

Core Logic New Zealand. 2011. Average House Size by Area. http://www.qv.co.nz/resources/news/article?blogId=61. Accessed on April 7, 2014.

Cox, J. 2011. "US Housing Crisis Is Now Worse Than Great Depression." *CNBC News.* http://www.cnbc.com/id/43395857/US_Housing_Crisis_Is_Now_Worse_Than_Great_Depression. Accessed January 5, 2011.

Cox, W. 2008. "America Is More Small Town Than We Think." New Geography, September 10. http://www.newgeography.com/content/00242-america-more-small-town-we-think. Accessed July 6, 2012.

Coy, P. 2007. "How Houston Gets Along without Zoning." *Bloomberg Businessweek*, October 1. http://www.businessweek.com/the_thread/hotproperty/archives/2007/10/how_houston_gets_along_without_zoning.html. Accessed March 21, 2012.

Cozens, P., and D. Hillier. 2012. "Revisiting Jane Jacobs's 'Eyes on the Street' for the Twenty-First Century: Evidence from Environmental Criminology." In *The Urban Wisdom of Jane Jacobs*, edited by S. Hirt with D. Zahm, 196–214. London and New York: Routledge.

Crane, R. 2007. "Is There a Quiet Revolution in Women's Travel? Revisiting the Gender Gap in Commuting." *Journal of the American Planning Association* 73, no. 3: 298–316.

Crawford, A. 1920. "What Zoning Is." In *Zoning as an Element in City Planning, and for Protection of Property Values, Public Safety and Public Health*, edited by L. Purdy, H. Bartholomew, E. Bassett, A. Crawford, and H. Swan, 1–7. Washington, D.C.: American Civic Association.

Cullen, J. 2003. *The American Dream: A Short History of an Idea that Shaped a Nation.* Oxford: Oxford University Press.

Cullingworth, B. 1993. *The Political Culture of Planning: American Land Use Planning in Comparative Perspective*. New York: Routledge.

Cullingworth, B., and V. Nadin. 2006. *Town and Country Planning in the UK*. London: Routledge.

Davidoff, P., and M. Brooks. 1976. "Zoning out the Poor." In *Suburbia: American Dream and Dilemma*, edited by P. Dolce, 156–161. Garden City: Anchor.

Dale, V. 1997. "The Relationship between Land-Use Change and Climate Change." *Ecological Applications* 7, no. 3: 753–769.

Davis, J. 1932. "A Banker's Philosophy of City Planning." In *Planning Problems of Town, City and Region Presented at the Twenty-Fourth National Conference on City Planning Held at Pittsburg, Pennsylvania*, 94–97. Philadelphia: Fell

De Boer, S. R. 1937. *Shopping Districts*. New York: American Planning and Civic Association.

Delafons, J. 1969. *Land-Use Controls in the United States*. Cambridge: MIT Press.

Delafons, J. 2005. *Politics and Preservation: A Policy History of the Built Heritage 1882–1996*. London: Routledge.

Demographia. 2013. "Demographia World Urban Areas." http://www.demographia.com/db-worldua.pdf. Accessed February 28, 2012.

———. N.d. "Australia & USA Have Largest Houses." http://www.demographia.com/db-hsize.pdf. Accessed December 7, 2012.

Deng, L., Q. Shen, and L. Wang. 2009. "Housing Policy and Finance in China: A Literature Review." Paper prepared for the U.S. Department of Housing and Urban Development. http://www.chinaplanning.org/Publications/Lan%20Deng%20-%20Housing%20Policy%20and%20Finance%20In%20China.pdf. Accessed February 24, 2012.

Dol, K., and M. Haffner, eds. 2010. *Housing Statistics in the European Union 2010*. The Hague: Ministry of the Interior and Kingdome Relations. http://abonneren.rijksoverheid.nl/media/00/66/040531/438/housing_statistics_in_the_european_union_2010.pdf. Accessed March 5, 2012.

Dolan, T. 2012. *Live-Work Planning and Design: Zero-Commute Housing*. Hoboken, N.J.: Wiley.

Dolce, P., ed. 1976. *Suburbia: American Dream and Dilemma*. Garden City: Anchor Books.

Donoghue, J., B. Tranter, and R. White. 2002. "Homeownership, Shareownership and Coalition Policies." *Journal of Australian Political Economy* 52. http://espace.library.uq.edu.au/eserv.php?pid=UQ:10783&dsID=bt_ajpe-03.pdf. Accessed July 3, 2012.

Dornette, J. and I. van Veen. N.d. *The Use of Public Ground Lease in European Cities*. City of Amsterdam: Development Corporation Amsterdam.

Downing, A. [1850] 2006. "The Architecture of Country Houses." In *The Suburb Reader*, edited by B. Nicolaides and A. Wiese, 18–23. New York and London: Routledge.

Downs, A. 1973. *Opening Up the Suburbs: An Urban Strategy for America*. New Haven, Conn.: Yale University Press.

Duany, A., E. Plater-Zyberk, and J. Speck. 2000. *Suburban Nation: The Rise of Sprawl and the Decline of the American Dream*. New York: North Point.

Duany, A., and E. Talen. 2002. "Making the Good Easy: The Smart Code Alternative." *Fordham Law Journal* (April): 1445–1468.

Ducas, S. 2000. *Case Study of the City of Stockholm and the Greater Stockholm Area*. Montreal: La Ville de Montréal.

Dursteler, E. 2006. *Venetians in Constantinople: Nation, Identity, and Coexistence in the Early Modern Mediterranean*. Baltimore, Md.: Johns Hopkins University Press.

Dutt, B. 1925. *Town Planning in Ancient India*. Calcutta: Thacker, Spink & Co.

Düwell, J., and N. Gutschow. 2001. *Städtebau in Deutschland im 20. Jahrhundert*. Stuttgart: Teuben.

Duxbury, R. 2009. *Telling & Duxbury's Planning Law and Procedure*. Oxford: Oxford University Press.

Economic Development Research Group. 2005. *The Cost of Congestion to the Economy of the Portland Region*. Boston, MA: Economic Development Research Group.

The Economist. 2011. "Life in the Slow Lane." *The Economist*, April 28. http://www.economist.com/node/18620944. Accessed December 27, 2012.

Elazar, D. 1988. "Land and Liberty in American Civil Society." *Publius* 18: 1–29.

Ellickson, R. 1973. "Alternatives to Zoning: Covenants, Nuisance Rules, and Fines as Land Use Controls." *University of Chicago Law Review*: 681–781.

Ellin, N. 2006. *Integral Urbanism*. New York: Routledge.

Elliott, D. 2008. *A Better Way to Zone: Ten Principles to Create More Livable Cities*. Washington, D.C.: Island Press.

Emerson, R. W. [1841] 2010. "Self-Reliance." In *Self-Reliance and Other Essays*, 29–48. Nashville: American Renaissance Books.

Encyclopedia of the Nations. N.d. "France: Local Government." http://www.nationsencyclopedia.com/Europe/France-LOCAL-GOVERNMENT.html. Accessed July 6, 2012.

Energy Information Administration. 1999. "A Look at Residential Energy Consumption in 1997." http://eber.ed.ornl.gov/pub/RECS%200632-97.pdf. Accessed February 6, 2014.

Engels, F. 1942 [1845]. *The Condition of the Working-Class in England in 1844, with a Preface written in 1892*. Translated by F. Wischnewetzky. Transcribed from the 1942 George Allen & Unwin reprint of the 1892 edition by D. Price. http://www.gutenberg.org/files/17306/17306-h/17306-h.htm. Accessed March 24, 2014.

European Commission. 1999. *The EU Compendium of Spatial Planning Systems and Policies: Germany*. Luxemburg: European Commission.

———. 2000. *The EU Compendium of Spatial Planning Systems and Policies: Sweden*. Luxemburg: European Commission.

European Mortgage Federation. 2013. Hypostat 2013: A Review of Europe's Mortgage and Housing Markets. http://www.hypo.org/PortalDev/Objects/6/Files/HYPOSTAT_2013.pdf. Accessed April 4, 2014.

Eurostat. 2012. "Living Conditions and Social Protection." European Commission. http://epp.eurostat.ec.europa.eu/cache/ITY_OFFPUB/CH_06_2012/EN/CH_06_2012-EN.PDF. Accessed April 1, 2014.

Eurostat (2014a). Distribution of Population by Degree of Urbanisation, Dwelling type and Income group. [for 2011 total, detached, semi-attached, flat, other] http://epp.eurostat.ec.europa.eu/statistics_explained/index.php/Housing_statistics. Accessed April 7, 2014.

Eurostat. 2014b. Distribution of Population by Tenure Status, Type of Household and Income Group. [for 2012 owner, owner with mortgage or loan, owner without loan, renter] http://epp.eurostat.ec.europa.eu/statistics_explained/index.php/Housing_statistics#Tenure_status. Accessed April 7, 2014.

Evenson, N. 1979. *Paris: A Century of Change.* New Haven, Conn.: Yale University Press.

Fedako, J. 2006. "Zoning Is Theft." Ludwig von Mises Institute, March 9. http://mises.org/daily/2077. Accessed October 9, 2013.

Fetzer, J. 2000. *Public Attitudes toward Immigration in the United States, France, and Germany*. Cambridge, UK: Cambridge University Press.

Fiévé, N. and P Waley, P., eds. 2013. *Japanese Capitals in Historical Perspective: Place, Power and Memory in Kyoto, Edo and Tokyo*. Routledge.

Fifoot, C. 1949. *History and Sources of the Common Law: Tort and Contract*. London: Stevens & Sons.

Fischel, W. 1999. "Does the American Way of Zoning Cause the Suburbs of Metropolitan Areas to Be Too Spread Out?" In *Governance and Opportunity in Metropolitan America*, edited by A. Altshuler, M. Morill, H. Wolman, and F. Mitchell, 149–191. Washington, D.C.: National Academy.

———. 2001a. "An Economic History of Zoning and a Cure for Its Exclusionary Effects." Unpublished paper. http://www.americandreamcoalition.org/housing/econofzoning.pdf. Accessed October 12, 2012.

———. 2001b. *The Homevoter Hypothesis: How Home Values Affect Government Taxation, School Finance and Land-Use Policies*. Cambridge, Mass.: Harvard University Press.

———. 2010. *The Evolution of Zoning since the 1980s: The Persistence of Localism*. Cambridge: Lincoln Institute of Land Policy.

Fischer, C. 2010. *Made in America: A Social History of American Culture and Character*. Chicago: University of Chicago Press.

Fischler, R. 1998a. "Health, Safety, and the General Welfare: Markets, Politics, and Social Science in Early Land-Use Regulation and Community Design." *Journal of Urban History* 24 (November): 675–719.

————.1998b. "The Metropolitan Dimension of Early Zoning: Revisiting the 1916 New York City Ordinance. *Journal of the American Planning Association 64,* no. 2: 170–188.

————. 1998c. "Toward a Genealogy of Planning: Zoning and the Welfare State." *Planning Perspectives* 13, no. 4: 389–410.

————. 2007. "Development Controls in Toronto in the Nineteenth Century." *Urban History Review* 36, no. 1: 16–31.

Fischler, R., and K. Kolnick. 2006. "American Zoning: German Import or Home Product?" Paper presented at the 2nd World Planning Schools Congress, Mexico City, July 11–16.

Fishman, R. 1982. *Urban Utopias in the Twentieth Century: Ebenezer Howard, Frank Lloyd Wright, Le Corbusier.* Cambridge: MIT Press.

————. 1987. *Bourgeois Utopias: The Rise and Fall of Suburbia.* New York: Basic Books.

————. 2000. *The American Planning Tradition: Culture and Policy.* Washington, D.C.: Woodrow Wilson Center Press.

Fitzgerald, F. S. [1925] 1993. *The Great Gatsby.* New York: Columbia University Press.

Fogelson, R. 2005. *Bourgeois Nightmares: Suburbia, 1870–1930.* New Haven, Conn.: Yale University Press.

Fogg, A. 1974. *Australian Town Planning Law: Uniformity and Change.* Brisbane: University of Queensland Press.

Forman, S. 2011. "The American Dream: Sick but Not Dead." *The Examiner,* September 16. http://www.examiner.com/political-buzz-in-new-york/the-american-dream-sick-but-not-dead. Accessed February 17, 2012.

Forrest, Tuomi J. n.d. "William Penn Plans the City." William Penn: Visionary Proprietor. http://xroads.virginia.edu/~cap/PENN/pnplan.html. Accessed February 24, 2012.

Foucault, M. 1972. *The Archeology of Knowledge.* New York: Pantheon Books.

————. 1980. *Language, Counter-Memory, Practice: Selected Essays and Interviews.* Ithaca, N.Y.: Cornell University Press.

French, R., and Hamilton, F. 1979. *The Socialist City: Spatial Structure and Urban Policy.* New York: Wiley.

Freund, E. 1926. "Discussion." In *Planning Problems of Town, City, and Region: Papers and Discussions of the Eighteenth National Conference on City Planning Held at St. Petersburg and Palm Beach, Florida,* 73–82. Philadelphia: Fell.

————. 1929. "Some Inadequately Discussed Problems of the Law of City Planning and Zoning." In *Planning Problems of Town, City, and Region: Papers and Discussions of the Twenty-First National Conference on City Planning Held at Buffalo and Niagara Falls, New York,* 79–96. Philadelphia: Fell.

Frug, J. 1996. "The Geography of Community." *Stanford Law Review* 48, no. 5: 1047–1108.

Gale, W., J. Gruber, and S. Stephens-Davidowitz. 2007. "Encouraging Homeownership through the Tax Code." *Tax Notes* (June 18): 1171–1189. http://economics.mit.edu/files/6425. Accessed March 27, 2012.

Garnett, N. 2000. "On Castles and Commerce: Zoning Law and the Home-Business Dilemma." *William and Mary Law Review* 42, no. 4: 1191–1244.

Garvin, A. 2002. *The American City: What Works and What Doesn't.* New York: McGraw-Hill.

Gates, C. 2010. "City: Historical Overview and Theoretical Issues." In *The Oxford Encyclopedia of Ancient Greece and Rome,* vol. 2, edited by M. Gagarin, 151–161. Oxford: Oxford University Press.

Gates, P. 1996. *The Jeffersonian Dream: Studies in the History of American Land Policy and Development.* Albuquerque: University of New Mexico Press.

Gerckens, L. 1994. "American Zoning & the Physical Isolation of Uses." Planners Web, July 15. http://plannersweb.com/1994/07/american-zoning-the-physical-isolation-of-uses/. Accessed February 4, 2014.

German, A. 2010. "Japan Residential Zoning Laws Explained." http://www.realestate. co.jp/2010/11/18/japan-residential-zoning-laws-explained/. Accessed April 23, 2012.

Gillis, L. 2010. "Homeownership in Russia Gets an American-Style Boost." AOL Real Estate, June 15. http://realestate.aol.com/blog/2010/06/15/homeownership-in-russia-gets-an-american-style-boost/. Accessed July 3, 2012.

Glaeser, E., and J. Gyorko. 2002. "The Impact of Zoning on Housing Affordability." NBER Working Papers no. 8835, National Bureau of Economic Research, Cambridge, Massachusetts. http://ideas.repec.org/p/nbr/nberwo/8835.html. Accessed June 29, 2012.

Godschalk, D., D. A. Rodríguez, P. Berke, and E. J. Kaiser. 2006. *Urban Land Use Planning*. 5th ed. Chicago: University of Illinois Press.

Goldstein, J. 2011. "Obama Administration: Not Everybody Should Own a Home." NPR Planet Money, February 11. http://www.npr.org/blogs/money/2011/02/11/133680256/obama-administration-not-everybody-should-own-a-home. Accessed January 14, 2012.

Golubchikov, O. 2004. "Urban Planning in Russia: Towards the Market." *European Planning Studies* 12, no. 2: 229–247.

Goodrich, E. 1928. "Mass and Density of Buildings in Relation to Open Spaces and Traffic Facilities." In *Planning Problems of Town, City and Region: Papers and the Discussions at the Twentieth National Conference on City Planning Held at Dallas and Fort Worth, Texas*, 8–18. Philadelphia: Fell.

Gosniak, G., and A. Stevens. 2006. "Local Government in Germany Shaped by Regional Differences." City Mayors. http://www.citymayors.com/government/germany_government.html. December 1, 2012.

Goto, T. 1999. "Land Use Control Regulation in Japan." Summary of presentation made at the Asian City Development Strategy, Tokyo, July. http://www.gdrc.org/uem/observatory/land-regulation.html. Accessed July 10, 2012.

Gould, S. 1989. *Wonderful Life: The Burgess Shale and the Nature of History*. New York: Norton.

Government of Australian Capital Territory. 2008. "Territory Plan." ACT Government. http://www.legislation.act.gov.au/ni/2008-27/current/default.asp#Residential+Zones. Accessed July 10, 2012.

Government of British Columbia. 1996. "Local Government Act." http://www.bclaws.ca/EPLibraries/bclaws_new/document/ID/freeside/96323_30. Accessed July 12, 2012.

Government of Western Australia. 2005. "Planning and Development Act of 2005." Western Australia Consolidated Acts. http://www.austlii.edu.au/au/legis/wa/consol_act/pada2005236/. Accessed March 3, 2013.

Government of Western Australia. 2013. "An Introduction to the Western Australia Planning System." http://www.planning.wa.gov.au/dop_pub_pdf/intro_to_planning_system.pdf. Accessed on April 4, 2014.

Grant, J. 2002. "Mixed Use in Theory and Practice: Canadian Experience in Implementing a Planning Principle." *Journal of the American Planning Association* 68, no. 1: 71–84.

———. 2005. *Planning the Good Community: New Urbanism in Theory and Practice*. New York: Routledge.

Great Britain. 1844. *Metropolitan Buildings Act*. With notes and an index by David Gibbons. London: John Weale.

Greater London Regional Planning Committee. 1933. *Second Report of the Greater London Regional Planning Committee*. London: Greater London Regional Planning Committee.

Green, N. 2011. "A Chronicle of Urban Codes in Pre-Industrial London's Streets and Squares." In *Urban Coding and Planning*, edited by S. Marshall, 14–32. London and New York: Routledge.

Green, R. 1999. "Nine Causes of Sprawl." *Illinois Real Estate Letter* (Fall): 10–13.

Gries, J., and J. Ford. 1932. *Planning for Residential Districts*. Washington, D.C.: The President's Conference on Home Building and Home Ownership.

Grinnalds, J. 1920. "Zoning for Real Estate Protection." *Baltimore Municipal Journal* (November 19): 2.

———. 1921. "The Housing Survey Is Necessary before Zoning." *Baltimore Municipal Journal* (October 21): 2.

Guo, Q. 2011. "Prescribing the Ideal City: Building Codes and Planning Principles in Beijing." In *Urban Coding and Planning*, edited by S. Marshall, 101–119. London: Routledge.

Gutkind, E. 1972. *Urban Development in Eastern Europe, Bulgaria, Romania and the USSR*. Vol. 8 of *International History of City Development*. New York: Free Press.

Haar, C., ed. 1984. *Cities, Laws, and Social Policy: Learning from the British*. Lexington: Lexington Books.

———. 1989. "Reflections on Euclid: Social Contract and Private Purpose." In *Zoning and the American Dream: Promises Still to Keep*, edited by C Haar and J. Kayden, 333–354. Chicago: Planners Press, 1989.

———. 1996. *Suburbs under Siege*. Princeton, N.J.: Princeton University Press.

Haar, C., and J. Kayden, eds. 1989. *Zoning and the American Dream: Promises Still to Keep*. Chicago: Planners Press.

Habermas, J. 1996. "Modernity: An Unfinished Project." In *Habermas and the Unfinished Project of Modernity*, edited by M. Passerin d'Entrèves, 38–58. London: Polity Press, 1996.

Hakim, B. 2001. "Julian of Ascalon's Treatise of Construction and Design Rules from Sixth-Century Palestine." *Journal of the Society of Architectural Historians* 60, no. 1: 4–25.

Hall, E. 2007. "Divide and Sprawl, Decline and Fall: A Comparative Critique of Euclidean Zoning." *University of Pittsburgh Law Review* 68: 915–952.

Hall, P. 1996. *Cities of Tomorrow: An Intellectual History of Urban Planning and Design in the Twentieth Century*. London: Blackwell.

———. 2002. *Urban and Regional Planning*. London: Routledge.

Hall, P., and R. Taylor. 1996. "Political Science and the Three New Institutionalisms." *Political Studies* 44, no. 5: 936–957.

Hall, T. 2009. *Planning Europe's Capital Cities: Aspects of Nineteenth-Century Development*. London: Taylor & Francis.

Hamilton, A. 1797. *Report to Congress on the Subject of Manufactures*. http://nationalhumanitiescenter.org/pds/livingrev/politics/text2/hamilton.pdf. Accessed May 5, 2014.

Hamnett, S., and A. Freestone, eds. 2000. *The Australian Metropolis: A Planning History*. London: Allen & Unwin.

Hason, N. 1977. *The Emergence and Development of Zoning Controls in North American Municipalities: A Critical Analysis*. Toronto: Department of Urban and Regional Planning, University of Toronto.

Hatzfeld, J., and A. Aymard. 1996. *History of Ancient Greece*. Translated by A. Harrison and E. Goddard. New York: Norton.

Haverfield, F. 1913. *Ancient Town-Planning*. Oxford: Clarendon.

Hayden, D. 1981. *The Grand Domestic Revolution: A History of Feminist Designs for American Homes, Neighborhoods and Cities*. Boston: MIT Press.

Heights of Buildings Commission, City of New York. 1913. *Report of the Heights of Buildings Commission to the Committee on the Height, Size and Arrangement of Buildings of the Board of Estimate and Apportionment of the City of New York*. New York: Board of Estimate and Apportionment.

Hicks, J., and G. Allen. 1999. "A Century of Change: Trends in UK Statistics since 1900." Research Paper 99/111. Social and General Statistics Section, House of Commons Library, London. http://www.parliament.uk/documents/commons/lib/research/rp99/rp99-111.pdf. Accessed April 1, 2012.

Hirt, S. 2005. "Toward Post-Modern Urbanism: Evolution of Planning in Cleveland, Ohio." *Journal of Planning Education and Research* 25, no. 1: 27–42.

———. 2007a. "The Devil Is in the Definitions: Contrasting American and German Approaches to Zoning." *Journal of the American Planning Association* 73, no. 4: 436–450.

———. 2007b. "The Mixed-Use Trend: Planning Attitudes and Practices in Northeast Ohio." *Journal of Architectural and Planning Research* 24, no. 3: 224–244.

———. 2012. "Mixed Use by Default: How the Europeans (Don't) Zone." *Journal of Planning Literature* 27, no. 4: 375–393.

———. 2013a. "Form Follows Function: How America Zones." *Planning Practice and Research* 28, no. 1: 204–230.

———. 2013b. "Home, Sweet Home: American Residential Zoning in Comparative Perspective." *Journal of Planning Education and Research* 33, no. 3: 292–309.

Hirt, S., and K. Stanilov. 2009. *Twenty Years of Transition: The Evolution of Urban Planning in Eastern Europe and the Former Soviet Union, 1989–2009*. Nairobi: United Nations Human Settlements Programme.

Hofstede, G. 2001. *Culture's Consequences: Comparing Values, Behaviors, Institutions and Organizations across Nations*. Thousand Oaks, Calif.: Sage.

Hogue, C. 2013. *Government Organization Summary Report: 2012*. http://www2.census.gov/govs/cog/g12_org.pdf. Accessed on February 25, 2014.

Home, R. 1992. "The Evolution of the Use Classes Order." *Town Planning Review* 63, no. 2: 187–200.

———. 2009. "Land Ownership in the United Kingdom: Trends, Preferences and Future Challenges." *Land Use Policy* 26, supplement 1 (December): S103–S108.

Hoover, H. [1922] 1992. Excerpt from *American Individualism*. Herbert Hoover Presidential Library Association. http://www.hooverassociation.org/hoover/americanindv/american_individualism_chapter.php. January 2, 2012.

———. 1931. "Address to the White House Conference on Home Building and Home Ownership." The American Presidency Project. http://www.presidency.ucsb.edu/ws/index.php?pid=22927&st=home+ownership&st1. Accessed November 23, 2012.

Horsfall, T. 1905. *The Improvement of the Dwellings and Surroundings of the People: The Example of Germany. Supplement to the Report of the Manchester and Salford Citizens' Association for the Improvement of the Unwholesome Dwellings and Surroundings of the People*. Manchester: Manchester University Press.

Howard, E. [1898] 1965. *Garden Cities of To-Morrow: A Peaceful Path to Reform*. Cambridge, Mass.: MIT Press.

Howe, F. 1911. "The Municipal Real Estate Policies of German Cities." In *Proceedings of the Third National Conference on City Planning Held at Philadelphia, Pa.*, 14–26. Boston: National Conference on City Planning.

Howells, W. 1871. *Suburban Sketches.* Boston: Houghton, Mifflin.

Hubbard, T., and H. Hubbard. 1929. *Our Cities To-Day and To-Morrow: A Survey of Planning and Zoning Progress in the United States.* Cambridge, Mass.: Harvard University Press.

Hugo-Brunt, M. 1972. *The History of City Planning: A Survey.* Montreal: Harvest House.

Huron, A. 2014. "Planning and Politics." In *Cities of North America: Contemporary Challenges in U.S. and Canadian Cities.* Edited by L. Benton-Short, 193–220. Lanham, MD: Rowman & Littlefield.

Ifs School of Finance. 2008. Young Business Writer of the Year 2009. Accessed on March 5, 2012 at http://www.ifslearning.ac.uk/aboutus/newsandmedia/08-10-29/ifs_Young_Business_Writer_of_the_Year_2009.aspx.

Ihlder, J. 1922. *City Zoning Is Sound Business.* Cleveland: The Realty Record.

———. 1927. "How City Planning Affects Real Estate Values." In *Proceedings of the Nineteenth National Conference on City Planning Held at Washington, D.C.,* 73–84. Philadelphia: Fell Co.

INSEE (Institut national de la statistique et des études économiques). 2010. "Zonage en aires urbaines 2010 de Paris (001)." http://www.insee.fr/fr/methodes/nomenclatures/zonages/zone.asp?zonage=AU2010&zone=001. Accessed July 8, 2012.

———.2012. Évolution et structure de la population: Marseille (13055 - Commune). http://www.statistiques-locales.insee.fr/FICHES/DL/DEP/13/COM/DL_COM13055.pdf. Accessed April 3, 2014.

International Transport Forum. 2012. "IRTAD Database, December 2012—Risk Indicators." http://internationaltransportforum.org/irtadpublic/pdf/risk.pdf. Accessed October 18, 2013.

Jackson, K. 1985. *Crabgrass Frontier: The Suburbanization of the United States.* Oxford: Oxford University Press.

Jacobs, A. 2011. "Japan's Evolving Nested Municipal Hierarchy: The Race for Local Power in the 2000s." *Urban Studies Research.* http://www.hindawi.com/journals/usr/2011/692764/. Accessed December 2, 2012.

Jacobs, J. 1961. *The Death and Life of Great American Cities.* New York: Random House.

Jacobs, H. 2006. *The "Taking" of Europe: Globalizing the American Ideal of Private Property.* Cambridge: Lincoln Institute of Land Policy.

———. 2009. "An Alternative Perspective on United States–European Property Rights and Land Use Planning: Differences without Any Substance." *Planning and Environmental Law* 61, no. 3: 3–12.

Jameson, M. 1990. "Domestic Space in the Greek City-State." In *Domestic Architecture and the Use of Space,* edited by S. Kent, 92–113. Cambridge: Cambridge University Press.

Jefferson, T. [1805] 1884. "To Mr. Volney." In *The Works of Thomas Jefferson.* Vol. 4. Edited by H. Washington. New York: Townsend Mac.

Jillson, C. 2004. *Pursuing the American Dream: Opportunity and Exclusion over Four Centuries.* Lawrence: University of Kansas Press.

Kalnay, E., and M. Cai. 2003. "Impact of Urbanization and Land-Use Change on Climate." *Nature* 423 (May 29): 528–531.

Kayden, J. 1986. *Incentive Zoning in New York City: A Cost-Benefits Analysis.* Cambridge: Lincoln Institute of Land Policy.

———. 1999. "National Land-Use Planning in America: Something Whose Time Has Never Come." *Washington Law Review* 3: 445–472.

———. 2000. *Privately Owned Public Spaces: The New York Experience.* New York: New York City Department of City Planning and the Municipal Art Society of New York.

————. 2004. "Reconsidering Zoning: Expanding an American Land-Use Frontier." *Zoning Practice* 1 (January): 2–13.

————. 2011. "Meet Me at the Plaza." *New York Times*, October 19.

Kelly, B. 1993. *Expanding the American Dream: Building and Rebuilding Levittown.* Albany: State University of New York Press.

Kelly, E., and B. Becker. 2000. *Community Planning: An Introduction to the Comprehensive Plan.* Washington, D.C.: Island Press.

Kendig, L., S. Connor, C. Byrd, and J. Heyman. 1980. *Performance Zoning.* Washington, D.C.: Planners Press.

Kennon, J. 2010. "Nearly 1 out of 3 Homeowners Have No Mortgage." Joshua Kennon Weblog, November 2. http://www.joshuakennon.com/nearly-1-out-of-3-homeowners-have-no-mortgage/. Accessed March 5, 2010.

King Phillip II of Spain (and others). 1573. *The Laws of the Indies.* http://cbp.arc.miami.edu/Resources/Laws%20of%20the%20Indies.html. Accessed March 26, 2014.

Kitchen, J. 1926. *What It Means to Zone.* Ottawa: Town Planning Commission.

Kiviat, B. 2010. "The Case against Homeownership." *Time*, September 11. http://www.time.com/time/magazine/article/0,9171,2013850,00.html. Accessed January 5, 2011.

Knaap, G., E. Talen, R. Olshansky, and C. Forrest. 2001. *Government Policy and Urban Sprawl.* Paper prepared for the Illinois Department of Natural Resources. http://dnr.state.il.us/orep/pfc/balancedgrowth/pdfs/government.pdf. Accessed June 29, 2012.

Knack, R., S. Meck, and I. Stollman. 1996. "The Real Story behind the Standard Planning and Zoning Acts of the 1920s." *Land Use Law* (February): 3–9.

Knox, P., and L. McCarthy. 2005. *Urbanization: An Introduction to Urban Geography.* Upper Saddle River, N.J.: Pearson Prentice Hall.

Kolnik, K. 2008. "Order before Zoning: Land Use Regulation in Los Angeles 1880–1915." Ph.D. diss., University of Southern California.

Kopf, K. 1996. "An Alternative Approach to Zoning in France: Typology, Historical Character and Development Control." *European Planning Studies* 4, no. 6: 717–737.

Kosareva, N., A. Puzanov, and A. Tumanov. 2010. "Moving towards a More Integrated Approach to Russian Housing Policies." Unpublished paper. http://www.cchpr.landecon.cam.ac.uk/Conference2010/Downloads/Papers/Puzanov%20A%20Paper.pdf. Accessed February 27, 2012.

Kostof, S. 1987. *America by Design.* New York: Oxford University Press.

————. 1991. *The City Shaped: Urban Patterns and Meanings through History.* London: Thames and Hudson.

Krauthammer, C. 2012. "Did the State Make You Great?" *Washington Post*, July 19. http://www.washingtonpost.com/opinions/charles-krauthammer-did-the-state-make-you-great/2012/07/19/gJQAbZOiwW_story.html. Accessed August 4, 2012.

Krier, L. 1988. "Traditional Ideas for Today's Towns." *City Magazine* 10, no. 2: 20–23.

Kunstler, J. 1996. *Home from Nowhere: Remaking our Everyday World for the 21st Century.* New York: Simon & Schuster.

Kwartler, M. 1989. "Legislating Aesthetics." In *Zoning and the American Dream: Promises Still to Keep*, edited by C. Haar and J. Kayden, 187–220. Chicago: Planners Press.

Ladd, B. 1990. *Urban Planning and Civic Order in Germany, 1860–1914.* Cambridge, Mass.: Harvard University Press.

Lahanas, M. N.d. "Town Planning in Ancient Greece." Hellenica. http://www.mlahanas. de/Greeks/CityPlan.htm. Accessed July 19, 2012.

Langsdorf, A. 1931. "Discussion." In *Planning Problems of Town, City and Region: Papers and the Discussions at the Twenty-Third National Conference on City Planning*, 99–107. Philadelphia: Fell.

Laurence, R. 1996. *Roman Pompeii: Society and Space*. London: Taylor & Francis.

Le Corbusier, C. [1929] 1987. *The City of Tomorrow and Its Planning*. New York: Dover.

Lees, Martha A. 1994. "Preserving Property Values—Preserving Proper Homes— Preserving Privilege: The Pre-Euclid Debate over Zoning for Exclusively Private Residential Areas, 1916–1926." *University of Pittsburgh Law Review* 56: 367–440.

Le Goix, R., and D. Callen. 2010. "Production and Social Sustainability of Private Enclaves in Suburban Landscapes: French and US Long-Term Emergence of Gated Communities and Private Streets." In *Gated Communities: Social Sustainability in Contemporary and Historical Gated Developments*, 93–114. London: Earthscan.

Lefcoe, G. 1979. *Land Development in Crowded Places: Lessons from Abroad*. Washington, D.C.: The Conservation Foundation.

LeGates, R. [1935] 2004. *Early Urban Planning*. Vol. 9. New York: Routledge.

Legifrance. 2011. "Code de l'Urbanisme." Legifrance. http://www.legifrance.gouv.fr/ affichCode.do?cidTexte=LEGITEXT000006074075. Accessed September 29, 2011.

Levine, J. 2006. *Zoned Out: Regulation, Markets and Choices in Transportation and Metropolitan Land Use*. Washington, D.C.: Resources for the Future.

Levine, J., J. Grengs, Q. Shen, and Q. Shen. 2012. "Does Accessibility Require Density or Speed? A Comparison of *Fast* versus *Close* in Getting Where You Want to Go in U.S. Metropolitan Regions." *Journal of the American Planning Association* 78, no. 2: 157–172.

Levy, J. 2006. *Contemporary Urban Planning*. Upper Saddle River, N.J.: Pearson Prentice Hall.

Lewis, H. 1939. *City Planning: Why and How?* New York: Longmans, Green and Co.

Lewis, N. 1916. *The Planning of the Modern City*. New York: Wiley.

Lewyn, M. 2005. "How Overregulation Creates Sprawl (Even in a City without Zoning)." *Wayne Law Review* 50: 1171–1208.

Liebmann, G. 1996. "Modernization of Zoning: A Means to Reform." *Regulation* 2: 71–77. http://www.cato.org/pubs/regulation/regv19n2/v19n2-8.pdf. Accessed September 21, 2011.

Light, M. 1999. "Different Ideas of the City: Origins of Metropolitan Land-Use Regimes in the United States, Germany, and Switzerland." *Yale Journal of International Law* 24: 577–612.

Loew, S. 1998. *Modern Architecture in Historic Cities: Policy Planning and Building in Contemporary France*. London: Routledge.

Logan, T. 1976. "The Americanization of German Zoning." *Journal of the American Institute of Planners* 42, no. 4: 377–385.

London City Council. 1894. *The London Building Act*. London: James Sears and Sons. http://archive.org/stream/londonbuildinga01coungoog#page/n11/mode/2up. Accessed December 23, 2012.

Lowenthal, J., and M. Curzan. 2011. "Dismantling the American Dream." Politico, August 24. http://www.politico.com/news/stories/0811/61953. html#ixzz1VwsaPBZI. Accessed January 15, 2012.

Lucy, W. 2010. *Foreclosing the Dream: How America's Housing Crisis Is Reshaping Our Cities and Suburbs*. Chicago: Planners Press.

Magnusson, L. 2000. *An Economic History of Sweden*. London: Routledge.

Mairie de Paris. 2011. Documents d'urbanisme. http://www.paris.fr/pratique/documents-d-urbanisme-plu/dossier-cartes-et-textes-du-p-l-u/documents-graphiques-du-plan-local-d-urbanisme/plan-de-zonage/rub_7042_dossier_21701_port_16186_sheet_3276. Accessed April 3, 2014.

Manco, J. 2009. "History of Building Regulations." Researching Historic Buildings in the British Isles. http://www.buildinghistory.org/regulations.shtml. Accessed May 2, 2012.

Marschner, F. 1958. *Land Use and Its Patterns in the United States*. Agriculture Handbook no. 153. Washington, D.C.: Department of Agriculture.

Marsh, B. 1909. *An Introduction to City Planning: Democracy's Challenge to the American City*. New York: Privately published.

Marshall, S., ed. 2009. *Cities Design and Evolution*. London: Routledge.

———. 2011. *Urban Coding and Planning*. London: Routledge.

Martinez-Vazquez, J., and A. Timofeev. 2009. "Decentralization Measures Revisited." International Studies Program Working Papers 09–13. Andrew Young School of Policy Research, Georgia State University, Atlanta, Georgia.

Marwedel, J. 1998. "Opting for Performance: An Alternative to Conventional Zoning for Land Use Regulation." *Journal of Planning Literature* 13, no. 2: 220–231.

Marx, L. 1991. "The American Ideology of Space." In *Denatured Visions: Landscape and Culture in the Twentieth Century*, edited by Stuart Wrede and William Adams, 62–68. New York: Museum of Modern Art.

Mathews, J. 2006. "The Effect of Proximity to Commercial Uses on Residential Prices." Ph.D. diss., Georgia State University.

Mattocks, R. 1935. "Review of Harvard City Planning Studies Volume I—Transition Zoning." *Town Planning Review* 16, no. 3: 243–244.

McCahill, C., and N. Garrick. 2012. "Automobile Use and Land Consumption: Empirical Evidence from 12 Cities." *Urban Design International* 3, no. 17: 221–228.

McCann, B., and R. Ewing. 2003. *Measuring the Health Effects of Sprawl: A National Analysis of Physical Activity, Obesity and Chronic Disease*. Washington, D.C.: Smart Growth America.

McDuffie, D. 1916. "A Practical Application of the Zone Ordinance." *Berkeley Civic Bulletin* 5, no. 1: 10–17.

McGinn, D. 2008. *House Lust: America's Obsession with Our Homes*. New York: Doubleday.

McKenzie, B., and M. Rapino. 2011. *Commuting in the United States: 2009*. Washington, D.C.: American Community Survey Reports.

McKenzie, E. 1994. *Privatopia: Homeowners Associations and the Rise of Residential Private Government*. New Haven, Conn.: Yale University Press.

Miao, P. 1990. "Seven Characteristics of Traditional Urban Form in Southeast China." *Traditional Dwellings and Settlements Review* 1: 35–47. http://iaste.berkeley.edu/pdfs/01.2d-Spr90miao-sml.pdf. Accessed July 18, 2012.

Micklow, A. 2008. "The Gender Implications of Euclidian Zoning." MA thesis, Virginia Tech.

Mieszkowski, P., and E. Mills. 1993. "The Causes of Metropolitan Suburbanization." *Journal of Economic Perspectives* 7 (Summer): 135–147.

Miller, R. 1929. "Discussion." In *Planning Problems of Town, City and Region: Papers and Discussions at the Twenty-Third National Conference on City Planning Held at Buffalo and Niagara Falls, New York*, 96–101. Philadelphia: Fell.

Mitchel, J. 1916. *Speech of Hon. John Purroy Mitchel, Mayor of the City of New York*. New York: M. B. Brown.

Monnett, J. 1927. "Zoning Scored as Communistic." *Cleveland Plain Dealer,* January 27).

Moomaw, D. 1931. "Administration of the Zoning Ordinance." In *Planning Problems of Town, City and Region Presented at the Twenty-Fourth National Conference on City Planning Held at Rochester, New York,* 85–92. Philadelphia: Fell.

Morag-Levine, N. 2011. "Is Precautionary Regulation a Civil Law Instrument? Lessons from the History of the Alkali Act." *Journal of Environmental Law* 23, no. 1: 1–43.

Morgenthau, H. 1909. "A National Constructive Programme for City Planning." In *Proceedings of the First National Conference on City Planning,* 59–60. Washington, D.C.: Government Printing Office. http://archive.org/stream/proceedingsoffir00nati/proceedingsoffir00nati_djvu.txt. Accessed November 21, 2012.

Morris, A. 1979. *History of Urban Form before the Industrial Revolution.* New York: Wiley.

Morris, M. 2000. *Incentive Zoning: Meeting Urban Design and Affordable Housing Objectives.* Chicago: Planners Press.

Mullen, J. 1976. "American Perceptions of German City Planning at the Turn of the Century." Unpublished paper. http://scholarworks.umass.edu/cgi/viewcontent.cgi?article=1034&context=larp_faculty_pubs. Accessed February 4, 2014.

Mumford, L. 1938. *The Culture of Cities.* New York: Harcourt Brace.

Munjee, N. N.d. "Homeownership Trends Worldwide." *Housing Finance International,* 17–28. http://www.housingfinance.org/uploads/Publicationsmanager/9512_Hom.pdf. Accessed April 1, 2012.

Munro, W. 1931. "A Danger Spot in the Zoning Movement." *Annals of the American Academy of Political and Social Sciences* 155 (May): 202–206.

Musterd, S. 2005. "Social and Ethnic Segregation in Europe: Levels, Causes, and Effects." *Journal of Urban Affairs* 27, no. 3: 331–348.

Nadin, V., and D. Stead. 2008. "European Spatial Planning Systems, Social Models and Learning." *disP–The Planning Review* 44, no. 172: 35–47.

Nacionalnoe Agentstvo Razvitiya Jiliyshtnyih Fondov. N.d. Analiz Izmeneniyh Jiliyshtnyih Fondov Rosiyskoi Federatsii. http://russocnaim.ru/i35/. Accessed April 1, 2014.

National Board of Fire Underwriters. 1907. *Building Code.* New York: National Board of Fire Underwriters.

National Board of Housing, Building and Planning. 2006. *Legislation—The Planning and Building Act.* Karlskrona, Sweden: Boverket. https://wcd.coe.int/wcd/com.instranet.InstraServlet?command=com.instranet.CmdBlobGet&InstranetImage=1279003&SecMode=1&DocId=1427506&Usage=2. Accessed October 5, 2011.

National Housing and Town Planning Council. 1914. *Summary and Text of the Ruislip-Northwood Town Planning Scheme, 1914.* London: National Housing and Town Planning Council.

National Multifamily Housing Council. 2012. "Quick Facts: Residential Demographics." National Multifamily Housing Council. http://www.nmhc.org/Content/ServeContent.cfm?ContentItemID=1152. Accessed March 5, 2012.

Natural England and the Campaign to Protect Rural England. 2010. *Greenbelts: A Greener Future.* N.p.: Campaign to Protect Rural England. http://www.ruaf.org/ruaf_bieb/upload/3284.pdf. Accessed April 12, 2012.

Nelson, A. 2004. *Planner's Estimating Guide: Projecting Land-Use and Facility Needs.* Chicago: American Planning Association.

———. 2012. *Reshaping Metropolitan America: Trends and Opportunities to 2030.* Washington, D.C.: Island Press.

Nelson, R. 1977. *Zoning and Property Rights: An Analysis of the American System of Land-Use Regulation.* Cambridge, Mass.: MIT Press.

———. 2005. *Private Neighborhoods and the Transformation of Local Government.* the Washington, DC: Urban Institute.

Nevett, L. 2010. *Domestic Space in Classical Antiquity.* Cambridge: Cambridge University Press.

New York City Board of Estimate and Apportionment. 1917. *New York City Building Zone Resolution Restricting the Height and Use of Buildings and Prescribing the Minimum Sizes of Their Yards and Courts.* New York: New York Board of Estimate and Apportionment.

New York City Board of Estimate and Apportionment (Commission on Building Districts and Restrictions). 1916. *Final Report.* New York: New York City Board of Estimate and Apportionment.

New York City Board of Estimates and Apportionment (Heights of Buildings Commission). 1913. *Report of the Heights of Buildings Commission to the Committee on the Height, Size and Arrangement of Buildings of the Board of Estimate and Apportionment of the City of New York.* New York, New York Heights of Buildings Commission.

Newman, P., and A. Thornley. 1996. *Urban Planning in Europe: International Competition, National Systems and Planning Projects.* London: Routledge.

Newsweek Staff. 2006. "Hail to the Suburban Oasis." *Newsweek,* December 3.

Nichols, P. 1943. *The Massachusetts Law of Planning and Zoning.* Boston: Massachusetts Federation of Planning Boards.

Nicolaides, B., and A. Wiese, eds. 2006. *The Suburb Reader.* London and New York: Routledge.

Nightingale, C. 2012. *Segregation: A Global History of Divided Cities.* Chicago: University of Chicago Press.

Nivola, P. 1999. *Laws of the Landscape: How Policies Shape Cities in Europe and America.* Washington, D.C.: Brookings Institution Press.

Nordregio. 2004. "Regional Planning in Finland, Iceland, Norway and Sweden." Ministry of Environment, Forest and Nature Agency, Spatial Planning Department of Denmark. http://www.naturstyrelsen.dk/NR/rdonlyres/C0C24D17-46A3-49FC-9667-09D69A31ECEE/6998/regional_planning_in20Nordic_UK.pdf. Accessed October 14, 2013.

Novak, W. 1996. *The People's Welfare: Law and Regulation in Nineteenth-Century America.* Chapel Hill: University of North Carolina Press.

Nuyten, T. 2012. Home Based Business Statistics in America. Business for Home. http://www.businessforhome.org/2012/07/home-based-business-in-america/ Accessed April 2, 2014.

ODPM (Office of the Deputy Prime Minister). 2005. "Changes of Use of Buildings and Land." ODPM circular 03/2005. Office of the Deputy Prime Minister, Eland House, London. http://www.planning-applications.co.uk/odpm_plan_036810.pdf. Accessed September 23, 2011.

OECD (Organisation for Economic Cooperation and Development). 2011. "An Overview of Growing Income Inequalities in OECD Countries: Main Findings." http://www.oecd.org/dataoecd/40/12/49499779.pdf. Accessed June 25, 2012.

Office of the Deputy Prime Minister (United Kingdom). 1997. "The Planning System: General Principles." http://webarchive.nationalarchives.gov.uk/20120919132719/ http://www.communities.gov.uk/documents/planningandbuilding/ pdf/147396.pdf. Accessed February 3, 2014.

Ohm, B., and R. Sitkowski. 2003. "The Influence of New Urbanism in Land Use, Planning and Zoning." *Urban Lawyer* 35: 783–943.

Oshugi, S. 2010. "Local Government Planning in Japan." Papers on the Local Governance System and Its Implementation in Selected Fields in Japan No.15. Unpublished paper. http://www.clair.or.jp/j/forum/honyaku/hikaku/pdf/BunyabetsuNo15en.pdf. Accessed July 10, 2012.

Pagonis, T., and A. Thornley. 1999. "Urban Development Projects in Moscow: Market/State Relationships in the New Russia." *European Planning Studies* 8, no. 6: 751–766.

Panayi. P. 1994. *Immigration, Ethnicity, and Racism in Britain, 1815–1945*. Manchester: Manchester University Press.

Parolek, D., K. Parolek, and P. Crawford. 2008. *Form-Based Codes: A Guide for Planners, Urban Designers, Municipalities and Developers*. Hoboken: Wiley.

Pendall, R., R. Puentes, and J, Martin. 2006. *From Traditional to Reformed: A Review of the Land Use Regulations in the Nation's Largest Metropolitan Areas*. Washington, D.C.: Brookings Institution.

Perrin, C. 1977. *Everything in Its Place: Social Order and Land Use in America*. Princeton, N.J.: Princeton University Press.

Perry, C. 1939. *Housing for the Machine Age*. New York: Russell Sage Foundation.

Pichler-Milanovic, N. 2007. "European Urban Sprawl: Sustainability, Cultures of (Anti)Urbanism and Hybrid Cityscapes." Unpublished paper.

Platt, R. 2004. *Land Use and Society: Geography, Law, and Public Policy*. Rev. ed. Washington, D.C.: Island Press.

Plato. 360 BCE. *The Republic.* Book VIII (translated by B. Jowett). Accessed on January 3, 2012 at http://classics.mit.edu/Plato/republic.9.viii.html. Accessed January 3, 2012.

Plunz, R. 1990. *A History of Housing in New York City*. New York: Columbia University Press.

———. 1993. Zoning and the New Horizontal City. In *Planning and Zoning New York City: Yesterday, Today and Tomorrow*, edited by T. Bressi, 27–47. New Brunswick, N.J.: Rutgers University Press

Polakowski, H., D. Ritchay, and Z. Weinrobe. 2005. "Effects of Mixed-Income, Multi-Family Rental Housing Developments on Single-Family Housing Values." Center for Real Estate, MIT, Cambridge, Massachusetts. http://community-wealth.org/sites/clone.community-wealth.org/files/downloads/paper-pollatowski-et-al.pdf. Accessed June 29, 2012.

Polanyi, K. 1944. *The Great Transformation*. New York: Rinehart.

Pollak, P. 1994. "Rethinking Zoning to Accommodate the Elderly in Single Family Housing." *Journal of the American Planning Association* 60, no. 4: 521–531.

Pollock, A. 2010. *Housing Finance in International Perspective*. Washington, D.C.: American Enterprise Institute.

Pollard, W. 1931. "Outline of the Law of Zoning in the United States." *Annals of the American Academy of Political and Social Science* 155, Part 2, Zoning in the United States: 15–33.

Pravitelstvo Sankt-Peterburga. 2011. "Pravila zemlepolzvaniya i zastroiki." http://www.kgainfo.spb.ru/pzz/pravila.html. Accessed October 6, 2011.

Proudfoot, H. 2000. "Founding Cities in Nineteenth-Century Australia." In *The Australian Metropolis: A Planning History*, edited by S. Hamnett and R. Freestone, 11–26. London: Spon.

Purdue, M. 2006. "The Law on Compensation Rights for Reduction in Property Values Due to Planning Decisions in the United Kingdom." *Washington Law Review* 5, no. 3: 493–512.

Purdy, L. 1911. "Condemnation, Assessments and Taxation in Relation to City Planning." In *Proceedings of the Third National Conference on City Planning Held at Philadelphia, Pa*, 118–125. Boston: National Conference on City Planning.

Putnam, R. 1993. *Making Democracy Work: Civic Traditions in Modern Italy*. Princeton, N.J.: Princeton University Press.

Rabin, Y. 1989. "Expulsive Zoning: The Inequitable Legacy of Euclid." In *Zoning and the American Dream: Promises Still to Keep*, edited by C. Haar and J. Kayden, 101–121. Chicago: Planners Press.

Rasmussen, S. 1937. *London: The Unique City*. London: Macmillan.

Reed, D. 2011. "More Homeowners Want Walkable, Transit-Served Communities." Greater Greater Washington, August 18. http://greatergreaterwashington.org/post/11722/more-homebuyers-want-walkable-transit-served-communities/. Accessed February 16, 2012.

Ren, C., and S. Tong. 2008. "Health Effects of Ambient Air Pollution—Recent Research Development and Contemporary Methodological Challenges." *Environmental Health* 7, no. 1. http://www.ehjournal.net/content/7/1/56. Accessed December 26, 2012.

Reps, J. 1964. "Requiem for Zoning." *Zoning Digest* 16, no. 2: 33–56.

———. 1965. *The Making of Urban America: A History of City Planning in the United States*. Princeton, N.J.: Princeton University Press.

Reynard, P. 2002. "Public Order and Privilege: Eighteenth-Century French Roots of Environmental Regulation." *Technology and Culture* 43, no. 1: 1–28.

Rich, B., and M. Wailes. 1920. *American Law Reports Annotated, Volume 9*. Rochester, N.Y.: The Lawyers Co-operative Publishing Company.

Richter, K. 2003. "Compensable Regulation in the Federal Republic of Germany." In *Comparative Urban Planning Law: An Introduction to Urban Land Development Law in the United States through the Lens of Comparing the Experience of Other Nations*, edited by J. Kushner, 66–67. Durham, N.C.: Carolina Academic Press.

Rifkin, J. 2004. *The European Dream: How Europe's Vision of the Future Is Quietly Eclipsing the American Dream*. Cambridge: Polity.

Robinson, C. [1904] 1970. *Modern Civic Art or the City Made Beautiful*. New York: Putnam.

Robinson, O. [1922] 1994. *Ancient Rome: City Planning and Administration*. London: Routledge.

Rodgers, D. 1998. *Atlantic Crossings: Social Politics in a Progressive Age*. Cambridge, Mass: Harvard University Press.

Rogers, I. 1991. *Canadian Law of Planning and Zoning*. Scarborough: Carswell.

Rohe, W., and H. Watson. 2007. *Chasing the American Dream: New Perspectives on Affordable Homeownership*. Ithaca, N.Y.: Cornell University Press.

Roos, J. 2011. "Nicolas Sarkozy et sa Mission Civilisatrice." Roarmag.org, April 12. http://roarmag.org/2011/04/nicolas-sarkozy-et-sa-mission-civilisatrice/. Accessed February 6, 2014.

Rosen, C. 2003. "'Knowing' Industrial Pollution: Nuisance Law and the Power of Tradition in a Time of Rapid Economic Change, 1840–1864." *Environmental History* 8, no. 4: 565–597.

Rosiyskaya Federatsiya. 2011. *Gradostroitelnyi Kodeks*. Moscow: Prospect.

Rowe, P. 1991. *Making a Middle Landscape*. Cambridge: MIT Press.

Sachweh, P., and S. Olafsdottir. 2010. "The Welfare State and Equality? Stratification Realities and Aspirations in Three Welfare Regimes." *European Sociological Review* 28, no. 2: 149–168.

Salkin, P. 2003. "From Euclid to Growing Smart: The Transformation of the American Local Land Use Ethic into Local Land Use and Environmental Controls." *Pace Environmental Law Review* 20, no. 1: 109–148.

Samuelson, R. 2010. "How a Homeownership Fetish Hurt the American Dream." *Washington Post*, August 23. http://www.washingtonpost.com/wp-dyn/content/article/2010/08/22/AR2010082202273.html. Accessed January 5.

Schmidt, R., and R. Buehler. 2007. "The Planning Process in the US and Germany: A Comparative Analysis." *International Planning Studies* 12, no. 1: 55–75.

Schmidt, V. 2008. "Discursive Institutionalism: The Explanatory Power of Ideas and Discourse." *Annual Review of Political Science* 11: 303–326.

Schmidt-Eichstaedt, G. 2001. "National-Level Planning Institutions and Decisions in the Federal Republic of Germany." In *National-Level Planning in Democratic Countries: An International Comparison of City and Regional Policy-Making*, edited by R. Alterman, 127–147. Liverpool: Liverpool University Press.

Schroeder, F. 1993. *Front Yard America: The Evolution and Meanings of a Vernacular Domestic Landscape.* Bowling Green, Ohio: Bowling Green State University Popular Press.

Schuiling, D., and J. van der Veer. 2004. "Governance in Housing in Amsterdam and the Role of Housing Associations." Paper presented at the International Housing Conference in Hong Kong, February 2–4. http://www.housingauthority.gov.hk/hdw/ihc/pdf/svv.pdf. Accessed July 5, 2012.

Schulz, S. 1989. *Constructing Urban Culture: American Cities and City Planning, 1800–1920.* Philadelphia: Temple University Press.

Schwartz, J. 1976. "Evolution of the Suburbs." In *Suburbia: The American Dream and Dilemma*, edited by P. Dolce, 1–36. Garden City: Anchor Books.

Scott, J. 1998. *Seeing Like a State: How Certain Schemes to Improve the Human Condition Have Failed.* New Haven, Conn.: Yale University Press.

Scott, M. 1971. *American City Planning since 1890.* Berkeley: University of California Press.

Sennett, R. 1970. *The Uses of Disorder: Personal Identity and City Life.* New York: Knopf.

Shibata, K. 2008. "The Origins of Japanese Planning Culture: Building a Nation-State, 1868–1945." Research Papers in Environmental and Spatial Analysis no. 128. http://www2.lse.ac.uk/geographyAndEnvironment/research/Researchpapers/128%20shibata%20update%20.pdf. Accessed July 10, 2012.

Shlay, N. 1986. "Taking Apart the American Dream: The Influence of Income and Family Composition on Residential Evaluations." *Urban Studies* 23: 253–270.

Silver, C. 1997. "The Racial Underpinnings of Zoning in American Cities." In *Urban Planning and the African American Community: In the Shadows*, edited by J. Manning and M. Ritzdorf, 23–42. Thousand Oaks: Sage.

Siy, E. 2004. *Learning from Abroad: The European Approach to Smarter Growth and Sustainable Development.* Coral Gables, Fla.: Funders' Network for Smart Growth and Sustainable Development.

Skaler, R., and T. Keels. 2008. *Philadelphia's Rittenhouse Square.* Chicago: Arcadia.

Small Business Administration. 2012. Frequently Asked Questions. http://www.sba.gov/sites/default/files/FAQ_Sept_2012.pdf. Accessed April 2, 2014.

Sonstelie, J., and P. Portney. 1978. "Profit Maximizing Communities and the Theory of Local Public Expenditures." *Journal of Urban Economics* 5 (April): 263–277.

Sorensen, A. 2002. *The Making of Urban Japan: Cities and Planning from Edo to Twenty-First Century.* London: Routledge.

Southworth, M., and E. Ben-Joseph. 2003. *Streets and the Shaping of Towns and Cities.* Washington, D.C.: Island.

———. 2004. "Reconsidering the Cul-de-Sac." *Access 2004: Transportation Research at the University of California* (Spring). http://web.mit.edu/ebj/www/access24.pdf. Accessed September 5, 2012.

Spain, D. 2001. *How Women Saved the City*. Minneapolis: University of Minnesota Press.

Spencer, J. 1989. "Public Nuisance—A Critical Examination." *Cambridge Law Review* 48: 55–55.

Stanilov, L., and L. Sykora. 2012. "Planning, Markets and Patterns of Residential Growth in Metropolitan Prague." *Journal of Architectural and Planning Research* 29, no. 4: 278–291.

Statistical Bureau of Japan. 2010. 2008 Housing and Land Survey. http://www.e-stat.go.jp/SG1/estat/ListE.do?bid=000001025163&cycode=0. Accessed April 4, 2014.

Statistics Canada. 2001. "Number of Municipalities (Census Subdivisions) and Percentage Distribution by Province, Territory and Type of Region." http://www.statcan.gc.ca/pub/91f0015m/2007008/t/4054804-eng.htm. Accessed December 3, 2012.

———. 2006. "Community Profiles." http://www12.statcan.ca/census-recensement/2006/dp-pd/prof/92-591/index.cfm. Accessed August 4, 2012.

———. 2010. "Selected Dwelling Characteristics and Household Equipment." http://www40.statcan.ca/l01/cst01/famil09a-eng.htm. Accessed March 5, 2012.

Statistics Japan. 2010. Chapter IX: Household and Housing Status. http://www.stat.go.jp/english/data/kokusei/2010/poj/pdf/2010ch09.pdf. Accessed April 7, 2014.

Statistics New Zealand. 2009. "Review of Housing Statistics Report 2009." http://www.stats.govt.nz/browse_for_stats/people_and_communities/housing.aspx. Accessed March 5, 2012.

Stearns, Peter. *The Industrial Revolution in World History*. Boulder, Colo.: Westview Press, 1993.

Stern, M. 1931. "Discussion." In *Planning Problems of Town, City and Region: Papers and the Discussions at the Twenty-Third National Conference on City Planning*, 99–107. Philadelphia: Fell.

Stern, S. 2009. "Residential Protectionism and the Legal Mythology of Home." *Michigan Law Review* 107, no. 7: 1093–1144.

Streitfeld, D., and M. Thee-Brenna. 2011. "Despite Fears, Owning Home Retains Allure, Poll Shows." *New York Times*, June 29. http://www.nytimes.com/2011/06/30/business/30poll.html. Accessed January 14, 2012.

Stull, W. 1975. "Community Environment, Zoning, and the Market Value of Single-Family Homes." *Journal of Law and Economics* 18, no. 2: 535–558.

Rossiskoya Imperia. *Svod zakonov Rosiikoi Imperie poveleniem Gosudaria Imperatora Nikolaia Pervago, Tom dvanadctii, Chast I, Ustav Stroitelnyi* (Summary of laws of the Russian Empire under the reign of Emperor Nikolai I, Volume 12, Part I, Building Law). 1900. St. Petersburg; Author.

Swan, H. 1913. "The English and Swedish Town Planning Acts." In *Report of the Heights of Buildings Commission to the Committee on the Height, Size and Arrangement of Buildings of the Board of Estimate and Apportionment of the City of New York*, 155–160. New York: Board of Estimate and Apportionment.

———. 1920. *Zoning as an Element in City Planning, and for Protection of property Values, Public Safety, and Public Health*. Washington, D.C.: American Civic Association.

Swann, B. and A. Krupat. *Recovering the Word, Essays on Native American Literature*. Berkeley: University of California Press (1987).

Szelenyi, I. 1996. "Cities after Socialism—and After." In *Cities after Socialism: Urban and Regional Change and Conflict in Post-Socialist Societies*, edited by G. Andrusz, M. Harloe, and I. Szelenyi, 286–317. Malden: Blackwell.

Talen, E. 2005. *New Urbanism and American Planning: The Conflict of Cultures*. London: Routledge.

———. 2009a. "Americans, Urbanism and Sprawl: An Exploration of Living Preferences." In *Fleeing the City: Studies in the Culture and Politics of Antiurbanism*, edited by M. Thompson, 161–208. New York: Palgrave-Macmillan.

———. 2009b. "Design by the Rules: The Historical Underpinnings of Form-Based Codes." *Journal of the American Planning Association* 75, no. 2: 144–160.

———. 2012a. *City Rules: How Regulations Affect Urban Form*. Washington, D.C.: Island Press.

———. 2012b. "Zoning and Diversity in Historical Perspective." *Journal of Planning History* 11, no. 4: 330–347.

Talen, E., and G. Knaap. 2003. "Legalizing Smart Growth: An Empirical Study of Land Use Regulation in Illinois." *Journal of Planning Education and Research* 22, no. 4: 345–359.

Tarn, J. 1980. "Housing Reform and the Emergence of Town Planning in Britain before 1914." In *The Rise of Modern Urban Planning, 1800–1914*, edited by A. Sutcliffe, 71–97. New York: St. Martin's Press.

Tax Policy Center. 2013. "Local Property Taxes as a Percentage of Local Tax Revenue." Tax Facts, September 30. http://www.taxpolicycenter.org/taxfacts/displayafact. cfm?Docid=518. Accessed July 7, 2012.

Tiebout, C. 1956. "A Pure Theory of Local Expenditures." *Journal of Political Economy* 64, no. 5: 416–424.

Thompson, M. 2009. *Fleeing the City: Studies in the Culture and Politics of Antiurbanism*. New York: Palgrave Macmillan.

Thoreau. H. D. [1849] 2000. *Civil Disobedience*. Bedford: Applewood.

Thornley, A., and Newman, P. 1996. *Urban Planning in Europe: International Competition, National Systems, and Planning Projects*. London: Routledge.

Tocqueville, A. de. [1838] 1966. *Democracy in America*. New York: Harper & Row.

Toll, S. 1969. *Zoned American*. New York: Grossman.

Tosics, I. 2010. "National Spatial Planning Policies and Governance Typology." Plurel deliverable report 2.2.1, June. http://www.plurel.net/images/D221.pdf. Accessed October 14, 2013.

Town of Brookhaven. n.d. "Zoning Analysis." http://www.brookhaven.org/portals/12/ documents/Chapter%205%20-%20Zoning%20Analysis%20%285MB%29.pdf. Accessed October 9, 2013.

Town of Concord. n.d. "Chapter 2: Land Use." http://www.concordma.gov/pages/ concordma_finance/clrp/chapter_2.pdf. Accessed October 9, 2013.

Truslow, J. A. [1931] 1941. *The Epic of America*. Garden City, N.J.: Blue Ribbon Books.

Trutnev, E., and L. Bandorin. 2010. *Azbuka zemlepolzvaniya i zastroiki: Glavnoe o Pravila zemlepolzvaniya i zastroiki v populyarno izlojenii*. Moscow: Institute for Urban Economics.

Turner, F. [1893] 2008. *The Significance of the Frontier in American History*. Charleston: Bibliobazzar.

UNECE (United Nations Economic Commission for Europe). 2004. "Chapter III: The Housing Stock." In *Country Profiles on the Housing Sector: Russian Federation*. http://www.unece.org/fileadmin/DAM/hlm/prgm/cph/countries/russia/ Chapter%20III.pdf. Accessed March 5, 2012.

Unger, S. 2005. "Ancient Lights in Wrigleyville: An Argument for the Unobstructed View of a National Pastime." *Indiana Law Review* 38: 532–564.

United Cities and Local Governments and the World Bank. 2008. *Decentralization and Local Democracy in the World: First Global Report by United Cities and Local Governments*. Washington, D.C.: United Cities and Local Governments and the World Bank.

United Kingdom. 1932. "Town and Country Planning Act." legislation.gov.uk. http://www.legislation.gov.uk/ukpga/1932/48/section/21/enacted. Accessed October 15, 2012.

Urban Audit. Accessed on February 28, 2012; Data queries via http://www.urbanaudit.org/

U.S. Bureau of the Census. 1932. *Fifteenth Census of the U.S. Population*. Vol. 6, *Families*. Washington, D.C.: Government Printing Office.

———. 2010a. Interactive Population Map: Most Populous Places. http://www.census.gov/2010census/popmap/. Accessed April 7, 2014.

———. 2010b. State & County Quick Facts. http://quickfacts.census.gov/qfd/index.html. Accessed April 5, 2012.

———. 2010c. Tenure, Household Size, and Age of Householder: 2010. American Fact Finder. 2010 Census Summary File 1. U.S. Census Bureau. http://factfinder2.census.gov/faces/tableservices/jsf/pages/productview.xhtml?pid=DEC_10_SF1_QTH2. Accessed April 7, 2014.

———. 2011a. American Housing Survey for the United States: 2009. https://www.census.gov/prod/2011pubs/h150-09.pdf. Accessed April 3, 2014.

———. 2011b. Metropolitan Summary Report - AHS 2009: Individual Tables. http://www.census.gov/programs-surveys/ahs/data/2009/h170-09.html.Accessed April 30, 2014.

———. 2012a. *Calculating Migration Expectancy Using ACS Data*. https://www.census.gov/hhes/migration/about/cal-mig-exp.html. Accessed May 23, 2014.

———. 2012b. *Largest Urbanized Areas with Selected Cities and Metro Areas*. http://www.census.gov/dataviz/visualizations/026/508.php. Accessed April 6, 2014.

———. n.d. a. "Census 2000 Summary File 1 (SF 1)." http://www.census.gov/census2000/sumfile1.html. Accessed February 28, 2012.

———. n.d. b Physical Housing Characteristics for Occupied Housing Units. 2008–2012 American Community Survey. http://factfinder2.census.gov/faces/tableservices/jsf/pages/productview.xhtml?pid=ACS_12_5YR_S2504. Accessed April 7, 2014.

U.S. Department of Commerce. 1998. Census Brief: Increase in At-Home Workers Reverses Earlier Trend. Statistical Briefs: Public Information Office. http://www.census.gov/prod/3/98pubs/cenbr982.pdf. Accessed April 2, 2014.

U.S. Department of Commerce, Advisory Committee on City Planning. 1926. *A Zoning Primer*. Washington, D.C.: Government Printing Office.

U.S. Department of Commerce, Advisory Committee on Zoning. 1926. *A Standard State Zoning Enabling Act*. Washington, D.C.: Government Printing Office. https://www.planning.org/growingsmart/pdf/SZEnablingAct1926.pdf. Accessed March 23, 2012.

———. 1928. *A City Planning Primer*. Washington, D.C.: Government Printing Office.

U. S. Department of Housing and Urban Development and U.S. Department of Commerce. 2009. "American Housing Survey for the Washington Metropolitan Area: 2007." http://www.census.gov/housing/ahs/files/washington07.pdf. Accessed March 7, 2013.

———. 2011a. "American Housing Survey 2009." http://www.census.gov/prod/2011pubs/h150-09.pdf. Accessed March 5, 2012.

———. 2011b. "American housing survey for selected metropolitan areas: 2009." http://www.census.gov/prod/2011pubs/h170-09.pdf. Accessed March 5, 2012.

U.S. General Accounting Office. 1999. *Community Development: Extent of Federal Influence on 'Urban Sprawl' Is Unclear: Response to Congressional Requesters*. Washington, D.C.: United States General Accounting Office.

Vance, J. 1990. *The Continuing City: Urban Morphology in Western Civilization*. Balti-more, Md.: John Hopkins University Press.

Van der Krabben, E., and H. Jacobs. 2013. "Public Land Development as a Strategic Tool for Redevelopment: Reflections on the Dutch Experience." *Land Use Policy* 30, 1: 774–783.

Van Nus, W. 1979. "Towards the City Efficient: The Theory and Practice of Zoning, 1919–1939." In *The Usable Urban Past: Planning and Politics in the Modern Canadian City*, 226–246. Toronto: MacMillan.

Vazquez, L. 2006. "Thomas Jefferson: The Founding Father of Sprawl?" *Planetizen*, February 20. http://www.planetizen.com/node/18841. Accessed August 31, 2012.

Veiller, L. 1910. *The National Housing Association: A New Organization to Improve Housing Conditions Both Urban and Suburban in Every Practical Way*. New York: National Housing Association.

———. 1914. "Protecting Residential Districts." In *Proceedings of the Sixth National Conference on City Planning*, 92–111. Boston: Boston University Press.

Von Hoffman, A. 1998. *The Origins of American Housing Reform*. Cambridge, Mass.: Harvard Joint Center for Housing Studies.

Warner, S. 1962. *Streetcar Suburbs: The Process of Growth in Boston, 1870–1900*. New York: Atheneum.

———. [1972] 1995. *The Urban Wilderness: A History of the American City*. Berkeley: University of California Press.

Wasik, J. 2009. *The Cul-de-Sac Syndrome: Turning around the Unsustainable American Dream*. New York: Bloomberg.

Weaver, C., and R. Babcock. 1979. *City Zoning: The Once and Future Frontier*. Chicago: Planners Press.

Weber, M. [1930] 2005. *The Protestant Ethic and the Spirit of Capitalism*. London: Routledge.

Weinstein, A. 2005. *Homeowners Associations*. https://plannersweb.com/2005/04/homeowners-associations/. Accessed May 6, 2014.

Wheaton, W. 1989. "Zoning and Land Use Planning: An Economic Perspective." In *Zoning and the American Dream: Promises Still to Keep*, edited by C. Haar and J. Kayden, 319–330. Chicago: Planners Press.

White, J. 2007. *London in the Nineteenth Century: "A human awful wonder of God."* London: Viking Press.

Whittemore, A. 2012. "How the Federal Government Zoned America: The Federal Housing Administration and Zoning. *Journal of Urban History* 39 no 4: 620–642.

Whitten, R. 1921. *"Zoning and Living Conditions."* In *Proceedings of the Thirteenth National Conference on City Planning held in Pittsburgh, May 9–11*, 22–30. Philadelphia: W. Fell.

———. "Zoning in Atlanta." *Journal of the American Institute of Architects*, 1922 (10), 205.

Wickersham, J. 2001. "Jane Jacobs's Critique of Zoning: From Euclid to Portland and beyond." *Boston College Environmental Affairs Law Review* 28, no. 4: 547–563.

Wiegandt, C. 2000. *Urban Development and Urban Policy in Germany: An Overview*. Bonn: Federal Office for Regional Planning and Building.

Wightman, A. 1999. "Land Reform: Politics, Power and the Public Interest." http://www.caledonia.org.uk/land/wightman.htm#THE%20POLITICS%20OF%20LAND%20REFORM. Accessed June 28, 2012.

Williams, F. 1913. "The German Zone Building Regulations." In *Report of the Heights of Buildings Commission to the Committee on the Height, Size and Arrangement of Buildings of the Board of Estimate and Apportionment of the City of New York*, 94–119. New York: Board of Estimate and Apportionment.

———. 1914a. *Building Regulation by Districts: The Lessons of Berlin*. New York: National Housing Association Publications.

———. 1914b. "Housing and City Planning." *Journal of the American Institute of Architects* (January): 27–28.

———. 1920. "Zoning and the Law of the One-family House District." *Community Leadership*. New York: American City Bureau.

———. [1916] 1929. "Public Control over Private Real Estate." In *City Planning: A Series of Papers Presenting the Essential Elements of a City Plan*, edited by J. Nolen. New York: Appleton.

———. 1922. *The Law of City Planning and Zoning*. New York: Macmillan.

Williams, R. 1989. "Euclid's Locherian Legacy." In *Zoning and the American Dream: Promises Still to Keep*, edited by C. Haar and J. Kayden, 278–295. Chicago: Planners Press.

Willis, C. 1993. "A 3D CBD: How the 1916 Zoning Law Shaped Manhattan's Central Business Districts." In *Planning and Zoning New York City: Yesterday, Today and Tomorrow*, edited by T. Bressi, 3–26. New Brunswick, N.J.: Rutgers University Press.

Wilson, A., and J. Boehland. 2005. "Small Is Beautiful: U.S. House Size, Resource Use and the Environment." GreenBiz.com, July 12. http://www.greenbiz.com/news/2005/07/12/small-beautiful-us-house-size-resource-use-and-environment. Accessed December 7, 2012.

Wissink, G. 1962. *American Cities in Perspective*. Assen: Royal Vangorcum.

Wolf, M. 1989. "The Prescience and Centrality of *Euclid v. Ambler*." In *Zoning and the American Dream: Promises Still to Keep*, edited by C. Haar and J. Kayden, 252–277. Chicago: Planners Press.

———. 2008. *The Zoning of America: Euclid v. Ambler*. Lawrence: University of Kansas Press.

World Values Survey. N.d. Data queries via http://www.wvsevsdb.com/wvs/WVSAnalizeQuestion.jsp. Accessed May 22, 2012.

Wright, F. L. 1932. *The Disappearing City*. New York: Payson.

Xie, J. 2012a. "Diversity and Mixed Use: Lessons from Medieval China." In *The Urban Wisdom of Jane Jacobs*, edited by S. Hirt with D. Zahm, 150–167. London: Routledge.

———. 2012b. "The Diversity of Urban Life and Form: A Historical Study of the Urban Transformation in Tang-Song China and Nineteenth-Century England." Ph.D., University of New South Wales.

Yen, H. 2012. "US Growth of Distant Suburbs Falls to Historic Low." Associated Press, April 5. http://news.yahoo.com/us-growth-distant-suburbs-falls-historic-low-040346997.html. Accessed April 10, 2012.

Young, D. 1996. "Common Interest Developments: A Historical Review of CID Development." Public Law Research Institute. http://www.uwec.edu/geography/ivogeler/w270/cids.htm. Accessed March 10, 2013.

Zelinsky, W. 1973. *A Cultural Geography of the United States*. Englewood Cliffs, N.J.: Prentice-Hall.

Zuckerman, M. 2010. "The American Dream of Home Ownership Has Become a Nightmare." *U.S. News*, September 23. http://www.usnews.com/opinion/mzuckerman/articles/2010/09/23/the-american-dream-of-home-ownership-has-become-a-nightmare. Accessed February 6, 2014.

Zweigert, K., H. Kötz, and T. Weir. 1998. *An Introduction to Comparative Law*. Oxford: Oxford University Press.

Index

www.ingramcontent.com/pod-product-compliance
Lightning Source LLC
Chambersburg PA
CBHW030400270326
41926CB00009B/1203